W9-BKV-484

Junctures
in Women's Leadership

⟨ Social Movements ⟩

Junctures

Case Studies in Women's Leadership
Alison R. Bernstein, Series Editor

The books in this series explore decisions women leaders make in a variety of fields. Using the case study method, the authors focus on strategies employed by each woman as she faces important leadership challenges in business, various social movements, the arts, the health industry, and other sectors. The goal of the series is to broaden our conceptions of what constitutes successful leadership in these changing times.

Junctures
in Women's Leadership

⟨ Social Movements ⟩

Edited by Mary K. Trigg and Alison R. Bernstein

RUTGERS UNIVERSITY PRESS

NEW BRUNSWICK, NEW JERSEY, AND LONDON

Library of Congress Cataloging-in-Publication Data

Junctures in women's leadership : social movements / edited by Mary K. Trigg
and Alison R. Bernstein.
    pages cm.—(Junctures: case studies in women's leadership)
    Includes bibliographical references and index.
    ISBN 978-0-8135-6600-9 (hardcover : alk. paper)—
ISBN 978-0-8135-6599-6 (pbk. : alk. paper)—ISBN 978-0-8135-6601-6 (e-book
(web pdf))—ISBN 978-0-8135-7543-8 (e-book (epub))
    1. Leadership in women. 2. Women executives. 3. Women's rights. I. Trigg,
Mary K., 1955- editor. II. Bernstein, Alison R., 1947- editor.

HQ1236.J86 2016
305.42—dc23
2015024449

A British Cataloging-in-Publication record for this book is available from the
British Library.

Copyright © 2016 by Rutgers, the State University
All rights reserved
No part of this book may be reproduced or utilized in any form or by any
means, electronic or mechanical, or by any information storage and retrieval
system, without written permission from the publisher. Please contact Rutgers
University Press, 106 Somerset Street, New Brunswick, NJ 08901. The only
exception to this prohibition is "fair use" as defined by U.S. copyright law.

Visit our website: http://rutgerspress.rutgers.edu

Manufactured in the United States of America

Contents

Foreword to the Series

Junctures: Case Studies in Women's Leadership

Throughout history, women have always been leaders in their societies and communities. Whether the leadership role was up-front such as hereditary queens and clan mothers, as elected officials, or as business executives and founders of organizations, women have participated at the highest levels of decision making. Yet, up through most of the twentieth century, we seldom associated the word *leader* with women. I might even argue that the noun *leader* was one of the most masculinized words in the English language. When we thought of leaders, our minds seldom conjured up a woman.

Fortunately, there has been a recent shift in our thinking, our images, and our imaginations. In the United States, credit may go to those women in the public eye like Gloria Steinem, Oprah Winfrey, Cecile Richards, and even Eleanor Roosevelt, who have blazed new trails in politics, media, and statecraft. Now leadership is beginning to look more gender neutral. That said, it is important to remember that, in many parts of the world, women leaders, including prominent feminists, have risen to power more rapidly than seems to be the case here. I think of Gro Bundtland in Norway, Helen Clarke in New Zealand, Michelle Bachelet in Chile, and others. These leaders certainly raise new and interesting questions about linking feminism with powerful political leadership. We in the United States also have Sheryl Sandberg to thank for using the word *feminist* in the same sentence as *leadership*.

Despite progress in the past few decades, women have not reached any kind of rough parity with men in terms of positional leadership—that is, the form of leadership that is appointed or elected and recognized as powerful and influential in coeducational public life. Women continue to be dramatically underrepresented in all major domains of leadership from politics to Fortune 500 companies, to labor unions, to academic administration, and even in fields where they are the majority, like in health care professions, teaching, or the arts. Scholars like Deborah Rhode and Nannerl O. Keohane note that, at the rate the United States is going, there will not be a convergence toward parity for an additional three centuries. Given the need for outstanding leadership at all levels and sectors of society, and given the huge waste of talent that exists when so many capable women are not encouraged to move into senior leadership positions, we cannot afford to wait for parity even three decades, let alone three centuries!

If we wish to accelerate the process of gender parity in producing leaders in the twenty-first century, what steps might we take, and what role can academia play in helping to increase the pool and percentage of women leaders? Historically, women's colleges, according to pioneering research by Elizabeth Tidball and others, graduated disproportionate numbers of women leaders up through the 1970s. More recently, business schools, which were largely male bastions, have educated a share of women leaders.

Today, in interdisciplinary fields such as women's and gender studies, examining the concept of leadership and teaching women students to be more effective leaders in a given profession or context is highly contested. For example, *Ms.* magazine noted in 2011, "Only a handful of the more than 650 women's studies programs at colleges and universities provide practical and theoretical knowledge necessary for the next generation to make a significant impact on their communities and world" as leaders. Many feminists and women scholars have negative associations with traditional ideas of leadership, arguing that the concept is elitist, individualistic, and hierarchical and justifies putting work ahead of family and parenting. Moreover, traditional leadership studies often have failed to take account of structural and contextual frameworks of unequal power and privilege, especially around gender and race. And yet approaching the study of leadership with a gender-sensitive lens is crucial if we are to make more progress toward a fairer and more just distribution of power and opportunity for women and men alike.

Which brings me to the genesis of this series, Junctures: Case Studies in Women's Leadership. The volumes in the series are designed to provide insights into the decision-making process undertaken by women leaders, both well-known and deserving to be better known. The case studies run the gamut from current affairs to past history. The Rutgers Institute for Women's Leadership (IWL) consortium, a group of nine separate units at the university, including Douglass Residential College, the Department of Women's and Gender Studies, and the Center for American Women in Politics, is sponsoring this series as a way to provide new pedagogical tools for understanding leadership that has been exercised by women. Each volume will consist of a dozen or so case studies of leaders in a specific field of endeavor. The focus is not on the woman leader per se but rather on the context that surrounded her decision, the factors she considered in making the decision, and the aftermath of the decision. Also, even though the series is focused on decision making by women leaders, it is not designed to demonstrate that all decisions were good ones or yielded the results expected.

The series does not promote the notion that there are biologically determined differences between women's and men's decision-making practices. There is no such thing as a "women's" approach to leadership. Nothing universally characterizes women's approaches to leadership as opposed to men's. Neither gender is genetically wired to be one kind of leader as opposed to another. That kind of biologically determined, reductionist thinking has no place in this series. Nor does the series suggest that women make decisions according to a single set of "women's values or issues," though there is some evidence to suggest that once women reach a critical mass of decision makers, they tend to elevate issues of family and human welfare more than men do. This evidence, collected by the Rutgers University's Center for American Women in Politics, also suggests that women are more likely to seek compromise across rigid ideologies than are men in the same position.

Our series of case studies on women in leadership is not designed to prove that simply electing or appointing women to leadership positions will miraculously improve the standard-of-living outcomes for all people. Few of us believe that. On the other hand, it is important to examine some questions that are fundamental to understanding the values and practices of women leaders who, against the odds, have risen to shape the worlds in which we all live. The series employs the "case study" method because it provides a concrete, real-life example of a woman leader in action. We hope the case studies will prompt many questions, not the least of which is, What fresh perspectives and expanded insights do these women bring to leadership decisions? And, more theoretical and controversial, is there a feminist model of leadership?

In conclusion, the IWL is delighted to bring these studies to the attention of faculty, students, and leaders across a wide range of disciplines and professional fields. We believe it will contribute to accelerating the progress of women toward a more genuinely gender-equal power structure in which both men and women share the responsibility for forging a better and more just world for generations to come.

Alison R. Bernstein
Director, Institute for Women's Leadership (IWL) Consortium
Professor of History and Women's and Gender Studies
Rutgers University / New Brunswick
April 2015

Preface

Women have a long history of leadership in social movements. Whether as mothers, community members, heads of organizations, political representatives, or grassroots activists, women in the United States and around the world have not hesitated to step forward and take a stance in support of rights.

This volume in the Junctures: Case Studies in Women's Leadership series highlights twelve progressive women leaders in social movements at decision-making junctures in their activist or professional lives. The women profiled here were (or are) leaders in social justice movements that span the 1940s to the present, including the civil rights and women's rights movements in the United States and encompass questions of racism, reproductive rights, labor rights, Indigenous rights, environmental rights, lesbian and gay rights, health advocacy, and global human rights. These case studies capture moments in time—what we might call a *movement moment*—and they include examples from Nicaragua, South Africa, and Kenya, as well as the United States. They ask us to consider women's leadership in action and the ways that gender and women's leadership influence movements for social change.

The historian Linda Gordon has described social movement leaders as gifted, hardworking artists whose own self-recognition often comes second to the visibility of their cause or of their followers in the movement. In her estimation, social movements are "not just an emanation of beauty, or of justice, or of rage, but a product of art, even artifice—that is, of craft, skill, strategy, hard work, and discipline."[1] She also notes that in some ways, "the more effective the leader, the less the recognition, because it may well be that the most effective leaders teach and lead in such a way as to promote others rather than themselves."[2]

Promoting others rather than themselves seems to characterize a number of the women leaders profiled here. Whether because of modesty, manners, a collaborative philosophy, a desire to share the limelight, or a fear of criticism, women have been more reluctant to take center stage. The global human rights leader Charlotte Bunch talks here of being raised to be humble and facing a very real internal struggle when she decided to step up and become a media spokesperson for the global human rights movement. The feminist icon Gloria Steinem believes she is a more adept listener than a public speaker and is reluctant to embrace her own public image as a feminist superstar. For decades, she has insisted that other women join her at the podium. Colleagues and friends of Steinem describe her ability to truly listen, with empathy, as one of her great attributes.

Women have also been silenced, sidelined, and gender stereotyped in social movements, which has motivated them to organize. The Caribbean American lesbian poet Audre Lorde, profiled in these pages, describes how she and the iconic singer Lena Horne were given the job of making coffee for the male speakers at the 1963 March on Washington. "Because that is what most Black women did in the 1963 March on Washington," Lorde noted.[3] The civil rights leader Daisy Bates was also relegated to the background at the 1963 march.

What prepared the women in this volume for leadership varies. For example, Daisy Bates, who in 1957 led the racial integration of Central High School in Little Rock, Arkansas, stated simply, "Nothing prepared me [for leadership] more than my anger." Bates's anger was fueled by her experiences and witnessing of racism in the segregated US South of the 1950s. Audre Lorde wrote of her experiences a decade earlier: "Growing up Fat Black Female and almost blind in America requires so much surviving that you have to learn from it or die." The US labor activist Bhairavi Desai was motivated by what she called "the sacrifice of the working men and women in the country, of the immigrants in this country." She believed she owed them, as well as her hardworking South Asian immigrant parents, something in return. The lawyer and public protector Thuli Madonsela credits growing up poor and Black during apartheid in South Africa as fueling her social justice commitments.

Many, if not all, of the activist leaders profiled here came of age participating in social change movements and then helped push them forward. Their parents or educations often introduced them to these movements. The HIV/AIDS organizer Dázon Dixon Diallo gained her sense of social justice as a child through the Episcopal church, her parents' activism and community service, and later her education at Atlanta's Spelman College. Being at Duke in the 1960s exposed Charlotte Bunch to the civil rights and Methodist student movements, which served as important catalysts for her. Aileen Hernandez first encountered the civil rights movement as a student at Washington, DC's Howard University, where she joined the NAACP and picketed against segregation at the National Theater, the Eisner Auditorium, and at Thomson restaurants. The Planned Parenthood director and reproductive rights activist Cecile Richards recalled her involvement in the anti–(South African) apartheid movement and her years as a student at Brown being more about "agitating" than studying. Wangari Maathai encountered both the civil rights movement and a more sexually liberal society when she studied in the United States in the early 1960s. Both Aileen Hernandez and Cecile Richards applied what they learned organizing workers in the trade union movement in their subsequent work in affirmative action and reproductive rights movements.

Courage, creativity, passion, and perseverance are some of the qualities that fuel leadership.[4] These qualities and many more are on display in these pages. The Kenyan environmental and democracy activist Wangari Maathai's public and political condemnation as a divorced, "wayward woman" only made her more resolute. After being beaten and imprisoned multiple times, she declared, "My skin is thick, like an elephant's." The Nicaraguan physician Mirna Cunningham was kidnapped, beaten, and raped by former members of Somoza's army yet went on to become a gifted mediator and Indigenous leader. Many of these social movement leaders asked critical questions, challenged injustice, and exhibited the will to act in the face of at-times virulent criticism and violence. They encouraged women (and men) to raise their voices together, from Maathai's exhortation to Kenyans to tell their story about their lives under Kenya's autocratic regime to Steinem's vision of her speaking events as community meetings that could continue after she left. The feminist theorist Audre Lorde entreated Black women and lesbians to break their silences, memorably proclaiming, "Your silence will not protect you."

Most of these leaders were also important movement builders and were skilled at organizing, were savvy at using media, and proved themselves astute political and grassroots campaigners. Between them, they launched numerous organizations. Aileen Hernandez cofounded Black Women Organized for Action in San Francisco in 1973, to develop leadership among Black women. Audre Lorde cofounded the first women-of-color press in the United States, Kitchen Table: Women of Color Press, in 1980. In 1989, Dázon Dixon Diallo began Sister Love, which focuses on women with HIV/AIDS in the Black community. Wangari Maathai founded the Green Belt Movement that inspired women and men to plant trees to address deforestation and malnutrition in rural Kenya. Bhairavi Desai cofounded the New York Taxi Workers Alliance and led a series of successful yellow cab strikes in 1998.

Gender conventions also influenced the ways some of these women practiced their leadership. In an examination of a number of women involved in the US labor, civil rights, and feminist movements of the twentieth century, the scholar Georgina Hickey has suggested that at times women activists have found themselves caught in a "respectability trap."[5] "In these moments," Hickey writes, "women have shaped, curtailed, or rearranged their behaviors or appearances to meet certain social connotations or normative gender expectations, even when those gender conventions contradict larger goals or ideologies held by these activists."[6] The historian Evelyn Brooks Higginbotham has described "the politics of respectability" adopted by Black women's rights activists in the Baptist church in the early twentieth century. In their efforts to work for the uplift and reform of their race, African American women at times endorsed the dominant white ideals.[7]

We can point to instances of "the politics of respectability" or the "respectability trap" in some of the case studies included here. When the widowed first lady Eleanor Roosevelt was appointed US delegate and chair to the United Nations Commission on Human Rights in 1948, she found herself outnumbered as a woman in an overwhelmingly male organization. Although she tried to negotiate the politics of gender by drawing on notions of gendered propriety, she still felt that she "walked on eggs" and received a largely chilly reception from her colleagues. Rather than hounding other delegates, she invited them to tea or to share a meal. Similarly, the civil rights activist Daisy Bates made it a point to dress immaculately, smile often, and be consistently courteous when she attended community hearings on the school integration plan in Little Rock, Arkansas, in the mid-1950s. As the author Bridget Gurtler writes of Bates, "Her leadership abilities are best understood as deeply embedded in the social relations and norms that shaped women's participation in the movement."

Some of these women turned the tables with gender-specific strategies, as other women before them have done in history. Wangari Maathai and "the Mamas" drew on Kenyans' traditional respect for motherhood to connect their political identity as mothers to their citizenship and demanded and won social justice on behalf of their imprisoned sons. Likewise, the labor activist Bhairavi Desai gained the acceptance and respect of male immigrant taxi drivers by lending her "female ear" to their struggles. The advocate of women's reproductive freedom Cecile Richards is often described as a proud mother of three, devoted wife, and gracious company.

The women chronicled here practiced different kinds of leadership. Eleanor Roosevelt's leadership style is described as "pragmatic," because she was able to negotiate between culturally diverse views to produce a human rights document. Like other women in the civil rights movement, Daisy Bates was a bridge leader, who provided the local leadership necessary to bridge, amplify, and transform the (civil) rights movement for potential recruits.[8] Mirna Cunningham, through her skillful mediation, created a bridge between the Sandinista nationalist project and Indigenous autonomy. Audre Lorde was a coalitional leader who strove to connect women of color throughout the world. Wangari Maathai was an inclusive leader who worked to reach the rural, grassroots women in Kenya and to inspire them to be courageous and self-confident in their own abilities and knowledge. Bhairavi Desai views her role as a conduit for the workers she leads, to empower them to build every part of the organization. Charlotte Bunch describes her leadership style as "collaborative." In her emphasis on collective and multilayered leadership and the importance of relationship building within organizations, with constituencies and with both allies and opponents, Bunch's approach exemplifies feminist leadership as Srilatha Batliwala has defined it.[9] Dázon Dixon Diallo describes her approach as "leading from behind," which means encouraging those who are directly affected (HIV-positive women) to find the voice and agency to lead a movement for their own needs. We have been inspired by the women leaders in this volume, and we hope you find their leadership challenges, dilemmas, and accomplishments instructive and thought provoking.

Mary K. Trigg
Alison R. Bernstein
April 2015

Notes

1 Linda Gordon, "Social Movements, Leadership, and Democracy: Toward More Utopian Mistakes," *Journal of Women's History* 14, no. 2 (2002): 104.

2 Ibid., 102.

3 Audre Lorde, "I Am Your Sister: Organizing Women across Sexualities," in *A Burst of Light: Essays* (Ann Arbor, MI: Firebrand Books, 1988), 23.

4 Gordon, "Social Movements," 104.

5 Georgina Hickey, "The Respectability Trap: Gender Conventions in 20th Century Movements for Social Change," *Journal of Interdisciplinary Feminist Thought* 7, no. 2 (2013): 1–12.

6 Ibid., 2.

7 Evelyn Higginbotham, *Righteous Discontent: The Women's Movement in the Black Baptist Church, 1880–1920* (Cambridge, MA: Harvard University Press, 1994).

8 Belinda Robnett, "African-American Women in the Civil Rights Movement, 1954–1965: Gender, Leadership, and Micromobilization," *American Journal of Sociology* 101, no. 6 (1996): 1686.

9 Srilatha Batliwala, *Feminist Leadership for Social Transformation: Clearing the Conceptual Cloud* (New Delhi, India: Creating Resources for Empowerment in Action, 2011), 65–66, http://www.uc.edu/content/dam/uc/ucwc/docs/CREA .pdf.

Acknowledgments

This volume, focused on women's leadership in social movements, is part of a projected eight-volume series that explores those critical junctures when twelve women—both well-known and deserving to be better known—made important decisions that they hoped would make a positive difference in the lives of others.

A volume of case studies examining women's leadership in the business context is being published simultaneously with this book. Case studies of leaders of corporations are familiar pedagogical terrain in business schools, but a whole volume focused on women's leadership is not. Lisa Hetfield, the associate director of the Institute for Women's Leadership (IWL) at Rutgers, and her coeditor, Dana Britton, the director of the Center for Women and Work at Rutgers, have shown us how to develop this kind of teaching tool with integrity and an eye for the telling detail. We are grateful that Lisa and Dana took this effort forward.

This volume represents the work of many individuals at Rutgers and beyond. We are especially indebted to Professors Beverly Guy-Sheftall at Spelman College and Blanche Wiesen Cook at John Jay College and the Graduate Center of the City University of New York (CUNY). They served as senior editors for the case studies of Audre Lorde and Eleanor Roosevelt, respectively. We thank our anonymous readers; you know who you are. In addition, we are especially indebted to several women leaders—Gloria Steinem, Mirna Cunningham, Dázon Dixon Diallo, Thuli Madonsela, and our colleague Charlotte Bunch, who agreed to be interviewed or otherwise offer input for this volume. They gave generously of their time and insights and even helped to revise the case study, which resulted in a more nuanced understanding of the leadership challenges each faced. Looking back, we benefited from the advice of scholars and teachers in deciding which leaders to profile in the volume and how to think about women leaders. Special thanks go to Jane Bennett, Gay Seidman, Jacklyn Cock, Joan W. Scott, Johanna Schoen, Mary Hartman, and the directors of the nine units of the IWL consortium who warmly embraced this idea. It would have remained just an idea if it had not been for Marlie Wasserman, the director of Rutgers University Press, who shepherded this effort from its earliest inception through to publication. Also, we are especially grateful to three undergraduate research assistants, Judy Wu, Marie Ferguson, and Kim LeMoon, for their meticulous and dedicated work in reading and preparing the manuscript.

Finally, we wish to thank two other sets of individuals whose commitment to the series made this volume possible. The first group are those talented graduate students who served as researchers and coauthors of the case studies: Bridget Gurtler (our guide to the process of case study writing), Carolina Alonso Bejarano, Jo Butterfield, Jeremy LaMaster, C. Laura Lovin, Rosemary Ndubuizu, Kathe Sandler, Stina Soderling, Miriam Tola, and Taida Wolfe. The volume would not exist without the hard work and willingness of these emerging scholars to get the job done. Additionally, we want to salute the donors to this series—our own Mary Hartman (founding director of the IWL), Donna Griffin, and Bernice Venable—whose early support was critical. They provided the funding that enabled us to give modest support to our graduate-student collaborators.

We hope the courage, persistence, and achievements of the women profiled in this volume prompt new questions regarding what constitutes leadership in these times and inspire young women like our students to take up the mantle of leadership in the journeys that lie ahead. In that spirit, we dedicate this book to our daughters: Emma, Julia, Laurel, and Sarah.

Junctures

in Women's Leadership

⟨ Social Movements ⟩

Eleanor Roosevelt
Negotiating the Universal Declaration of Human Rights

Jo E. Butterfield and Blanche Wiesen Cook

Background

Hailed as the "First Lady of the World," Eleanor Roosevelt was the most internationally recognized woman of the early postwar era. To this day, Roosevelt remains the public face of the 1948 Universal Declaration of Human Rights (UDHR). Drafted by the nascent United Nations in the aftermath of World War II, the UDHR continues to serve as the foundation of modern human rights standards. Roosevelt served as both the US delegate and chair to the UN Commission on Human Rights (CHR) charged by the United Nations to draft an International Bill of Rights. Between 1947 and 1948, the eighteen-member commission debated and compromised to craft a document that outlined the fundamental rights owed to all human beings, regardless of "race, color, sex, language, religion, political or other opinion, national or social origin, property, birth or other status." As chair of the commission and as the representative of the US government, Roosevelt's leadership shaped the UDHR drafting process in critical ways.

Cognizant of the League of Nations' failure to prevent the Second World War, Allied-aligned states drafted the 1945 UN Charter, setting forth the principles and purposes of the new international organization.[1] To secure a peaceful postwar order by promoting cooperation among member nations, the charter established the Economic and Social Council (ECOSOC) as one of the UN's primary entities. In 1946, at its first official meeting, the UN established Commission on Human Rights under ECOSOC's auspices.

Elected by the CHR's other national delegates, Roosevelt led a diverse commission that confronted challenging political and philosophical questions. Chief among them were settling on a guiding human rights theory (why human beings have rights) and how the international community could enforce human rights given the UN Charter's simultaneous guarantee of noninterference and the primacy of domestic jurisdiction. Already struggling to negotiate national and regional differences, emerging Cold War politics further complicated the commission's work. The United States and Soviet Union governments forwarded competing human rights visions. While US policy makers prioritized the civil and political rights of individuals, the Soviet delegation emphasized the state's responsibility to secure economic and social rights. At stake was the legitimacy of each superpower's claim to global leadership.

As chair, Roosevelt's task was to steer the commission toward agreement on a single document that reflected the aspirations of the international community. As the US delegate, Roosevelt's job was to advance US interests. The job required a difficult balancing act. Under Roosevelt's leadership, the commission bypassed declaring a single theory of human rights and grappled with whether to prioritize a declaration—a statement of principles and aims—or a covenant that would legally bind signatories. Ultimately the commission compromised by working simultaneously on a declaration, a covenant, and a study on implementation. Over the course of nearly two years, the CHR debated and negotiated. In the fall of 1948, however, the CHR produced only a draft declaration, setting aside the covenant for further debate. Before the United Nations adopted what came to be named the Universal Declaration of Human Rights, drafts of the document were negotiated by national delegates to the CHR, circulated to all fifty-five member states for comment, approved by the Economic and Social Council, and debated and reworked at more than eighty General Assembly committee and plenary meetings. In the end, the foundational human rights document included political and civil rights as well as economic and social rights. The UDHR thus endorsed an interdependent interpretation of human rights, advancing the idea that the guarantee of one type of right (e.g., political) worked to ensure the fulfillment of others (e.g., economic). Similarly, the denial of one type of right endangered others. Shortly before midnight on December 10, 1948, the General Assembly adopted the UDHR without a single negative vote and only eight abstentions.[2]

Scholars debate the legacy of Eleanor Roosevelt's postwar leadership. In the 1980s, newly emergent feminist historians resurrected Roosevelt's central political role, focusing on her international human rights work as well as her domestic efforts to promote racial and gender equality. The turn to historicizing human rights emphasized Roosevelt's pragmatic leadership in negotiating between culturally diverse views to produce a universal human rights document. While scholars continue to celebrate Roosevelt's life work, skeptics have questioned her commitment to promoting the rights of women and racial equality during the UDHR drafting process.[3]

How does one reconcile the incongruity between historical accounts that situate Roosevelt as a pragmatic heroine on the one hand and as political figure who faltered in the promotion of gender and racial justice at the UN on the other? Situating Roosevelt's human rights activism and political leadership in the specific context of both prevailing ideas about gender and Cold War geopolitics helps to explain (even if it does not exonerate) the difficult leadership choices made by the US delegate.

Advocating for Human Rights

Roosevelt framed her political activism as undertaken on behalf of others, not for self-interest.[4] She is widely known for applying her influence to ameliorate the suffering of individuals who sought her assistance. Roosevelt maintained a rigorous schedule, producing a nearly inconceivable amount of daily correspondence in addition to a syndicated column. She traveled widely both in the United States and abroad, bearing witness to the misery of people trapped in poverty and overwhelmed by war.

Roosevelt is also credited with her support for women's rights. She is perhaps best known for holding White House press conferences exclusively for female reporters, providing executive branch access.[5] She believed that women were men's equals, but she understood them to be fundamentally different, explaining in one of her columns, "you can't change the fact that men and women are different, and it is fortunate for us that this is the case."[6] Roosevelt worked closely with the Women's Trade Union League, which actively lobbied to improve labor conditions for working women. To this end, Roosevelt supported so-called protective labor legislation, such as measures to regulate the maximum number of hours, to shield working women from the excesses of industrial capitalism.[7] In doing so, Roosevelt was part of the feminist mainstream in the United States that opposed the Equal Rights Amendment to the US Constitution lest it obliterate hard-won gender-specific labor laws.

Roosevelt also enjoyed a reputation as a "friend of the Negro." While her husband juggled support for social justice with party politics, Eleanor Roosevelt rarely equivocated in her outspoken advocacy for racial justice. She is widely recognized for her efforts to help arrange Marion Anderson's concert at the Lincoln Memorial. She defied police instructions to abide by laws requiring segregated seating at the 1938 Southern Conference on Human Welfare in Alabama.[8] Roosevelt also labored on behalf of federal antilynching legislation, plying her influence to give the law's supporters access to the president.[9] In 1945, she formalized her relationship with the National Association for the Advancement of Colored People (NAACP), the most established organization working for racial equality in the nation, by joining its board of directors.

By appointing the recently widowed Roosevelt to the United Nations in 1946, Harry S. Truman (FDR's successor) hoped to maintain the link between the revered former president, his administration, and the new international organization. Internationally, Eleanor Roosevelt enjoyed considerable prestige and recognition, benefiting from her husband's popularity abroad. The UN delegate from Haiti, Emile Saint-Lot, addressed her as "the wife of the apostle of fundamental human rights and liberties."[10] Furthermore, Roosevelt attracted the attention of the international press corps and thus highlighted the US role in the human rights project. What she said and did mattered a great deal.

Roosevelt's previous work on behalf of racial and gender equality divided those who grasped the potential of the postwar UN human rights project to challenge the status quo. The executive secretary of the NAACP, Walter White, believed Roosevelt's appointment installed a powerful ally at the UN, even as others, particularly the renowned scholar and activist W.E.B. Du Bois, remained skeptical.[11] Democrats committed to maintaining white supremacy berated Truman for appointing a woman they felt sure would use the international arena to undermine Jim Crow, the US system of apartheid.[12] In fact, southern Democrats—termed Dixiecrats—revolted in 1948 by forming a distinctly segregationist party when Truman's election platform included civil rights provisions. Racial equality was a specter exacerbated, southern Democrats believed, by the prospect of an enforceable international human rights treaty.

Roosevelt's new position also divided women's rights activists. Leaders of the Women in World Affairs Committee, which labored to secure women's appointment to office, argued that "probably no woman in the country has a closer knowledge of domestic and foreign affairs" and asserted that Roosevelt had "the confidence of a great body of American women."[13] Labor-oriented feminists, who enjoyed Roosevelt's support, were nonetheless cautious. For example, feminist policy makers in the US Department of Labor's Women's Bureau believed that although Roosevelt was "sympathetic" to the "status of women," she was "more interested in the problem of race."[14] In contrast, feminists affiliated with the National Woman's Party, who opposed protective labor legislation as limiting women's economic opportunities, saw Roosevelt's selection as nothing less than catastrophic.[15] One feminist opponent lamented that "Mrs. R. is the most powerful person in the world!"[16] Although unusual in her prestige and influence, Roosevelt nevertheless served as a female delegate in an overwhelmingly male organization.

Gender and Postwar International Political Participation

By pointing to women's critical contributions and sacrifices on behalf of the Allied war effort, feminists enjoyed early and unprecedented, if still meager, success in gaining the appointment of women to the United Nations. They did so by mounting aggressive lobbying campaigns and, in an era marked by differentiating democracy from fascism, by linking women's participation to genuine democratic governance. During the war, Roosevelt actively advocated for the inclusion of women in postwar planning committees and for their appointment to international conferences. She wrote numerous columns and sponsored multiple White House meetings that stressed the significance of women's wartime contributions and their essential place in securing the postwar peace.[17]

Yet the new United Nations only hesitantly incorporated women into postwar international politics, a domain historically dominated by men. Women were both few in number and segregated by field at the United Nations. Although women served as support staff and attended UN conferences as consultants for nongovernmental organizations, only a handful of female delegates enjoyed full voting authority. Despite the presence of women as official delegates or advisers at the 1945 founding conference, only four women, Virginia Gildersleeve (United States), Bertha Lutz (Brazil), Wu Yi-Fang (China), and Minerva Bernardino (Dominican Republic), held high enough positions to be one of their nation's signatories. At the first UN General Assembly, the number of voting women delegates improved slightly. By 1949, however, their numbers had actually declined. Furthermore, of the fifty-six women who served as delegates to the UN from 1946 to 1949, only one served on a commission not affiliated with social, cultural, or humanitarian affairs.[18] This field was deemed appropriately feminine in nature and considered within the realm of women's expertise. Likened to social reforms and charitable measures, social, cultural, and humanitarian affairs were viewed as the domestic sphere of international politics.

Female delegates understood that their male counterparts considered women to be outsiders. Press accounts reinforced the novelty of women's presence by reports obsessed with female delegates' physical appearance (instead of their positions), musings about sex-based antagonisms, and gendered diplomatic approaches.[19] At the first UN General Assembly, ER hosted gatherings of female delegates who convened as an unofficial caucus and collectively crafted an Open Letter to the World. The Open Letter, read by Roosevelt at the General Assembly, justified women's international political participation and appealed to women the world over to take interest and for governments to appoint more female delegates.[20]

Roosevelt's advocacy reflected her long-held belief that sufficient participation by women in international politics could prevent future wars.[21] Female delegates regularly lamented what they understood to be patronizing, disinterested, and even hostile responses to their presence at the UN.[22] Yet they also held distinct and diverse politics, disagreeing about feminist approaches at the UN. Some, like the Australian delegate Jessie Street, insisted that women seize the opportunity to advance an explicitly feminist agenda. To do so, delegates like Street struggled to navigate between their feminist objectives and their obligations as national representatives. Others, like Virginia Gildersleeve, a US delegate to the 1945 conference, contended that a feminist-focused approach was bad politics. Gildersleeve argued that "at this stage of advancement" female delegates were better off "not [to] talk too much about abstract principles of women's rights but to do good work in any job they get, better work if possible than their male colleagues."[23] At the United Nations, Eleanor Roosevelt adopted positions more aligned with the Gildersleeve camp. Delegates who prioritized international feminist positions over national objectives often resigned in frustration, were marginalized, or, like Street, were forced by their governments out of the United Nations.

Negotiating the Politics of Gender

Domestically, Roosevelt was a polarizing figure, with public opinion drawn largely, but not exclusively, along partisan lines. Many people in the US foreign-policy establishment questioned Truman's judgment in nominating Roosevelt. Some opposed her because of alleged inexperience, while others did so because of her ties to the left-leaning New Deal. Across the board, male members of the bipartisan US delegation were skeptical of her—or any woman's—ability to carry out the tough political task of securing US interests at the new United Nations. The southern Democratic senator Tom Connally asked fellow members of the US delegation, "Would you like to have a woman in here dictating to us what to do?"[24] Initially, ER's conservative Republican counterparts, Arthur Vandenberg and John Foster Dulles, also vehemently opposed her nomination. At the outset, both because of—and despite—her politics, Roosevelt's so-called colleagues offered a chilly reception.

Roosevelt herself questioned her qualifications for the job and at first rejected Truman's offer to serve. In her autobiography, she recalled that she had accepted the position with "fear and trembling."[25] Roosevelt's apprehension was due, in part, to the fact that she recognized the precarious nature of women's induction into official intergovernmental politics. She remembered, "I walked on eggs. I knew that as the only woman on the delegation I was not very welcome. Moreover, if I failed to be a useful member, it would not be considered merely that I as an individual had failed but that all women had failed, and there would be little chance for others to serve in the near future."[26]

Ultimately Roosevelt chose to navigate the male-dominated sphere of international politics by both challenging and deploying gendered ideas about political women. She embraced her role as a professional despite the fact that she had not served as an official international delegate prior to her work at the United Nations. She quickly demonstrated that she could be an effective member of the delegation. Roosevelt was intellectually sharp and studied the delegate's material produced by her trusted State Department coaches prodigiously. She emerged as the only delegate adequately prepared to take on Andrei Vishinsky, the formidable Soviet delegate, on the refugee question. UN politics quickly revealed that social, cultural, and humanitarian issues were no less politically charged than those of the Security Council.

Roosevelt also employed a distinctly gendered approach to politics. She understood—given prevailing ideologies about gender—that charges of "petticoat rule" could readily undermine political projects, and she often worked to conceal her influence.[27] Her generous and persuasive hospitality contributed to her success as a US political operative. She did not strong-arm other delegations; she had them for tea or to dine. In the final push to adopt the Declaration, an outgoing adviser offered advice to his successor: "As you know, Mrs. Roosevelt makes it a practice of entertaining all the delegates. . . . This is done by small luncheon or evening sessions. . . . [You] should make sure that people are lined up for luncheon every day and you should also make plans for evening sessions. In each case the group invited must be carefully picked out so as to secure maximum efficiency in lining up votes. . . . [It] is a pattern which Mrs. Roosevelt has used in the past . . . successfully."[28]

The image of Roosevelt as "First Lady of the World" drew on both her role as a diplomat and as FDR's widow. This mixed characterization epitomized the postwar tensions between women's public and private roles. As both the niece and wife of former US presidents, Roosevelt's familial associations somewhat tempered anxieties about her wielding political power. In her syndicated "My Day" column, Roosevelt set out to allay residual fears by linking her UN service to FDR, writing that she hoped to contribute as an "individual and as my husband's widow."[29] Roosevelt fully grasped the gendered dynamics of the United Nations, and as one adviser noted, she performed her duties with the perfect blend of "cunning and naiveté."[30]

Roosevelt's blending of political acumen, traditional gender propriety, and international prestige helped US policy makers achieve their objectives at the United Nations, particularly regarding the postwar human rights project. One adviser commented on the advantage Roosevelt offered: "Always remember that there are some votes which can be secured only if Mrs. Roosevelt speaks to the delegates herself. This is a measure which must be sparingly used because if word gets around that Mrs. Roosevelt is talking to some of the delegates and not to others the others may be offended."[31]

Resolution

Those who endorsed—and condemned—Roosevelt's nomination did so because they hoped—or feared—that she would use the UN human rights project to agitate specifically for gender and racial equality. This was not an unfounded assumption. Indeed, prior to embarking on her first trip to the United Nations, Roosevelt requested the counsel of both women's and civil rights advocates.[32] Yet ultimately Roosevelt prioritized her responsibility as the US delegate over specific advocacy on behalf of racial and gender justice.

Given the challenges female delegates faced in gaining international appointments and the skepticism encountered by the few who managed to achieve these positions, it is perhaps not surprising that she chose not to position herself as an outside activist but instead to prove herself useful to the delegation.

Balancing Cold War Exigencies and Human Rights Advocacy

Although Roosevelt advanced US policy positions, she did not formulate them. An interdepartmental working group, led by the State Department, crafted the position papers to be used by US delegates.[33] Several agencies, including the Department of Labor's Women's Bureau, played significant roles in formulating policy. Roosevelt followed her instructions explicitly, often employing verbatim language from her detailed position papers. She had advisers at the ready. Roosevelt recalled, "[Durward] Sandifer was always seated just behind me to give me guidance. As time went on I could tell merely by his reactions whether the discussion was going well or badly. If I could feel him breathing down my neck I knew that there was trouble coming, usually from the Russians."[34] When unexpected developments occurred, Roosevelt rarely improvised; advisers promptly scribbled responses in the margins of her instructions.

When Roosevelt found a US policy position disagreeable, she kept it out of the public eye, voicing her concerns only behind the scenes. Roosevelt argued that if she disagreed with her instructions, she had the "right to say so and try to get the official attitude changed or modified." If that failed, her only option was to "appeal to the President to intervene," and if the dispute could not be resolved, she would "resign in protest."[35]

Although her advisers recalled that her public positions rarely diverged from those of the State Department, the promotion of economic and social rights was one area in which Roosevelt uneasily juggled her belief system and her obligations as the US delegate.[36] US reticence to support economic and social rights prompted Roosevelt to offer her resignation. Indeed, she insisted that one could not talk human rights to people who were hungry. Truman refused ER's resignation and urged her to follow her conscience.[37] Yet the Soviet Union's efforts to incorporate the state as the guarantor of economic and social rights ran counter to the US government's emphasis on the right of individuals to be free from state intrusion. The official US position therefore prioritized civil and political rights, which underpinned the US Constitution in theory if not practice. US policy makers understood civil and political rights as a feature that distinguished the US and Soviet systems. The divergent rights priorities of each superpower represented a philosophical divide with significant political implications. They were implications that grew in significance as the Cold War escalated and as the various types of rights came to symbolize the distinct, competing political and economic systems.

Roosevelt's long-standing commitment to and work on behalf of economic rights contrasted with US policy makers' refusal to incorporate an explicit state obligation to guarantee economic rights. She managed the tension between her national obligation and her personal beliefs by publicly reiterating the centrality of economic rights even as she worked to deemphasize the state's responsibility to ensure economic security. During one drafting session, for example, she insisted that "men in need were not free men."[38] Facilitating her ability to reconcile her role as the US delegate and her commitment to economic and social rights was a belief that economic and social rights should rest on a foundation of political freedom, not dictatorship. ER also understood that US opponents of the human rights project would capitalize on the concept of a state obligation to advance arguments that it was a socialist-inspired program.

Roosevelt also privately challenged US foot-dragging on an enforceable human rights covenant. From the beginning, Roosevelt argued that human rights had to be enforceable if they were to be meaningful. She questioned the decision to press for the UDHR's adoption before an enforceable covenant had been negotiated, understanding that with the declaration's passage, pressure to pursue the covenant would ease. Yet when assured by the State Department that the covenant would not be sidelined, Roosevelt accepted arguments that the covenant's delay best served both the US position and the human rights project. Roosevelt also worked on behalf of the government to insert a federal-state clause in the draft covenant, a move that would have allowed southern states to reject elements that ran counter to their commitment to white supremacy. Policy makers insisted that the clause was essential to securing domestic support for US participation in an international agreement.[39]

The Cold War contest between the United States and the Soviet Union played a significant role in Roosevelt's acquiescence to policies she might otherwise have protested and was a principle reason she did not publicize her reservations. Committed to the principle of individual rights, Roosevelt believed the US political model worthy of international emulation. She understood equality of opportunity promoted through legal measures as the key to empowering the oppressed. Thus, for Roosevelt, the attainment of human rights rested on democratic governance. Furthermore, she accepted the US narrative of racial progress, while acknowledging its flaws, assuaged by faith that conditions had improved and, given time, would improve still further. Roosevelt found Soviet party-line positions frustrating and obstructive. The former First Lady was not sympathetic to those who would complicate her task at the United Nations by inflaming what she held were already well-known shortcomings in the US political system. To do so, for Roosevelt, only made her difficult job more challenging.

Although Roosevelt supported advances in both racial and gender equality, she fashioned herself a pragmatist. She had championed the NAACP's legal approach to black equality, but her support waned when the NAACP took the national struggle to the international arena by petitioning the UN in 1947. The NAACP's *An Appeal to the World* catalogued the US government's failure to secure even the most basic rights for the black community, let alone to protect African Americans from violent acts perpetrated by racists. The NAACP's indictment, leaked to the press, demolished the US government's narrative of racial progress.[40]

Roosevelt believed that the Soviet delegation's predictable emphasis on the NAACP's petition compromised her ability to represent the US government. She insisted that as an individual, she would like to be present when the NAACP presented the petition, but as the US delegate, she could not. When the NAACP seemed poised to press the *Appeal*, Roosevelt submitted her resignation to the organization's board. If forced to choose, Roosevelt would elect to serve the UN as the US representative over supporting the petition, a tactic she believed was misguided.[41]

The activist position assumed by the UN's Commission on the Status of Women (CSW) also threatened to place Roosevelt's commitment to women's rights and her task as the US delegate in tension. The early CSW was composed of women who had been active in feminist circles both nationally and internationally during the interwar era. Women like Minerva Bernardino, who served the brutal right-wing Dominican dictator Raphael Trujillo, joined forces with the left-leaning Australian Jessie Street to forge a coalition among other UN feminists. Determined to use the human rights project to advance long-standing women's rights claims, CSW delegates adopted an agenda that advanced identical civil and political rights for men and women and incorporated particular economic and social rights for women as a social group. For instance, they insisted on universal suffrage and on the state's obligation to provide paid maternity leave and child care. The CSW advanced gender-specific, particular rights as necessary to achieve *equality* between men and women. For the majority of CSW delegates, employing the language of equality to advance women's status did not necessitate that the sexes be treated identically. This interpretation of equality stood in stark contrast to most US feminists, who held that the language of *equal rights* threatened to mandate *identical rights*.

US labor feminists feared that the CSW's commitment to the language of equal rights and equality would undermine gender-specific labor standards for women. Domestic feminists enjoyed the support of US policy makers who prioritized women's political and educational rights at the UN. Roosevelt carried the message. As an ex-officio delegate to early CSW meetings, she attempted to limit the scope of the commission's activity, arguing that the delegates should make specific recommendations on "rights to which [they] give priority and on which all other rights rest, . . . the fundamental right of women to political equality."[42]

For Roosevelt and her US feminist allies, references to the universality of rights by definition precluded the possibility of specific rights for women. For these US women, the term *universal* (like *equal*) implied identical treatment. ER initially held that the language of "all men" was sufficient but by June 1948 accepted arguments made by UN feminists like Hansa Mehta of India that "all human beings" was a more appropriate signifier for the UDHR. Feminist policy makers in the US Women's Bureau convinced their State Department colleagues to press for the removal of all specific references to women's rights. They did so primarily out of concern that mentioning women in one area threatened to undermine their rights claims elsewhere in the UDHR. During drafting sessions, Roosevelt forwarded US policy positions that sought to eliminate all specific mention of women's rights, including equal rights in marriage and divorce. This was despite her long-standing support for women's rights in this area.[43]

The fact that the Soviet Union offered consistent support for the CSW's agenda endeared neither US policy makers nor Roosevelt to its promotion. In the context of the nascent Cold War, Roosevelt prioritized the larger goal of US leadership and its emphasis on political democracy over CSW delegates' call for a "social revolution."[44] If the security of human rights hinged on democratic governance, the fact that nearly half of UN member states restricted women's right to vote helped to validate an emphasis on political rights at the same time that it reinforced the legitimacy of the US political model.

The human rights commission did not reach, as hoped, an agreement on a legally binding covenant immediately following the UDHR's adoption. The intractability of Cold War positions taken by US and Soviet Union policy makers mired the debate and eventually—if the covenant process were to proceed—required the abandonment of UDHR's explicitly interdependent approach to human rights. Thus, by early 1952, the CHR began drafting two distinct covenants, one on political and civil rights and another to promote economic, social, and cultural rights.

Although US policies designed to discredit economic and social rights as an integral part of the human rights project began under the Truman administration, they escalated following the election of Dwight Eisenhower in 1952.[45] As is customary with the election of a new president, Roosevelt offered her resignation, and to her disappointment, Eisenhower accepted. The secretary of state and Roosevelt's former associate at the UN, John Foster Dulles, led the charge to eradicate the UN human rights treaty project from the nation's policy objectives.[46] Not until 1966 did the UN General Assembly complete the two covenants, and not until 1992 under the administration of George H. W. Bush did the US government ratify the Covenant on Civil and Political Rights. The United States has yet to adopt the Covenant on Economic, Social, and Cultural Rights.

Conclusion

The leadership choices made by Eleanor Roosevelt during the creation of modern human rights standards have produced competing historical accounts. Roosevelt demonstrated a deep compassion for others and used her influence to ameliorate suffering. Although she did not formulate US policy positions at the United Nations, as the US delegate, Roosevelt executed them with skill and vigor. That she did so in the context of vocal doubts about women's competency as international political actors offers insight into the leadership decisions Roosevelt made. Furthermore, despite her often fierce anticommunism, it was likely Roosevelt's diplomatic craft, specifically her collegiality, that helped to usher the UDHR to passage with Soviet abstentions rather than negative votes.

Roosevelt's commitment to executing her responsibilities as a US delegate ran up against her traditional role as an outspoken advocate for gender and racial equality. In the context of the burgeoning Cold War, Roosevelt prioritized US influence over advocacy on behalf of the NAACP's *Appeal to the World* or the CSW's call to incorporate women's particular rights into the UDHR. In collaborating with the State Department to minimize the *Appeal*'s impact, Roosevelt held firm in her dedication to the US political model (in theory) and the power of individual political and civil rights to transform societies when exercised under a democratic system. This was despite the glaring US shortcomings in practice. Her adherence to US policy on women's rights aligned with domestic feminists' belief that the UDHR's claim to universality embraced rights for women, although it failed to include particular rights such as the government's obligation to provide child care and paid maternity leave, as CSW delegates had hoped.

What does this mean for Roosevelt's leadership legacy? The First Lady of the World employed her international prestige, congenial diplomacy, and political astuteness to advance the US position throughout the UDHR drafting process. At the UN, Roosevelt juggled her long-standing commitment to human rights—civil, political, economic, and social rights—with her obligations as a national delegate. Roosevelt reconciled the disparity by advancing democratic governance as the best option to secure human rights. It held, she believed, a better chance than the Soviet Union's one-party system, which subverted its citizens' political voice even if it purported to provide for basic human needs. Ultimately, US policy positions helped legitimize a human rights framework that privileged political and civil rights over economic and social rights and worked against a system that promoted their interdependence. Roosevelt's understanding of Cold War exigencies bolstered her willingness to advance US policy and thereby contributed to this situation.

In a world that has yet to embrace genuine civil and political rights for all, the concept of what we would today call structural inequality has also yet to become widely accepted. The long-term effects of slavery, failed education systems, and cycles of poverty spawned by landlessness, alongside prolonged disenfranchisement, will not be undone by the ballot alone. Societies built on the foundation of patriarchy, economic systems that devalue unpaid labor, particularly women's reproductive labor, and the concomitant economic disadvantages that perpetuated systems of dependency will not be overturned through the empowerment of individual women. Although conflict and rights violations pervade the global landscape today, human rights activists nonetheless persist in challenging the status quo. The end of the Cold War and renewed attention to human rights—in theory and practice—by organizations like the National Economic and Social Rights Initiative (NESRI) have underscored the interdependence of rights guarantees as essential to promoting the "fundamental freedoms and human rights" mandated by the UN Charter and enshrined in the Universal Declaration of Human Rights.[47]

Activists thus continue to press for a human rights regime with the power to remake the world, as Roosevelt had hoped.

Notes

1 For an interpretation that emphasizes the Allied-partner nations' activism in challenging the reticence of the Big Three (the United States, Britain, and the Soviet Union) to support human rights as a principle and purpose of the UN and the role of nongovernmental organizations and individual activists in pressing for the inclusion of the UN Charter's human rights provisions, see Paul Gordon Lauren, *The Evolution of International Human Rights: Visions Seen*, 3rd ed. (Philadelphia: University of Pennsylvania Press, 2011), 165–194. For the inclusion of human rights because of imperial powers' desire to avoid a system similar to the League of Nations' Minority Treaties, see Mark Mazower, "The Strange Triumph of Human Rights," *Historical Journal* 47, no. 2 (2004): 379–398.

2 The USSR and its allies (the Byelorussian Soviet Social Republic, Czechoslovakia, Poland, the Ukrainian Soviet Socialist Republic, and Yugoslavia) as well as Saudi Arabia and South Africa abstained.

3 Works analyzing Eleanor Roosevelt's leadership are voluminous. For early works, see, for example, Jason Berger, *A New Deal for the World: Eleanor Roosevelt and American Foreign Policy* (New York: Columbia University Press, 1981); Marjorie Lightman and Joan Hoff-Wilson, eds., *Without Precedent: The Life and Career of Eleanor Roosevelt* (Bloomington: Indiana University Press, 1984); Blanche Wiesen Cook, "Eleanor Roosevelt and Human Rights: The Battle for Peace and Planetary Decency," in *Women and American Foreign Policy: Lobbyists, Critics, and Insiders*, ed. Edward Crapol (New York: Greenwood, 1987), 91–119. For the call to historicize human rights, see Kenneth Cmiel, "The Recent History of Human Rights," *American Historical Review* 109, no. 1 (2004): 117–135. For Roosevelt's "pragmatic" leadership, see Mary Ann Glendon, *A World Made New: Eleanor Roosevelt and the Universal Declaration of Human Rights* (New York: Random House, 2001); Allida Black, "Are Women 'Human'? The UN and the Struggle to Recognize Women's Rights as Human Rights," in *The Human Rights Revolution: An International History*, ed. Akira Iriye, Petra Goedde, and William Hitchcock (New York: Oxford University Press, 2011), 133–155. For more skeptical approaches, see Carol Anderson, *Eyes off the Prize: The United Nations and the African American Struggle for Human Rights, 1944–1955* (Cambridge: Cambridge University Press, 2003); Jo Butterfield, "Gendering Universal Human Rights: International Women's Activism, Gender Politics, and the Early Cold War, 1928–1952" (Ph.D. diss., University of Iowa, 2012).

4 Lightman and Hoff-Wilson, introduction to *Without Precedent*, 13.

5 Blanche Wiesen Cook, *Eleanor Roosevelt*, vol. 2, *1933–1938* (New York: Viking Penguin, 1999), 40–41.

6 Eleanor Roosevelt, "My Day," 1 June 1946, folder "My Day, April–June 1946," Eleanor Roosevelt Papers, Franklin D. Roosevelt Presidential Library, Hyde Park, NY.

7   Cook, *Eleanor Roosevelt*, 77–80, 266.

8   Ibid., 563–568.

9   Ibid., 153–189.

10 UN Doc. A/PV/180 (9 December 1948).

11 Anderson, *Eyes off the Prize*, 102.

12 See the numerous letters in the White House Central Files: Office Files, Box 528, Folder J—Endorsement, United Nations General Assembly (1945–46), Harry S. Truman Library, Independence, MO.

13 Alice McDiarmid to Alger Hiss, 16 November 1945, State Department memo, Lot File 61-D-146, box 20, folder "General Assembly," Alger Hiss Papers, 1940–1946, General Records of the Department of State, Records Group 59, National Archives and Records Administration, College Park, MD.

14 Rachel Nason to Constance Williams, 21 March 46, box 7, folder A-37-143, Frieda Segelke Miller Papers, Arthur and Elizabeth Schlesinger Library, Radcliffe Institute, Harvard University, Cambridge, MA.

15 See, for example, Alice Morgan Wright to Alice Paul, 20 April 1946, Microfilm Records, reel 175, National Woman's Party Papers 1913–1973, ed. Thomas Pardo (Glenn Rock, NJ: Microfilming Corporation of American, 1977–1978), University of Iowa Libraries.

16 Amelia Himes Walker to Alice Paul, 17 January 1946, box 104, folder 1379, Alice Paul Papers, Arthur and Elizabeth Schlesinger Library, Radcliffe Institute, Harvard University, Cambridge, MA.

17 See, for example, Roosevelt's invitation to the Inter-American Commission of Women. "Las mujeres de las Américas afrontarán las responsabilidades en la postguerra," no date or publication information listed, series B, box 11, folder "Inter-American Commission of Women," People's Mandate Committee Records, Swarthmore Peace Collection; and "My Day," 5 December 1942, in *My Day by Eleanor Roosevelt: The Best of Eleanor Roosevelt's Acclaimed Newspaper Columns, 1936–1962*, ed. David Emblidge (New York: MJF Books, 2001), 73.

18 Special thanks to the University of Iowa Center for Human Rights intern Julia Julstrom-Agoyo for her work collecting the statistics on women in the United Nations. Statistics based on United Nations, "The Yearbook of the United Nations," http://unyearbook.un.org/. Several delegates who served on a commission also sat for General Assembly sessions. Yet not a single woman served on a United Nations International Court of Justice or a council (Economic and Social Council, Security Council, or Trusteeship Council), the other principle organs of the new international organization.

19 See, for example, "UN Women's Unit Chided on Ambition," *New York Times*, 15 May 1946; *Time*, 20 May 1946, 23, which describes various delegates as "the best-looking of commission members," "black-eyed and soft-spoken," "petite and brunette," and "tall, blue-eyed"; "Men Delegates Talk Too Much," *Washington Post*, 27 July 1946.

20 UN Doc. A/46 (12 February 1946).

21 Eleanor Roosevelt, *What I Hope to Leave Behind*, ed. Allida Black (New York: Carlson, 1995), 35.

22 Butterfield, "Gendering Universal Human Rights," 294–300, 314–322.

23 Virginia Crocheron Gildersleeve, *Many a Good Crusade: Memoirs of Virginia Crocheron Gildersleeve* (New York: Macmillan, 1952), 353.

24 Quoted in Steve Neal, introduction to chap. 2, in *Eleanor and Harry: The Correspondence of Eleanor Roosevelt and Harry S. Truman*, ed. Neal (New York: Scribner, 2002), 53.

25 Eleanor Roosevelt, *The Autobiography of Eleanor Roosevelt* (1961; repr., New York: Da Capo, 1992), 299.

26 Ibid., 305; Eleanor Roosevelt, *On My Own* (New York: HarperCollins, 1958), 47.

27 Marjorie Lightman and Joan Hoff-Wilson, introduction to *Without Precedent: The Life and Career of Eleanor Roosevelt*, ed. Lightman and Hoff-Wilson (Bloomington: Indiana University Press, 1984), vii.

28 James Hendrick to James Simsarian, 27 July 1948, confidential memo, box 8, folder "Human Rights General," Subject Files of Durward Sandifer: Department Assistant Secretary of State for United Nations Affairs, 1944–1954, United States National Archives and Records Administration, College Park, MD. Hereafter cited as Sandifer files.

29 Eleanor Roosevelt, "My Day," 13 September 1947, in *My Day by Eleanor Roosevelt*, 129.

30 James Hendrick to Dean Rusk, 7 July 1948, quoted in Anderson, *Eyes off the Prize*, 133.

31 Hendrick to Simsarian, 27 July 1948.

32 See, for example, Dr. Helen Wright Reid's reply to Roosevelt's query, 28 December 1945, box 4561, folder UN: General Correspondence, November–December, 1945, Eleanor Roosevelt Papers.

33 Truman established the International Social Policy Committee (ISP) to better coordinate UN policy in 1947. See Records Group 353, United States National Archives and Records Administration, College Park, MD. Hereafter cited as ISP records.

34 Roosevelt, *Autobiography*, 306.

35 Ibid., 306–307.

36 A. Glenn Mower, Jr., *The United States, the United Nations, and Human Rights: The Eleanor Roosevelt and Jimmy Carter Eras* (Westport, CT: Greenwood, 1979), 39.

37 Blanche Wiesen Cook, *Eleanor Roosevelt*, vol. 3 (New York: Penguin Random House, forthcoming).

38 UN Doc. E/CN.6/SR.64 (8 June 1948).

39 See, for example, Roosevelt's protest over passing the declaration without the covenant in Department of State Memorandum of Conversation, 24 August 1948, box 8, folder "Human Rights Council," Sandifer files.

40 For a persuasively argued account of the US government's and Roosevelt's handling of the NAACP petition, see Anderson, *Eyes off the Prize*, 93–148.

41 Roosevelt maintained her position on the board only after Walter White promised a more conciliatory approach. See Anderson, *Eyes off the Prize*, 112.

42 Helen Sater to Frieda Miller, 4 May 1946, Records Group 86, box 10, folder C-H-4-1-2-3, US Department of Labor, Women's Bureau Records, United States National Archives and Records Administration, College Park, MD.

43 UN Doc. E/CN.4/AC.1/SR.13 (20 June 1947); Supplement 2 to S/HRW D-35/48 Rev. 1 (10 May 1948), 13:4A Subcommittee 3, box 111, documents 2–35, 1948, ISP records.

44 Dorothy Kenyon, "Freedom and Equality," *Independent Woman*, March 1949, box 21 folder 3, Dorothy Kenyon Papers, Sophia Smith Collection, Smith College, North Hampton, MA.

45 Roger Normand and Sarah Zaidi, *Human Rights at the UN: The Political History of Universal Justice* (Bloomington: Indiana University Press, 2008), 197–246.

46 Dulles's pronouncement to Congress that the United States would withdraw from the treaty process was in an effort to kill the proposed Bricker Amendment to the US Constitution, which would have hampered the presidential prerogative to negotiate treaties.

47 See the National Economic and Social Rights Initiative website: https://www.nesri.org/.

Bibliography

Anderson, Carol. *Eyes off the Prize: The United Nations and the African American Struggle for Human Rights, 1944–1955*. Cambridge: Cambridge University Press, 2003.

Berger, Jason. *A New Deal for the World: Eleanor Roosevelt and American Foreign Policy*. New York: Columbia University Press, 1981.

Black, Allida. "Are Women 'Human'? The UN and the Struggle to Recognize Women's Rights as Human Rights." In *The Human Rights Revolution: An International History*, edited by Akira Iriye, Petra Goedde, and William Hitchcock, 133–155. New York: Oxford University Press, 2011.

Butterfield, Jo. "Gendering Universal Human Rights: International Women's Activism, Gender Politics, and the Early Cold War, 1928–1952." Ph.D. diss., University of Iowa, 2012.

Cmiel, Kenneth. "The Recent History of Human Rights." *American Historical Review* 109, no. 1 (2004): 117–135.

Cook, Blanche Wiesen. *Eleanor Roosevelt*. Vol. 2, *The Defining Years, 1933–1938*. New York: Viking Penguin, 1999.

———. *Eleanor Roosevelt*. Vol. 3 New York: Penguin Random House, forthcoming.

———. "Eleanor Roosevelt and Human Rights: The Battle for Peace and Planetary Decency." In *Women and American Foreign Policy: Lobbyists, Critics, and Insiders*, edited by Edward Crapol, 91–119. New York: Greenwood, 1987.

Department of State Memorandum of Conversation. 24 August 1948, box 8, folder "Human Rights Council," Subject Files of Durward Sandifer: Department Assistant Secretary of State for United Nations Affairs, 1944–1954, United States National Archives and Records Administration, College Park, MD.

Gildersleeve, Virginia Crocheron. *Many a Good Crusade: Memoirs of Virginia Crocheron Gildersleeve*. New York: Macmillan, 1952.

Glendon, Mary Ann. *A World Made New: Eleanor Roosevelt and the Universal Declaration of Human Rights*. New York: Random House, 2001.

Hendrick, James, to James Simsarian, 27 July 1948. Confidential memo, box 8, folder "Human Rights General," Subject Files of Durward Sandifer: Department Assistant Secretary of State for United Nations Affairs, 1944–1954, United States National Archives and Records Administration, College Park, MD.

Kenyon, Dorothy. "Freedom and Equality." *Independent Woman*, March 1949. Box 21, folder 3, Dorothy Kenyon Papers, Sophia Smith Collection, Smith College, North Hampton, MA.

"Las mujeres de las Américas afrontarán las responsabilidades en la postguerra." No date or publication information listed. Series B, box 11, folder "Inter-American Commission of Women," People's Mandate Committee Records, Swarthmore Peace Collection.

Lauren, Paul Gordon. *The Evolution of International Human Rights: Visions Seen*. 3rd ed. Philadelphia: University of Pennsylvania Press, 2011.

Lightman, Marjorie, and Joan Hoff-Wilson, eds. *Without Precedent: The Life and Career of Eleanor Roosevelt*. Bloomington: Indiana University Press, 1984.

Mazower, Mark. "The Strange Triumph of Human Rights." *Historical Journal* 47, no. 2 (2004): 379–398.

McDiarmid, Alice, to Alger Hiss, 16 November 1945. State Department memo, Lot File 61-D-146, box 20, folder "General Assembly," Alger Hiss Papers, 1940–1946, General Records of the Department of State, Records Group 59, National Archives and Records Administration, College Park, MD.

"Men Delegates Talk Too Much." *Washington Post*, 27 July 1946.

Mower, Alfred Glenn, Jr. *The United States, the United Nations, and Human Rights: The Eleanor Roosevelt and Jimmy Carter Eras*. Westport, CT: Greenwood, 1979.

Nason, Rachel, to Constance Williams, 21 March 46. Box 7, folder A-37-143, Frieda Segelke Miller Papers, Arthur and Elizabeth Schlesinger Library, Radcliffe Institute, Harvard University, Cambridge, MA.

Neal, Steve, ed. *Eleanor and Harry: The Correspondence of Eleanor Roosevelt and Harry S. Truman*. New York: Scribner, 2002.

Normand, Roger, and Sarah Zaidi. *Human Rights at the UN: The Political History of Universal Justice*. Bloomington: Indiana University Press, 2008.

Records Group 353. United States National Archives and Records Administration, College Park, MD.

Reid, Helen Wright. Reply to Roosevelt, 28 December 1945. Box 4561, folder UN: General Correspondence, November–December, 1945, Eleanor Roosevelt Papers.

Roosevelt, Eleanor. *The Autobiography of Eleanor Roosevelt*. 1961. Reprint, New York: Da Capo, 1992.

———. "My Day," 1 June 1946. Folder "My Day, April–June 1946," Eleanor Roosevelt Papers, Franklin D. Roosevelt Presidential Library, Hyde Park, NY.

———. *My Day by Eleanor Roosevelt: The Best of Eleanor Roosevelt's Acclaimed Newspaper Columns, 1936–1962*. Edited by David Emblidge. New York: MJF Books, 2001.

———. *On My Own*. New York: HarperCollins, 1958.

———. *What I Hope to Leave Behind*. Edited by Allida Black. New York: Carlson, 1995.

Sater, Helen, to Frieda Miller, 4 May 1946. Records Group 86, box 10, folder C-H-4-1-2-3, US Department of Labor, Women's Bureau Records, United States National Archives and Records Administration, College Park, MD.

Supplement 2 to S/HRW D-35/48 Rev. 1 (10 May 1948). 13:4A Subcommittee 3, box 111, documents 2–35, 1948, Records Group 353, United States National Archives and Records Administration, College Park, MD.

Time, 20 May 1946, 23.

UN Doc. A/46. 12 February 1946.

UN Doc. A/PV/180. 9 December 1948.

UN Doc. E/CN.4/AC.1/SR.13, 20 June 1947. Supplement 2 to S/HRW D-35/48 Rev. 1 (10 May 1948), 13:4A Subcommittee 3, box 111, documents 2–35, 1948, Records Group 353, United States National Archives and Records Administration, College Park, MD.

UN Doc. E/CN.6/SR.64. 8 June 1948.

United Nations. "The Yearbook of the United Nations." http://unyearbook.un.org/.

"UN Women's Unit Chided on Ambition." *New York Times*, 15 May 1946.

Walker, Amelia Himes, to Alice Paul, January 17, 1946. Box 104, folder 1379, Alice Paul Papers, Arthur and Elizabeth Schlesinger Library, Radcliffe Institute, Harvard University, Cambridge, MA.

White House Central Files: Office Files. Box 528, Folder J—Endorsement, United Nations General Assembly (1945–46), Harry S. Truman Library, Independence, MO.

Wright, Alice Morgan, to Alice Paul, 20 April 1946. Microfilm Records, reel 175, National Woman's Party Papers 1913–1973, edited by Thomas Pardo. Glenn Rock, NJ: Microfilming Corporation of American, 1977–1978. University of Iowa Libraries.

Daisy Bates

The NAACP

Bridget Gurtler

<h3>Background</h3>

On September 2, 1957, Daisy Bates sat in her home and watched the governor of Arkansas give a televised address. Governor Orval Eugene Faubus announced that he was concerned about violence in Little Rock, Arkansas. He had received such a quantity of vitriolic mail expressing "discord, anger and resentment" over the forced integration of Little Rock High School that he deemed it a veritable "deluge."[1] He announced, "the inevitable conclusion therefore, must be that the schools in Pulaski County must be operated in the same manner in which they have been operated in the past. . . . THE PUBLIC PEACE WILL BE PRESERVED!"[2] In direct opposition to a federal court order to integrate the schools and allow black students to enroll, Faubus stated that he was calling out the National Guard to surround the school on opening day (September 4) to prevent black students from entering and to keep the peace. Furthermore, the governor testified that white Little Rock citizens were arming themselves for the coming conflict.[3]

This crisis was the culmination of years of debate and negotiation in the Little Rock community and the nation over the effects of segregation on black children and what steps should be taken to alleviate harmful inequalities in schooling. Daisy Bates, the president of the Arkansas chapter of the National Association for the Advancement of Colored People (NAACP), a small but strong-willed, one-hundred-pound, five-foot-three woman, had been on the front lines for the battle to integrate Little Rock schools. But in the wake of Faubus's address, it became clear that it would not be just Bates and other adult leaders who would fall under fire; now it would be children. Some parents, fearing for their children's safety, had decided that their children would not enter Central High School on opening day. From the initial sixteen willing students, the number had dropped to nine as the day of integration approached. Bates would need to draw on all of her knowledge and powers of persuasion gleaned from her years leading the Arkansas NAACP chapter and her abilities to gauge how and when racial tensions might tip over into violence (developed over a lifetime of experiencing racism) and to weigh the potential gains of moving forward with the students against the prospective harm to herself, the children and their families, the Little Rock community, and the civil rights movement more broadly. How could she ethically, safely, and successfully lead in this pivotal moment?

The Early Years

From a small town in the very corner of southern Arkansas, Daisy Bates's early years were shadowed with debate and hardship. Bates was born in 1913 in Huttig, a small sawmill town in southeast Arkansas. A racially segregated town, it was like many others in the Delta—full of inadequate schools for black children, shotgun houses, and spoken and unspoken social rules governing relations between the races, sexes, and ages. Bates, whose official name was Daisy Lee Gatson, was raised by her foster mother and foster father, Susie and Orlee Smith. The identity of her birth parents has remained a subject of historical debate, as has her birth mother's fate. Bates herself believed that her birth mother had been raped and murdered and that her body was dumped in a local pond. Although local newspapers at the time never reported on the violent death of a woman listed on Bates's birth certificate, Millie Riley, the story is often repeated in popular renditions of Bates's childhood.[4] Bates herself also later referred to learning about her mother, as well as a critical event at age seven of being denied meat at the butcher's because she was black, as the catalyst for her intense anger for and resistance to all systems and expressions of racism. However, her foster father's experiences also played a formative role in Bates's identity development. In her memoir, Bates recalls the impact that her foster father, a veteran of World War I, had on her. "How I loved this strong man who all his life had not been able to use his strength in the way he wanted to. He was forced to suppress it and hold himself back, bow to the white yoke or be cut down."[5] In later years, Bates said, "I have been angry all of my life. . . . I was so tight inside . . . it gave me the strength. . . . My father encouraged me to channel it into something creative. . . . Nothing prepared me [for leadership] more than my anger."[6]

As a young woman, Bates married L. C. (Lucius Christopher) Bates, a family friend from Mississippi who was twelve years her senior. L. C. Bates was a man of education and life experience who was an insurance salesman and then newspaperman. However, their early years of courtship were, purposefully, veiled. L. C. Bates had a prior marriage, and historical records point toward the fact that it was unlikely dissolved in divorce until the early 1940s, around ten years after Daisy and L. C. had set up a home together in Little Rock, Arkansas. It was only in 1942, after L. C. decided to launch a newspaper, that the need to appear respectable to the community pushed the couple to solemnize their vows in the small town of Fordyce, outside of Little Rock.

Writing and Advocating in Little Rock

The *State Press*, in print from 1941 until 1959, was the primary love and brainchild of L. C. It, following in the footsteps of black papers like the *Chicago Defender* and *Kansas City Call*, offered its readers stories about the struggle for civil rights while they were also being entertained and informed about broader happenings in the black community—from beauty pageants to local municipal court cases.[7] Above all, however, the *State Press* was about advocacy. Whether about issues of black voting or discrimination on the job, its point of view was aimed at the black community and its uplift and, in so doing, was seen by many white community members as inflammatory. Indeed, at one point L. C. had to switch printing companies after a white-owned press objected to and refused to print one of his editions. Daisy Bates's biographer, Grif Stockley, argues that it was in the context of running the paper that Bates received much of her education.[8]

Through working with the paper, Daisy and L. C. began to know leaders in business, advocacy, and thought communities in the Little Rock area. One of the most significant friendships they formed in this manner was with Harold Flowers, a lawyer who founded his own antidiscrimination group, the Committee on Negro Organizations, after being unable to obtain help from the NAACP. The paper even ran a front-page story on Flowers's group in 1942 with the headline "He Founded a Movement."[9] Flowers's perspective on social change was that African Americans should exercise their political capital through the vote and should demand change (rather than accept what changes whites instituted)—a perspective that Daisy agreed with and brought to her work with the NAACP.

The NAACP was founded in 1909 and had been working toward desegregation and social justice for blacks nationwide for thirty years by the time Daisy Bates became acquainted with it. By the 1940s, it was undergoing significant upheaval as it struggled to decide how militant the NAACP should be while simultaneously attempting to expand its organizational base in the South. Leading the Arkansas chapter of the NAACP as its president was the Reverend Marcus Taylor, a conservative who also headed the Little Rock branch. Under Taylor, the chief organizer of branches was the Bateses' friend Harold Flowers. Echoing the larger battle over the nature of the organization, Bates and Flowers both attempted to oust Taylor and institute more aggressive (rather than merely reactive) policies. Flowers ran for president of the Arkansas chapter (successfully) in 1948. Bates attempted to form a new branch in Pulaski County and nominated herself as president. However, the national office refused since most of the required membership subscriptions (over fifty) she had gathered to begin a new branch actually held addresses in Little Rock and thus, it argued, should join that existing branch. Unbowed, Bates bided her time by first becoming the cochair of the NAACP State Conference Committee for Fair Employment Practices and then, in 1952, being elected as president of the State Conference of Branches. Now, she presided over all of the NAACP chapters in the southern state of Arkansas. Thus, unlike most other women of color in the civil rights movement, Bates held a formal position of power. At the same time, not everyone was comfortable with her (nontraditional) tactics and strategies, a charge often levied at women leaders in social movements. In the words of U. Simpson Tate, the NAACP counsel for the Southwest region, "[Bates] tends to go off the deep end at times on various issues. [Yet] there was no one else to be elected who offered any promise of doing any thing to further the work of the NAACP in Arkansas. I am not certain that she was the proper person to be elected, but I am certain that she was the most likely person of those present at the Conference."[10] Nevertheless, this was a major accomplishment for anyone, much less someone who had no more than two years of training beyond high school.

Integration and the "Little Rock Nine"

On May 17, 1954, the US Supreme Court handed down its decision in the *Brown v. Board of Education* case. Unanimously the court found that, in the words of Chief Justice Earl Warren, "to separate [children in grade and high schools] from others of similar age and qualifications solely because of their race generates a feeling of inferiority as to their status in the community that may affect their hearts and minds in a way unlikely to ever be undone." Educational opportunity was deemed a "right that must be made available to all on equal terms." The doctrine of "separate but equal" had "no place" in the United States. The Supreme Court found that "separate educational facilities are inherently unequal."[11] As important a decision as it was, its impact on the ground was not immediately apparent, neither nationally nor in Arkansas.

After the decision, Virgil Blossom, the superintendent for the Little Rock schools, informed the community via a series of talks to various groups (black and white) across the city about plans for integration, a plan that would by no means happen that year. Citing the need to complete the building of additional school buildings and for delay in order to "do the job right" of integrating an intended two to three hundred black students into Little Rock schools, Blossom appeared to think that the black community would accept his assurances in good faith. Many people did, but Daisy Bates and the NAACP did not.

As Blossom continued his presentations to the community, Bates attended as many of the events as possible. Bates recalled, "He made a speech at the YWCA: I was there. He made a speech in Pleasant Valley, I was there. And this burned him up. . . . And it tickled me to death. . . . He knew I was there, see, because he had been saying one thing to whites . . . and one thing to Negroes."[12] Beautifully and conservatively dressed, unfailingly courteous and smiling, Bates would stand up during question-and-answer sessions and ask Blossom about comments he had made at other speeches. For instance, when recalling her exchanges with Blossom, she said, "When you spoke for the group at the YWCA, . . . did you say this?" and he would respond embarrassedly, "I didn't say *that*."[13] One school board member was quoted as saying that the Blossom Plan was meant to "provide as little integration as possible for as long as possible legally."[14] In fact, it was not until a year later, in May 1955, that a plan for gradual integration was unanimously approved by the school board. The Little Rock school board was the first in the South to draw up a plan for the progressive (albeit slow) integration of schools.

The Bateses opposed the plan on the grounds that it was "vague, indefinite, slow-moving and indicative of an intent to stall further on public integration."[15] Despite the fact that a majority of people accepted the plan, the Bateses' view turned out to be correct, as changes were shortly made to the plan that allowed students to move out of the zones of attendance to which they were assigned. This constituted a gerrymandering of the districts, with the result that even though black students might live closer to Central High, they would be placed back into the black high school, Horace Mann.

Bates demanded that Blossom integrate the schools. But he refused to do so, and on February 8, 1956, the NAACP sued the school board. In the hearings that resulted, Bates was present and used not only legal arguments but also her femininity, respectability, and the social norms around address and polite behavior that were supposed to accompany them. More specifically, Bates became angered by the way in which the school board's lawyer, Leon Catlett, continually referred to the NAACP as possessing "nigger" leaders and to herself as "Daisy." Bates leaned forward in her chair in the courtroom and said, "Leon, it is true that my name is Daisy. But only my husband and my close personal friends may call me by that name. You are not a friend of mine. And you may either call me Mrs. Bates, or you may call me nothing at all!" Flustered, Catlett chose to not call her anything at all.[16] The judge ruled that Central High would have to be integrated by 1957. Blossom's next step was to begin to try to disqualify the students who had been selected by the NAACP to transfer, despite the fact that the very reason they had been selected was because of their high grades and good attendance records. However, political winds blew against the adoption of the Blossom Plan since Governor Faubus, elected in 1954, decided to take a segregationist stand on September 2, 1957. Claiming concerns about the potential for mob violence, the governor gave a speech announcing that the schools would continue to operate in a segregated manner and that the public peace would be preserved. He called out the Arkansas National Guard to surround Central High and help him to prevent black students from entering.

In an early draft of Bates's memoir, she recalled that her immediate reaction to Faubus's declaration was to verify it herself. At seven o'clock in the evening, guarded by a friend with a shotgun, Bates drove over to the high school: "Took off for Central . . . [and] parked a block away. Could see soldiers unloading, taking their places. Saw reporters going, trying to talk, soldiers wouldn't talk, Car radio, Flashed over, Natnl Guards around school. Nobody knew what meant. Governor to speak. Brown uniforms. Helmets. Full combat, boots, Canopied trucks, Just the regular thing, just like a war."[17] Bates spent all day on September 3 speaking with the students' parents, who were terrified that mob violence might erupt and that harm would come to their children. Bates believed (or wanted to encourage the public to believe), however, that Faubus would actually try to prevent damage to "life and property" and went on to publicly state in the papers, "No, it was inconceivable that troops, and responsible citizens, would stand by and let a mob attack children."[18]

Bates also used her femininity in support of her cause in her relationship with the media. Her biographer says, "she radiated tastefulness and dignity."[19] Reporters saw Bates as an ideal representative to interview on the segregation debates. She spoke on behalf of the children and their parents, and she was attractive, beautifully dressed, calm, and attuned to the needs of the media. She almost never said "no comment"; rather, she offered a humanization of what had prior been a battle conducted in the courts. She spoke of "kids" rather than plaintiffs.[20] In a sense, she effectively connected the private sphere (the experience of racism, especially by children) with the public sphere of the civil rights movement itself. Her words, however, were not just her own; many were carefully written for her by L. C. and others in the movement. She was also the center of a storm of information, as the Little Rock Nine member Ernest Green later pointed out. She and L. C. knew many reporters, as colleagues and as friends. Describing Daisy, Green stated, "She was the most media-savvy person around us. She had this wide array of newspaper reporters. . . . All of these people were close friends of theirs. Not only would they cover the story, but at the end of the day, they were always hanging out in Daisy's house smoking cigars, drinking liquor, and swapping stories. So that while she was the center of this [controversy], she was also the center of all of this information."[21] Daisy worked hard to keep the controversy in the news, but some people around her joked that she could not pass by a camera without stopping for an interview. Many people at the time, and after, noted that she was always smiling into the cameras.

Later in the evening of September 3, Superintendent Blossom called a meeting with the children's parents and other leading members of the African American community to tell them how he wanted September 4, the day to attempt to enter the school, to proceed. He did not invite Daisy Bates. However, Bates later wrote, "the parents asked me to be present." Blossom asked parents not to accompany their children, arguing that it would be easier to protect them if the adults were not present. Neither Bates nor the parents left the meeting assured that the children would be protected. Adding to her concern, at ten o'clock that evening, a reporter came to warn her of the gravity of the situation. As she recalled in her mem-oir, the reporter said,

> "Look, Daisy . . . I know about the Superintendent's instructions. I know he said the children must go alone to Central in the morning. But let me tell you this is murder!" [Daisy thought,] He knew how ugly the whites were going to be the next morning. "I heard those people today, I've never seen anything like it, people I've known all my life—they've gone mad. They're totally without reason. You must know you can't expect much protection—if any—from the city police. Besides, the city police are barred from the school grounds! . . . [And] new recruits are pouring into the city from outlying areas. Even from other states. By morning there could be several thousand."[22]

After hearing this report, Bates "sat huddled in her chair, dazed, try-ing to think, yet not knowing what to do."[23] Violence seemed almost inevitable, and the lives and safety of the children weighed on her heavily. Was there any way that the children could be protected? If not, should they go forward with the plan to enter the school in the morning? Who, if anyone, could she depend on and mobilize to help? She picked up the phone, knowing that all of her work and the safety of the children could depend on the decision she made now.

Resolution

Late on the evening before the children were to enter Central High, Bates thought of a new plan to offer some protection to the children while also following Blossom's orders to keep parents and other African American adults away from the procession into the school. She picked up the phone and called Dunbar Ogden, Jr., the presi-dent of the newly formed Interracial Ministerial Alliance and minis-ter of Little Rock's (white) Central Presbyterian Church. She asked him if he could rally fifteen other of his white ministerial colleagues to walk the children into Central High. Ogden was quite shocked to get the call but agreed to ask other ministers in the area if they would be willing. When he finally called her back, it was to say that most had not been receptive to the idea. But his mind had been made up, and he would keep trying to convince his colleagues: "God willing, I'll be there."[24] Bates did not stop there. She called the police and asked for a car to take the children and ministers to the school in the morning. Finally, she called all the parents to inform them of the plan and then fell exhausted into bed. As Carolyn Calloway-Thomas and Thurmon Garner have pointed out, the orchestration of the children's and their parents' movements (to the level of detail of planning when they should arrive at Bates's home, the route they should take to school, and what door they should use) was a feat of organizational prowess.[25]

The next day dawned, and amid planning how to counter lawsuits against the NAACP later in the afternoon, Bates got in the car to meet the students and ministers. On the way, the news on the radio announced that a "Negro girl is being mobbed at Central High."[26] One student, Elizabeth Eckford, without a phone at her house had not gotten the message about where to meet and to wait for the escort. L. C. jumped out of the car, and after Elizabeth was turned away from the school by the National Guard, L. C. (along with the *New York Times* reporter Benjamin Fine and Grace Lorch) sat on a bench with her, amid a jeering crowd, to wait for a bus and a ride to safety.

The other students, with four white ministers in front of them and four black ministers behind them, were also turned away from Central High by the National Guard under Faubus's orders. The whole group was told to report to the local FBI office. After national political wrangling between President Eisenhower and Faubus and further court orders, the attempted entrance to school was to be repeated on September 23, but this time without the protection of the National Guard. However, as the mob focused its rage on both black and white reporters that morning, the students were able to enter a side entrance to the school. The mob of more than a thousand, however, after throwing bottles at passing cars and screaming racial epithets, caused police chiefs to deem the situation too risky for the students, and they were escorted out of the school by noon.

The photographs of little Elizabeth Eckford being heckled by a mob and the inability of students to be safe in school were a public-relations nightmare on an international stage. Amid Cold War anxieties about the status of democracy, President Eisenhower finally took a stand. On September 24, he signed a proclamation ordering all persons in Arkansas who were willfully disobeying the federal district court's order to desegregate to "cease and desist." To force his proclamation to stand, Eisenhower federalized the Arkansas National Guard and ordered one thousand troopers from the 101st Airborne Division to be deployed to Little Rock. Soldiers would escort the nine students into Central High, and as one young Little Rock Nine member put it, "As they came to Mrs. Bates's house to pick me up for school, for the first time I felt like a true American."[27] Bates's reaction was more complicated and measured. She wondered, "As I watched history unfold before my eyes, I was frightened. Frightened to death. All the weeks of pressures, threats, intimidations, and sleepless nights came down on me. Had I made the right decision? In honestly seeking justice, had I helped my people? Or was this day the result of a vendetta I had made against all white people? I was suddenly a little girl again sitting on the banks of a mill pond filled with hatred and pain that no child of eight or adult of seventy should ever experience."[28]

Although later historical scholarship proved that Bates's memoir and indeed her memory of the events surrounding the Little Rock Nine were exaggerated, her idea of using ministers to escort the children into school on September 4 was inspired. Stockley believes that it may well have saved them from more egregious forms of intimidation or beatings. Even the superintendent of the school board, Blossom, said of Bates, "Mrs. Bates . . . was a woman of great energy with an aggressive, crusading spirit. She was an efficient organizer and enjoyed her role as a leading figure in the state's NAACP."[29] However, her choices did not please everyone. Trying to explain the hard feelings among the black community about her handling of the integration crisis, Bates said, "I was doing something [the Little Rock Community] couldn't. I was an outsider and stirring up trouble. And this 1957 activity showed them up."[30] Some of the parents got shut out of the process, and in interviews long after the event, it is clear that parents resented this. Some of the Little Rock Nine students thought, in fact, that their parents, many better educated and more connected in the community than Bates was, could have done better.

On a more personal level, in the aftermath of the crisis, the *Arkansas Press* was forced to close because segregationists in Little Rock had advertisers withdraw their advertisements. Neither of the Bateses could get a job in town because prospective employers feared that their businesses would be the focus of reprisals. Because of this, the Bates family was in financial straits. Campaigns popped up in Kansas City and Philadelphia calling for "Dollars for Daisy Bates," and the receipts were sent to the couple to enable them to continue their fight. Daisy Bates began penning her book *The Daisy Bates Story* to help raise additional funds for her and L. C.

Bates's decision to be the public face of integration had real and hard consequences for her and her husband. For instance, the African American Democratic congressman Charles C. Diggs, Jr., was a guest at the Bates home in December 1959, years after the integration of Central High occurred, and he described their living conditions as "Fortress America." He said that they were forced to live behind walls because they feared for their lives. The home itself had a spotlight on it all night, and the front picture window had a steel barricade put in to block bombs or other objects that might be thrown at the house. Furthermore, an armed guard (Ellis Thomas, the father of a black student who entered an all-white school and subsequently lost his job because of it) was present twenty-four hours a day. After Diggs's visit, he called a press conference denouncing the situation and wrote a letter to President Eisenhower and a detailed report of his findings to the Justice Department. He suggested that Ike appeal to the decency of adults by addressing joint assemblies at Central and Hill High Schools and at the University of Alabama. He was particularly horrified at the regular abuse the children were receiving from other children in the integrated schools— physical beatings and intimidation—"sneak" attacks that the children said they were unable to stop because they did not want to report it and be considered nuisances or cry babies.[31] He said the pupils were being called vile names, spit upon, threatened, elbowed in the corridors or on the stairs, struck and kicked from behind, tripped and otherwise molested in the cafeteria.

Bates continued to speak out and work for integration and civil rights, however. She joined the Central High parent-teacher organization and found ways to keep informed of what sorts of interactions the Little Rock Nine had with white students. She traveled widely supporting integration and also spoke at various events. For instance, in October 1959, she was the guest speaker for the Metropolitan Baptist Church's Annual Woman's Day in Newark, New Jersey. In her capacity as speaker on the theme of "love, sympathy, and understanding," she outlined not only the doings of the Little Rock Nine and the Arkansas NAACP but also the "many duties of our women to our homes, churches and communities."[32] Her leadership abilities are best understood as deeply embedded in the social relations and norms that shaped women's participation in the movement. She was in many ways what the sociologist Belinda Robnett has called a "bridge leader."[33] She was a woman whose extraordinary activism and willingness to take risks enabled her to emerge as an NAACP leader during a period of intense crisis around integration. She continued to be a leader and figure within the movement but because of gendered politics of exclusion never rose higher in the NAACP and even at one of the most important events in the history of the civil rights movement, the 1963 March on Washington, was relegated to the background. All of the above are hallmarks of bridge leadership—loosely defined as the situations and actions that black women leaders take and face within social movements. However, the legal, educational, and social legacy of Little Rock and Daisy Bates's work there remains—integrated schools in the United States and a pivotal shift in broad popular sentiment about the civil rights movement. Nationally and internationally, a large swath of the public supported the nine courageous students who faced down a mob to gain the right to an equal education and applauded the eloquent woman who helped them do so. In her own words, Bates thought her most important contribution was "the very fact that the kids went in Central. They got in. . . . And they remained there for the full year. And that opened a lot of doors that had been closed to Negroes, because this was the first time that this kind of revolution had succeeded without a doubt."[34] In the words of the NAACP officer Kwisi Mfume, "She was a true American hero. She was a model for all of us then and now. She was a heroine."[35]

Notes

1 Orval E. Faubus, "Speech of Governor Orval E. Faubus, September 2, 1957," available at Southern Colloquium on Rhetoric, http://southerncolloqrhetoric .net/web/resources/Faubus570902.pdf.

2 Ibid.

3 Grif Stockley, *Daisy Bates: Civil Rights Crusader from Arkansas* (Jackson: University Press of Mississippi, 2005), 113.

4 Ibid., 17.

5 Quoted in ibid., 19.

6 Daisy Bates, interview by Elizabeth Jacoway, October 11, 1976, G-0009, in the Southern Oral History Program Collection #4007, Southern Historical Collection, Wilson Library, University of North Carolina at Chapel Hill, http:// docsouth.unc.edu/sohp/G-0009/G-0009.html.

7 Stockley, *Daisy Bates*, 28.

8 Ibid., 28.

9 For more on Flowers, see John A. Kirk, "He Founded a Movement: W. H. Flowers, the Committee on Negro Organizations and Black Activism in Arkansas, 1940–1957," in *The Making of Martin Luther King and the Civil Rights Movement in America*, ed. Brian Ward and Tony Badter (London: Macmillan, 1996), 29–44.

10 Stockley, *Daisy Bates*, 58.

11 *Oliver Brown, et al. v. Board of Education of Topeka, et al.*, 347 US 483, 493, 495, 496 (1954).

12 Quoted in Stockley, *Daisy Bates*, 68.

13 Ibid., 68.

14 Roy Reed, *Faubus: The Life and Times of an American Prodigal* (Fayetteville: University of Arkansas Press, 1997), 184.

15 John A. Kirk, "The Little Rock Crisis and Postwar Black Activism in Arkansas," *Arkansas Historical Quarterly* 60 (2007): 239.

16 Friend of Daisy Bates, interview in the documentary film "Daisy Bates: First Lady of Little Rock," dir. Sharon La Cruise, *Independent Lens*, PBS (Sakkara Films, 2010), http://www.pbs.org/independentlens/daisy-bates/.

17 Daisy Bates, draft of *The Long Shadow of Little Rock: A Memoir* (Fayetteville: University of Arkansas Press, 2007), 61, quoted in Stockley, *Daisy Bates*, 115.

18 Bates, interview in "Daisy Bates: First Lady of Little Rock."

19 Stockley, *Daisy Bates*, 54.

20 Ibid., 132.

21 Ernest Green (Little Rock Nine member), interview in "Daisy Bates: First Lady of Little Rock."

22 Bates, *Long Shadow of Little Rock*, 63–64.

23 Stockley, *Daisy Bates*, 121.
24 Quoted in Bates, *Long Shadow of Little Rock*, 65.
25 Carolyn Calloway-Thomas and Thurmon Garner, "Daisy Bates and the Little Rock School Crisis Forging the Way," *Journal of Black Studies* 26, no. 5 (1996): 616–628.
26 Bates, *Long Shadow of Little Rock*, 66.
27 Minniejean Brown (Little Rock Nine member), quoted in Jean Edward Smith, *Eisenhower: In War and Peace* (New York: Random House, 2012), 726.
28 Bates, interview in "Daisy Bates: First Lady of Little Rock."
29 Virgil T. Blossom, *It Has Happened Here* (New York: Harper, 1959), 27.
30 Bates, interview by Jacoway.
31 "Congressman Reports on Facts of Southern Tour," *Chicago Defender*, December 26, 1959, 21; "Diggs Exposes Little Rock Terror," *Cleveland Call and Post*, December 26, 1959, 1c.
32 "Mrs. Daisy Bates Woman's Day Speaker in Newark N.J.," *New Journal and Guide*, October 31, 1959, 5.
33 Belinda Robnett, *How Long? How Long? African-American Women in the Struggle for Civil Rights* (New York: Oxford University Press, 1997), 19.
34 Bates, interview by Jacoway.
35 "Civil Rights Heroine Daisy Bates, 84, Succumbs in Little Rock," *Jet*, November 22, 1999, 59.

Bibliography

Bates, Daisy. Interview by Elizabeth Jacoway, October 11, 1976, G-0009. In the Southern Oral History Program Collection #4007, Southern Historical Collection, Wilson Library, University of North Carolina at Chapel Hill. http://dc.lib.unc.edu/cdm/compoundobject/collection/sohp/id/11102/rec/1.

———. *The Long Shadow of Little Rock: A Memoir*. Fayetteville: University of Arkansas Press, 2007.

Blossom, Virgil T. *It Has Happened Here*. New York: Harper, 1959.

Calloway-Thomas, Carolyn, and Thurmon Garner. "Daisy Bates and the Little Rock School Crisis Forging the Way." *Journal of Black Studies* 26, no. 5 (1996): 616–628.

"Civil Rights Heroine Daisy Bates, 84, Succumbs in Little Rock." *Jet*, November 22, 1999, 59.

"Congressman Reports on Facts of Southern Tour." *Chicago Defender*, December 26, 1959.

"Daisy Bates: First Lady of Little Rock." Directed by Sharon La Cruise. *Independent Lens*, PBS. Sakkara Films, 2010. http://www.pbs.org/independentlens/daisy-bates/.

"Diggs Exposes Little Rock Terror." *Cleveland Call and Post*, December 26, 1959.

Faubus, Orval E. "Speech of Governor Orval E. Faubus, September 2, 1957." Available at Southern Colloquium on Rhetoric. http://southerncolloqrhetoric.net/web/resources/Faubus570902.pdf.

Kirk, John A. "He Founded a Movement: W. H. Flowers, the Committee on Negro Organizations and Black Activism in Arkansas, 1940–1957." In *The Making of*

Martin Luther King and the Civil Rights Movement in America, edited by Brian Ward and Tony Badter, 29–44. London: Macmillan, 1996.

———. "The Little Rock Crisis and Postwar Black Activism in Arkansas." *Arkansas Historical Quarterly* 60 (2007): 273–293.

"Mrs. Daisy Bates Woman's Day Speaker in Newark N.J." *New Journal and Guide*, October 31, 1959.

Oliver Brown, et al. v. Board of Education of Topeka, et al., 347 US 483 (1954).

Reed, Roy. *Faubus: The Life and Times of an American Prodigal*. Fayetteville: University of Arkansas Press, 1997.

Robnett, Belinda. *How Long? How Long? African-American Women in the Struggle for Civil Rights*. New York: Oxford University Press, 1997.

Smith, Jean Edward. *Eisenhower: In War and Peace*. New York: Random House, 2012.

Stockley, Grif. *Daisy Bates: Civil Rights Crusader from Arkansas*. Jackson: University Press of Mississippi, 2005.

Wangari Maathai

Kenyan Environmental and Democratic Movements

Rosemary Ndubuizu and Mary K. Trigg

Background

It was January 1992, and fifty-two-year-old Wangari Maathai was hospitalized after another brutal stay in prison. Recently charged with treason, sedition, and malicious intent, the Kenyan environmental social justice advocate Maathai was imprisoned for calling on international advocates to plead with the Kenyan government and halt its plans to destroy most of Uhuru Park, one of Kenya's largest public lands. Kenyan president Daniel arap Moi and members of the Kenyan parliament publicly denounced her character, professing that true African women would never support her. These politicians sought to divide Kenyan women, claiming that Maathai's status as a divorcée should be enough evidence to stop women from rallying to her cause.

But Maathai's protest prevailed. Eventually, the Kenyan government scaled back its plans to redevelop Uhuru Park and also dropped the charges against Maathai. But her fight for a better Kenyan democracy was far from over. While in the hospital recuperating from injuries sustained from her imprisonment, Maathai was asked by mothers of political prisoners to join them in their quest to protest the government. The mothers demanded the immediate release of their grown sons, who had been accused of criticizing the president and the ruling party or "plotting to overthrow the Kenyan government."[1] These rural mothers said the government denied their children a fair trial and unjustly held them without bail.

Injured and culturally maligned, Maathai had to decide whether to join these women in their human rights fight. After being defamed as a disobedient African woman, could she unite with and lead women who were acting as mothers to challenge the government? Could she help rally thousands of Kenyan women in support of this human rights struggle? How could her experience as a movement leader inspire these women to speak against the Kenyan government's abusive practices and create a more democratic Kenya?

Kikuyu Girlhood and the British Occupation

Self-described as a "child of the soil," Wangari Maathai was born in 1940 in a Kenyan village called Ihithe, located in the central highlands of what was then colonial Kenya. As members of the Kikuyu ethnic community, Maathai and her family lived from the land. Her childhood memories were of running in the forest, sitting under fig trees, and swimming in nearby rivers. Women played a pivotal role in Maathai's cultural understanding and character development. As the oldest girl, she experienced an intimacy and friendship with her mother as her right-hand helper. Maathai cared for her siblings and assisted with the growing and harvesting of staple and cash crops.

Maathai's mother taught Maathai to respect and care for the land, a Kikuyu tradition. In interviews, Maathai narrated how her aunt and mother told her stories about the sacredness of trees, land, and water.[2] Kikuyus' relationship to the land grounded their identity as a community. As a small child, Maathai learned Kikuyu creation stories about God's formation of the first people, Gikuyu and Mumbi, who were told to settle west of Mount Kenya.[3] In the story, Gikuyu and Mumbi bore ten daughters, who prayed under a special fig tree when seeking marriage. Eventually, nine of the ten daughters married and each produced a clan. Maathai is a descendant of the Anjiru clan, which is associated with leadership. Each clan was matrilineal, but as time passed, inheritance and ownership of land, livestock, and staple crops became patrilineal privileges. Maathai noted that the Kikuyus' mythology of origin fails to account for why or when these privileges shifted from women to men.

Nevertheless Kikuyus' traditions are centralized around Mount Kenya and the fig tree. For instance, prayers, burials, and even households' doors faced toward Mount Kenya. But much of this slowly and irrevocably changed with the arrival of European imperialists, specifically the British, who colonized Kenya from the 1880s until independence in 1963. Western imperialism forever reshaped Kenyan people's cultural practices and economic ambitions.

Colonialism distorted, and to some extent exacerbated, Kenyans' traditional practices and attitudes toward gender, both in the home and in the community. Before colonization, elderly men headed Kenyan communities, while women worked in agriculture and tended to their children and homes. During the years of British colonization, colonial institutions as well as British control of Kenyans' land and economy promoted patriarchy. Women who had once been in control of land became increasingly dependent on men. Women's historic value as agricultural workers vanished as male-dominated, money-making cash crops prevailed. The Kenyan lawyer Claris Gatwiri Kariuki claims that women's dispossession of land entrenched domestic patriarchy, requiring women to economically depend on men. She contends that "as colonialism continued in Africa, the perceived importance of female agricultural contributions to the household diminished as their vital role in food production was overshadowed by the more lucrative male-controlled cash crop cultivation."[4] Few girls attended schools because families believed their gender would stand in the way of them holding professional positions. Although colonialism in Kenya officially ceased in 1963, patriarchy was entrenched.[5]

British colonialism also affected Maathai's childhood. Around 1943, Maathai's father moved with his family onto the farm of the British settler Mr. Neylan to work. Under British colonial rule, most Kenyans, like Maathai's father, were denied the opportunity to own their land. British colonials usually gave the land to British settlers, who then allowed Kenyans to live on the land as squatters. Even though Maathai had fond memories of her childhood, she critiqued the effects of colonialism: "Although my family could grow food for our household on the farm, if my father wanted to sell maize, for example, Mr. Neylan had a monopoly. To sell your harvest to a cooperative you had to be a member, a privilege afforded only to the settler."[6]

On daytrips Maathai took with her mother to Nakuru, a nearby city, she glimpsed another view of colonial Kenya. The city was segregated, and Europeans, Indians, and Africans lived in separate areas. But the segregation, Maathai recalled, never muted the beauty of Nakuru because the city was still filled with trees.

The political and social conditions of colonial Kenya were shaped by a complex history that governed the lives of the Maathai family and other Kenyans before independence. The boundaries that now define Kenya were constructed at the 1884–1885 Berlin Conference, in which European heads of state gathered to divide African land among European powers. In 1894, Britain claimed ownership over Kenya. European states deployed missionaries to Kenya in the late nineteenth century to promote state interests.[7] Missionaries created schools and offered medical care. Although British colonizers preferred indirect rule over the decades and even promoted eventual African self-determination, the British government exploited interethnic tensions and applied military force to maintain power. In turn, the missionaries enforced compulsory Christianity.

Frustrated and outraged over the inequities of colonial rule, in the mid-twentieth century Kenyans fought back, but they turned against each other. The journalist and historian John Reader has written, "In the highlands, impoverished and dispossessed Kikuyus were urged to take violent action—not against the whites and their colonial government directly, but against Kikuyus who were suspected of supporting the government plans. Outbreaks of arson, cattle-maiming, and personal violence became rife and in October 1952 a state of emergency was declared."[8] According to Reader, at least two thousand loyalist Kikuyus were murdered in the Kenyan-led insurrection that came to be known as the Mau Mau rebellion. Britain enlisted scores of military arsenal to quell the rebellion, even arresting Jomo Kenyatta, who eventually became Kenya's first postcolonial president.

The colonial mentality affected the educational system in the country. In Maathai's all-girls Catholic boarding school, students were reprimanded for not using English, the official language of colonial Kenya. When students were heard speaking their original language, they were forced to wear a button that stated, "I am stupid, I was caught speaking my mother tongue." In retrospect, Maathai admitted, "Now, as then, this contributes to the trivialization of anything African and lays the foundation for a deeper sense of self-doubt and an inferiority complex."[9]

Maathai was in her first year of boarding school when the Mau Mau rebellion began. Along with other Kenyans, she was indoctrinated by the British colonizers to believe that the Mau Maus were terrorists and the British were civilized leaders. The British conscripted as many able-bodied young Kenyans as possible, including two of Maathai's brothers, forcing them to join the Home Guard and protect British interests. When home for the holidays, Maathai and other girls would sleep together in one house so that if the Mau Maus or Home Guards came, the girls could easily escape. Suspicious of almost all Kenyans, the British colonialists not only set up detention centers arresting anyone they suspected of supporting the Mau Mau but also created "emergency villages" where women, children, and the elderly were confined and disease and overcrowding ran rampant.[10]

Maathai was put in one such detention center when she was sixteen or seventeen, although her father was able to use his connections to have her released. This was a period of trauma for most Kenyans, and yet this period of insurrection also proved to be a decisive moment in the Kenyan struggle for independence.

Following graduation from high school, Maathai trounced the prevailing convention that a young woman should marry and become a teacher or nurse. Instead, she traveled to the United States to earn a bachelor's of science degree. While in America, Maathai studied widely, observed a more sexually liberal society, and also encountered the civil rights movement and its response to racial segregation. From religion to politics, her understanding of the world was dramatically reshaped. Upon her return to Kenya, she began using her traditional name, Wangari, instead of her Christian name, Miriam. In addition to reclaiming pride in her ancestral name, she also learned about the importance of gender equality. Her American experiences instilled in her the desire to ask critical questions and challenge injustice. At the same time, Kenya was headed toward independence. In 1964, the Republic of Kenya was formed, and educated citizens became increasingly important to the Kenyan government.[11]

Maathai Builds a Pro-Women and Pro-Democracy Movement in Postcolonial Kenya

Armed with a master's degree in biological sciences from the University of Pittsburgh, in 1966 Maathai quickly found that although she was qualified for high-level jobs in the newly independent nation, she nonetheless faced a series of glass ceilings as a Kenyan woman. Simultaneously, the ethnic divisions proved to be an obstacle as well. Maathai returned from the United States with a promise of appointment as a research assistant to a Kenyan zoology professor at the University of Nairobi. However, she was promptly denied the position. The professor had decided to hire another assistant, someone from his own ethnic community. Maathai later commented on this time, saying, "What I did not know then was that tribalism and other forms of corruption were going to become some of the most divisive factors in our society, and they would frustrate the dreams of the Kenyan people after independence." Disappointed but undeterred, Maathai quickly found another job as an assistant for a professor in University of Nairobi's Department of Veterinary Anatomy. After some time teaching and researching, Maathai married in 1969 and left for Germany to earn a Ph.D. in veterinary anatomy. When she returned in 1976, she became a professor at the University of Nairobi, lecturing in the Department of Veterinary Anatomy. Her husband, Mwangi Mathai, also studied in the United States and returned to Kenya to become a businessman. A rising politician, he became a member of parliament in 1974. By then, Wangari Maathai was mother to three children.[12]

Despite the inequality that existed between Kenyan women and men, women were still honored and held in high regard for their potential or actual motherhood. Strong family values, both then and now, are at the core of Kenyan culture and customs. An obligation to children, concern with children's welfare and future, respect for elders, and preference for a way of life that emphasizes kin and family over the needs of the individual are among those values.[13] The old woman (mother/grandmother) in Kenyan tradition invokes history, wisdom, and knowledge—and is often called on as story-teller/historian, keeper of memory and the past.[14] Especially in rural areas, by being viewed as mothers, women could command respect. The institution of motherhood was one that could be adopted as a political force to bring about change.[15]

Maathai was a mother herself now, and it was in her faculty position that she first tested her skills at organizing women. She and her colleague Vertistine Mbaya began to protest unfair wage differentials between female and male academics. University officials defended their position, stating, "You should just take the basic salary because the rest of the services that men get you don't need. Your husband is getting those services from his place of work and he should have your benefit from them. If he does not, too bad." Annoyed but emboldened, Mbaya and Maathai got organized. They promptly joined the university's Academic Staff Association and created a union. They won a mixed victory—their personal salaries were raised to that of their male colleagues, but other women's salaries remained the same. This was an outcome produced not only by male officials but also by the unwillingness of other women to join the battle for wage equity. Maathai and Mbaya were shocked about the resistance they received from women when they tried to recruit them. Fellow female colleagues had listened to their husbands' exhortations not to join in a pay-equity campaign fought by "man-hating women." Maathai reflected that "fighting battles with women can be very difficult and sad, because both society and the women themselves often make it appear that most women are happy with the little they have and have no intention of fighting for their rights."[16] Nevertheless, in the face of injustice and public pressure, Maathai did not shrink away from the challenge to fight for her rights and those of (even resisting) others.

The Power of a Single Idea: Turning Ordinary Citizens into Extraordinary Global Leaders

In the 1970s, Maathai joined two organizations, the Environment Liaison Centre and the National Council of Women of Kenya (NCWK). Both organizations revolutionized her thinking, and she began to shift her focus to the relationship between health and the environment. The first focused on environmental issues, including biological diversity and the effect that environmental crisis has on women.[17] The second took up the problem of malnourished children in Kenya's central region. At the behest of the Kenyan government, many farmers had begun growing cash crops like coffee and tea instead of indigenous crops, causing the commercialization of cropland and dependence on store-bought, processed foods. In addition, indigenous tree species were replaced, affecting the water available for farmland. This caused certain crops that had offered local food security in the past to no longer thrive.[18] Due to this shift and the deforestation that accompanied it, women began feeding their children foods high in carbohydrates and low in nutrients. Maathai and others felt a responsibility to help these rural women and families change the conditions they were facing. For Maathai, the solution was simple: plant trees. She reasoned, "The trees would provide a supply of wood that would enable women to cook nutritious foods. They would also have wood for fencing and fodder for cattle and goats. The trees would offer shade for human and animals, protect watersheds and bind the soil, and, if they were fruit trees, provide food. They would also heal the land by bringing back birds and small animals and regenerate the vitality of the earth."[19]

In hindsight, Maathai's idea was profound, not only because the idea offered a simple solution to complex structural problems like deforestation, malnutrition, and poverty but also because planting trees offered a symbol of healing. Maathai beautifully captured this sentiment: "Since the beginnings of human culture, the tree has been not only a source of food, medicine, and building material but a place of healing, consolation, and connection—with other human beings and with the divine."[20] The ability to reshape and rebuild the land so it can continue to nourish the bodies of the land's inhabitants proved to be a powerful concept. Maathai's idea signified hope too—the hope that postcolonial Kenya could be a place where ordinary Kenyans could change their future, preserve their culture, protect their environment, and thrive.

But not all good ideas come to immediate fruition. Maathai's first attempt to get her idea off the ground failed. She created Envirocare Ltd. as an attempt to employ poor Kenyans planting trees and maintaining gardens of rich Kenyans. Unfortunately, the project collapsed because rich residents did not want poor people maintaining their gardens, and these clients rarely paid in advance for services. Never one to give up when faced with setbacks, Maathai took her tree-planting idea to NCWK. In 1977, the National Council of Women of Kenya invited Maathai to speak about the learning she gained from attending the first United Nations conference on human settlements, known as Habitat I. In her speech, she argued that Kenya could address its deforestation issue and nutrition challenges by starting a tree-planting program. Soon after, the NCWK membership elected Maathai to its executive committee and its Standing Committee on Environment and Habitat and began to implement her tree-planting idea. She named this new NCWK program the Green Belt Movement (GBM).

The Green Belt Movement's first two tree-planting ceremonies were tied to international events like World Environment Day and the UN Conference on Desertification. Word traveled quickly—NCWK's connections led to farmers, schools, and churches asking for seedlings to plant trees. But many of these trees died from vandalism and the surrounding population's need for firewood. Maathai later commented, "I learned that if you do not have local people who are committed to the process and willing to work with their communities, the projects will not survive." In order to get local investment in tree planting, Maathai used Kenyan culture to motivate rural women's involvement. In her talks with women farmers, she would say, "I don't think you need a diploma to plant a tree. Use your woman sense. These tree seedlings are very much like the seeds you deal with—beans and maize and millet—every day. Put them in the soil. If they're good, they'll germinate. If they're not, they won't. Simple."[21] With the knowledge base of these women as farmers affirmed, they gained confidence planting trees and cultivating seedlings. Maathai demonstrated herself to still be a child of the soil. Despite her degrees from abroad and her job as a professor, she willingly got on her knees and planted trees, earning these women's respect.

Wangari Maathai also fought for her own rights as a Kenyan wife and mother. Her husband, Mwangi Mathai, was increasingly displeased with her activism. He divorced her in the early 1980s, describing her as an adulterer. Wangari Maathai suggested that the real reason for the divorce was that she was "too educated, too strong, too successful, too stubborn, and too hard to control." When the divorce court found against her and the judge determined that Wangari Maathai was not entitled to any support or belongings, she accused the judges of incompetence and corruption and was sentenced to six months in jail for contempt (she was released three days later after she agreed to apologize).[22] During the divorce proceedings, Mwangi Mathai demanded that Wangari drop her married last name. True to her contrarian disposition, Wangari modified her last name, adding an extra *a*, and officially became Wangari Maathai.[23]

Maathai's personal setbacks like her widely publicized divorce, unsuccessful bid to run for a parliament seat, and failure to win back her academic position at the University of Nairobi (after being required to leave it as she considered a parliament run) never thwarted her desire to help Kenya's environment and people.[24] By 1981, forty-one-year-old Maathai decided to redouble her efforts with the Green Belt Movement. With international funding, she was able to work full-time as GBM's executive director. She implemented several changes that had a direct impact on GBM's expansion. First, she enforced a new incentive system to make sure that the trees thrived. Only when trees survived for six months would Kenyan women be paid. Next, GBM decided to employ the women's husbands and sons as nursery attendants and required that they (along with the women tree planters) speak in their local languages. This simple requirement had tremendous impact on the expansion of the organization. No longer culturally encumbered by legacies of colonialism, rural women and their families were able to talk to and recruit others in languages that made them feel comfortable.

Eventually, the idea of planting trees was not enough—Maathai wanted to implant ideas. She recalled, "We held seminars with the communities in which Green Belt worked, in which I encouraged women and men to identify their problems. . . . They would put all the blame on the government. . . . I felt strongly that people needed to understand that the government was not the only culprit. Citizens, too, played a part in the problems the communities identified. One way was by not standing up for what they strongly believed in and demanding that the government provide it."[25] In order to convey this message, Maathai and other GBM staff taught Kenyans about the "Wrong Bus Syndrome." She used the bus analogy because it had a widely understood meaning. In these seminars, she would explain that when Kenyans get on the wrong bus, they end up at the wrong place. But Maathai implored the Kenyans, instead of lamenting about being at the incorrect location, to ask questions and to take action. GBM's workshop inspired Kenyans to become problem solvers and not simply fault finders. This activity helped Kenyans recognize their collective power—which meant that the future of their villages, Kenya, and the environment rested in their hands. They could create the world they desired if they learned how to solve problems and fight for a better future. Maathai knew that knowledge would awaken ordinary Kenyans' sense of worth and confidence when she said, "You cannot enslave a mind that knows itself, that values itself, that understands itself." Maathai argued that once Kenyans had the courage to question, then they could take action and become leaders. Anastasia Njeri, a Kenyan woman, agreed: "After Wrong Bus Syndrome, I have tried a lot to go and talk to women here and there to have groups. We try to encourage ourselves because if we do not do that, our country will come to expire. Now, I have the courage to say anything."[26]

Maathai's ability to inspire rural women in Kenya was one of her most valuable leadership qualities. This asset served her well as she transitioned her national focus from planting trees to advocating democracy. Even though GBM was gaining international acclaim for its success, domestically Maathai was often vilified. Maathai suspected that the government did not like the press GBM garnered. Police and government officials began to harass GBM's tree planters and Maathai. By the late 1980s, a culture of corruption had become endemic in Kenya. Maathai wrote, "People were jailed for voicing dissenting political opinions, demonstrators were shot by police, and Kenya was ruled like a dictatorship."[27] Several high-profile public-works scandals revealed the Kenyan government to be corrupt and President Daniel arap Moi to be caught up in unethical financing deals.[28] Maathai could not idly sit by and let the Kenyan government brutalize its citizens. Moreover, she realized that GBM's efforts to preserve the environment were intricately linked to Kenyan governance over the land. Consequently, like the rural women she worked with at GBM, she put her words about courage into practice and protested.

In 1989, Maathai learned about President Moi's plans to redevelop Kenya's largest park, the Uhuru Park, which was located in Nairobi, the country's capital. President Moi planned to build a sixty-two-story tower alongside a four-story statue of himself. She wrote letters to Kenyan officials, appealed to international authorities, and filed an injunction in court to stop the development. Filled with conviction, Maathai and a small group of women also staged a protest against the development. They were beaten and ordered to disperse.

Maathai's outspokenness earned her the ire of the Kenyan parliament. Members of parliament sought to ban GBM as a subversive group after Maathai petitioned international authorities for support. Parliament members claimed that she was a "wayward" and unhappy divorced African woman who did not know her proper place. In speeches, President Moi denounced Maathai's campaign to save the park, explaining, "According to African traditions women must respect their men. I ask you women, can't you discipline your own, one who has crossed the line?"[29]

Officials even evicted GBM from its office since the space was owned by the government. Ordinary citizens started to shy away from Maathai. The few who spoke to her reproached her, saying, "Why are you putting yourself in this situation? It's not your land. Why are you bothered?" She retorted, "Because after they are done with what is owned by the public, they'll come for what is mine and yours."[30] Maathai's public and political condemnation only made her more resolute. She dismissed the government's character attacks, telling parliament members that "they need to focus on the anatomy that matters—from the neck up."[31] She later remarked, "The Parliament was just being mean, chauvinistic, and downright dirty. Fortunately, my skin is thick, like an elephant's. The more they abused and ridiculed me, the more they hardened me. I know I was right, and they were wrong."[32]

Maathai's courageous act to speak against this injustice was met with swift retribution. The Kenyan government often enacted violent repression on citizens who challenged the government. When Maathai spoke out against a coup supported by President Moi, a ploy she believed would maintain Moi's power, the police promptly issued a warrant for her arrest. After a tense and internationally publicized three-day standoff in 1992, the police broke into Maathai's home, arrested her, and threw her into a holding cell. Maathai described her prison conditions as bleak. She was forced to sleep on a cold, wet, and hard floor without any covers. She stated, "I was also fifty-two years old, arthritic in both knees, and suffering from back pain. In that cold, wet cell my joints ached so much that I thought I would die. The lights were kept on twenty-four hours a day, so it was impossible to sleep. . . . By the time of my court hearing, my legs had completely seized up. Crying from the pain and weak from hunger, I had to be carried by four strong policewomen into the courtroom."[33]

While Maathai was in the hospital recovering from her jail-induced injuries, she was visited by Terry Kariuki, a widow of a murdered politician, J. M. Kariuki. She represented the mothers of political prisoners who were unjustly jailed and was there to ask Maathai to join their cause for justice. The previous December, President Moi had announced the repeal of section 2a of the Kenyan constitution, which had made it illegal to oppose the ruling party. Now with political debate allowed and Kenyans given the right to criticize the government publicly, these mothers claimed that their sons—no longer guilty of treason for speaking out against the Moi government—should be released. One of the mothers stated, "Why should my son continue to languish in prison while what he was fighting for (multi-partyism) is already here? He should not be held any longer." She added, "The pain of bearing a child does not allow me to let my son continue suffering in prison."[34] "The Mamas," as they came to be known, were between the ages of sixty and seventy, all Kikuyu and from rural areas, and had never previously been involved in activism or national politics.[35]

But the choice to join the protesting mothers presented many difficulties for Maathai. The first were about physical safety and well-being—Maathai was weak, released on bail, and politically maligned. The second was about her duty to her own cause for democracy—would the larger battle be lost if her voice was directed more narrowly toward the injustice suffered by political prisoners and their mothers' concerns? Finally, she was concerned about whether her presence would help or hinder the mothers' cause—people, and most especially women, feared being associated with Maathai. They knew she was being watched by Kenyan government officials and that the reprisal would be swift and likely violent for her supporters and collaborators. Her past efforts to organize women had not always been successful. Yet she deeply believed in the idea that ordinary Kenyans could change their futures, their communities, and their culture. She also understood the importance of perseverance and persistence in any movement for social change. As Maathai pondered the words and request of Terry Kariuki, all of these concerns crossed her mind. Should she simply decline their request and not fight this battle? If she accepted, would she be able to inspire rather than discourage other women to support these mothers? What goals should she have? Would she be able to mobilize women's knowledge and status in society for change? Could she successfully encourage Kenyan men to rally to this movement of mothers? Did she have the strength?

Resolution

After careful consideration, Maathai decided to join the mothers' cause after she was released from the hospital. Although this decision to continue with political protesting was against the requirements of her bail, Maathai felt that the unethical nature of the government made the charges of treason false and that, thus, she needed to continue, in her words, "pursuing the truth."[36] Her own experiences with Kenyan autocracy, the repression of political dissent, and her desire for a transparent and inclusive democracy fueled her. In addition, her long belief in the importance of citizens taking a stance and women believing in themselves motivated her to join their cause. All of these things represented truth to Maathai.

The women activists began to formulate a strategy. Maathai first advised the women to attempt the "legal" route to change—to petition the attorney general about the legality of indefinitely imprisoning their sons. After a meeting with Attorney General Amos Wako, who told the mothers he would review their sons' cases, the women—feeling impotent and infuriated—began a hunger strike. They began their strike at "Freedom Corner," the section of Uhuru Park where Moi and his KANU government had planned on building a skyscraper, the one that Maathai had successfully organized to block.[37] The Mamas, along with Maathai, began their hunger strike in protest on February 28, 1992. The mothers remained in the Nairobi park, sleeping in tents. By nightfall, more than fifty women came, most of them mothers or relatives of political prisoners. The protest spread like wildfire. Hundreds of Kenyans poured in, sharing their stories of government-sponsored torture and harassment. All day long they sang, drank water, prayed, and exchanged resources and hope.[38] On March 2, the police broke up a demonstration that had gathered in support of the protesting mothers. On March 3, the police returned to forcefully evict the mothers from Freedom Corner and to disperse their supporters. Many of the mothers were beaten or trampled, including Wangari Maathai, who had to be hospitalized once again.

The secret to the protest's success was in its concept. Maathai encouraged the women to share their stories of suffering with one another—and to learn from one another. This echoed their past and tradition of sharing their knowledge of the plants and fields with each other, as well as her own role teaching women in rural communities to come together to plant trees. In the Green Belt Movement's political education workshops, Maathai frequently asked Kenyan women to use their voices to champion for a better government and a better environment. In her earlier activism for wage equity at the University of Nairobi, she had encouraged women to raise their voices together against inequity. Her own history of courageous acts was contagious. Women started to speak up about the pain they endured under Kenya's autocratic, antidemocratic regime. This had a ripple effect. The protest grew exponentially because these women created a safe space for truth telling—a confessional space—and therefore a liberatory space. Maathai shared a similar conclusion when she described the emancipatory fervor of the protest: "For the very first time in this country, people narrated the torture they had gone through. And men [not just women] would cry tears as they narrated that story. People felt courageous enough to say, 'Let me tell you my story.'" The power of truth telling compelled many Kenyans to come out and build, heal, and connect with others. In meeting others, they transformed their individual pain into a collective pain—an emotional move that inspired them to fight for democratic reforms.[39]

Yet the women's emotional and physical strength was tested almost immediately, when the police violently tried to disperse the crowd. On March 4, 1992, the day of the attack by the police, three elderly women stripped naked in response to the brutality. The *Nation* reported, "Women wailed and stripped and ran screaming. . . . What kind of government is this that beats women! Kill us! Kill us now! We shall die with our children!"[40] The policemen walked away from the naked women. Interpreting the symbolic importance of that moment, Maathai explained, "In the African tradition, every woman who is about your mother's age is also your mother and you must treat her with the same respect. If men beat women, it is like sons violating their mothers, and the mothers respond by cursing them. And they cursed them by showing them their nakedness."[41] Many Kenyans believed that by stripping, the mothers put a curse on the Moi regime and even on the entire nation.[42] Their nakedness became a protest within a protest. These women exposed the brutality of postcolonial Kenya by demonstrating how the police officers blindly inflict violence on anyone, even elderly women—their cultural mothers. Dramatizing this inhumanity, women used their bodies to shame the police and forced them to question the immorality of their abusive methods.

In response to the severe treatment of the mothers and their many followers, uprisings broke out in Nairobi.[43] There was no stopping these women. Shortly after they were forced to leave the park and while Maathai was in the hospital convalescing, the mothers decided to go to nearby All Saints Cathedral and continue their protest. For almost an entire year, women remained in this cathedral demanding the release of their loved ones. President Moi reportedly commented, "There are some women whose heads are not okay. They are defending criminals, people who have broken the laws of the land. . . . They do not know what they are doing."[44] Still, the general public supported the mothers' activism. Ruth Wangari, one of the mothers who led the campaign, recounted, "Moi tried every way to get rid of us. Because we women were driving him crazy. But we were determined we'd never leave that place until we got our children back."[45] After Maathai was released from the hospital, she spent most of her time with the women at the cathedral. The women's protest eventually attracted international headlines, shining a light on state-sponsored torture and undemocratic denial of rights. The United States and Germany responded to the beating of the mothers by criticizing Moi's regime for human rights abuses.[46] When four prisoners were set free on June 24, 1992, and four more on January 19, 1993, Kenyans celebrated the success of the mothers' protest. Over fifty political prisoners—many of them sons of these activist mothers—were eventually released. This group of rural Kikuyu women strategically claimed a public, political identity as mothers, while at the same time they acted as citizens concerned about issues such as justice and equality, issues that had always been central to Wangari Maathai's long-standing fight for a more democratic Kenya.[47]

Undoubtedly, Maathai and the Mamas embodied courage in 1992. Their act of courage helped spark and awaken Kenya's pro-democracy movement, which directly contributed to Kenyans eventually ousting Moi through multiparty presidential elections held in 2002. These powerful women showed Kenya—and the world—that courage in this case meant that their fear of the painful possibility of losing their sons greatly overshadowed their fear of state repression.[48] Maathai's strategic involvement and courageous leadership helped raise the visibility of the atrocities that "the Mamas" and their sons faced while also inspiring these women to share their truth publicly—and to demand justice.

These mothers and their families helped create a powerful civil society that demanded a more accountable and democratic government, and Wangari Maathai played a key role in inspiring them. Ruth Wangari stated, "Wangari [Maathai] has given me the strength to know if I fight for something, I can make it happen." Lilian Wanjiru Njehu, a member of the Green Belt Movement, concurred, saying Maathai taught them that "the little, little grassroots people—they can change this world."[49] She encouraged women to claim their political voice and take control of their futures by planting trees and advocating justice. Maathai inspired women—the Kenyan people—to see themselves as seedlings of justice. They planted justice wherever they witnessed acts of injustice taking place. They learned the power of their collective voice in a democratic and civil society. They learned that they can lead themselves. But most importantly, these women learned courage. They had the courage to challenge gender conventions. They had the courage to rewrite the legacies of colonialism and reclaim their land. They had the courage to fight for a different postcolonial Kenya. Maathai concluded, "Courage. I guess that the nearest it means is not having fear. Fear is the biggest enemy you have. I think you can overcome your fear when you no longer see the consequences. When I do what I do, when I am writing letters to the president, accusing him of every crime on this earth, of being a violator of every right I know of, especially violating environmental rights and then of violence to women, I must have courage."[50] Maathai and the women she inspired had the courage to question and the will to act—and as a result of their persistence, the Kenyan country became a shining example of a successful pro-democracy movement.[51]

After thirty years of caring for the environment and fighting for democracy, in 2004 Wangari Maathai was awarded the Nobel Peace Prize. In her acceptance speech, she called on not only Kenya but the entire international community to redirect its efforts toward creating just policies so that African nations and developing countries are no longer exploited and depleted of their resources. Later in her life, Maathai became widely recognized as a global champion of environmental justice and peace, advocating for all human beings' right to have a better world and a better environment. Maathai's simple idea to plant trees had revolutionary reach. She moved from planting trees to advocating democracy and gave Kenyan women a stirring example of courage in the face of an autocratic government. Her ideas and intrepid leadership changed the direction of an entire nation.

Notes

1 Alexandra Tibbetts, "Mamas Fighting for Freedom in Kenya," *Africa Today* 41, no. 4 (1994): 27.
2 *Taking Root: The Vision of Wangari Maathai*, dir. Alan Dater and Lisa Merton (Marlboro Productions, 2008), DVD.
3 Wangari Maathai, *Unbowed: A Memoir* (New York: Knopf, 2006), 4–5; Thomas Spear, "Oral Traditions: Whose History?," *History in Africa* 8 (1981): 165–181.
4 Claris Kariuki, "Women Participation in the Kenyan Society," *African Executive: Free Africa's Ultimate Capital* 296 (2010): 2, http://www.africanexecutive.com/modules/magazine/articles.php?article=5609&magazine=314.
5 Maathai, *Unbowed*, 101.
6 Maathai, *Unbowed*, 15.
7 John Reader, *Africa: A Biography of the Continent* (New York: Knopf, 1998).
8 Ibid., 647.
9 Maathai, *Unbowed*, 59, 60.
10 Because missionaries were usually unable to establish schools on white settlers' land, Kenyan parents who were able to afford to send their oldest children to school sent them to boarding schools in nearby towns. Maathai was one of the few girls of her region to be educated, a fact influenced not only by distance and finances but also by conflict. Ibid., 61, 64, 65.
11 Ibid., 78, 79, 81, 73.
12 Ibid., 101, 106.
13 Neal Sobania, *Culture and Customs of Kenya* (Westport, CT: Greenwood, 2012), 147, 157.
14 Obioma Nnaemeka, *The Politics of (M)othering: Womanhood, Identity, and Resistance in African Literature* (London: Routledge, 1997), 5, 9.
15 Rosaline Achieng, *Kenya Reconstructing? Building Bridges of Peace: Post-Conflict Transformation Processes and Human Security Mechanisms* (Berlin: LIT Verlag, 2012), 89.
16 Maathai, *Unbowed*, 115, 116.
17 Ibid., 120, 176.
18 Wangari Maathai, "Bottlenecks to Development in Africa," The Green Belt Movement, August 30, 1995, http://www.greenbeltmovement.org/wangari-maathai/key-speeches-and-articles/bottleknecks-to-development-in-africa.
19 Maathai, *Unbowed*, 125.

20 Wangari Maathai, *Replenishing the Earth: Spiritual Values for Healing Ourselves and the World* (New York: Doubleday, 2010), 79.

21 Maathai, *Unbowed*, 132, 136.

22 "Can One Woman Save Africa?," *Independent*, September 28, 2009, http://www.independent.co.uk/news/world/africa/can-one-woman-save-africa-1794103.html; Maathai, *Unbowed*, 146.

23 Maathai, *Unbowed*, 147.

24 Ibid., 11, 161–162.

25 Ibid., 173.

26 *Taking Root.*

27 Maathai, *Unbowed*, 181.

28 Susan Hawley, *Turning a Blind Eye: Corruption and the UK Export Credits Guarantee Department* (London: Corner House, 2003), 28–32, http://www.thecornerhouse.org.uk/resource/turning-blind-eye. Moi, the second president of Kenya, was in office from 1978 through 2002.

29 *Taking Root.*

30 Maathai, *Unbowed*, 195.

31 *Taking Root.*

32 Wangari Maathai, "Speak Truth to Power," in *Speak Truth to Power: Human Rights Defenders Who Are Changing Our World*, ed. Kerry Kennedy Cuomo and Eddie Adams (New York: Umbrage Editions, 2000), 42–43.

33 Maathai, *Unbowed*, 214.

34 Jemimah Marakisha, "When Women Bared All," *Nation (Nairobi)*, March 8, 1992, 5, quoted in Tibbetts, "Mamas Fighting for Freedom," 29. The woman was Glady Thiitu.

35 Tibbetts, "Mamas Fighting for Freedom," 31.

36 Maathai, *Unbowed*, 216.

37 Tibbetts, "Mamas Fighting for Freedom," 31.

38 *Taking Root.*

39 Maathai, *Unbowed*, 216–226; *Taking Root.*

40 "Mothers Strip as Riot Police Charge," *Nation (Nairobi)*, March 4, 1992, 1, quoted in Tibbetts, "Mamas Fighting for Freedom," 31–32.

41 *Taking Root.*

42 Tibbetts, "Mamas Fighting for Freedom," 32.

43 Ibid.

44 "Quote of the Day," *Nation (Nairobi)*, March 5, 1992, 7, quoted in Tibbetts, "Mamas Fighting for Freedom," 33.

45 *Taking Root.*

46 "US and Germany Riled by Brutality," *Standard (Nairobi)*, March 5, 1992, 3, cited in Tibbetts, "Mamas Fighting for Freedom," 33.

47 Tibbetts, "Mamas Fighting for Freedom," 28–29, 35.

48 Maathai, "Speak Truth to Power," 43.

49 *Taking Root.*

50 Maathai, "Speak Truth to Power," 43.

51 *Taking Root.*

Bibliography

Achieng, Rosaline M. *Kenya Reconstructing? Building Bridges of Peace: Post-Conflict Transformation Processes and Human Security Mechanisms.* Berlin: LIT Verlag, 2012.

"Can One Woman Save Africa?" *Independent*, September 28, 2009. http://www.independent.co.uk/news/world/africa/can-one-woman-save-africa-1794103.html.

Hawley, Susan. *Turning a Blind Eye: Corruption and the UK Export Credits Guarantee Department.* London: Corner House, 2003. http://www.thecornerhouse.org.uk/resource/turning-blind-eye.

Kariuki, Claris. "Women Participation in the Kenyan Society." *African Executive: Free Africa's Ultimate Capital* 296 (2010): 1–8. http://www.africanexecutive.com/modules/magazine/articles.php?article=5609&magazine=314.

Maathai, Wangari. "Bottlenecks to Development in Africa." The Green Belt Movement, August 30, 1995. http://www.greenbeltmovement.org/wangari-maathai/key-speeches-and-articles/bottleknecks-to-development-in-africa.

———. *Replenishing the Earth: Spiritual Values for Healing Ourselves and the World.* New York: Doubleday, 2010.

———. "Speak Truth to Power." In *Speak Truth to Power: Human Rights Defenders Who Are Changing Our World*, edited by Kerry Kennedy Cuomo and Eddie Adams, 38–43. New York: Umbrage Editions, 2000.

———. *Unbowed: A Memoir.* New York: Knopf, 2006.

Marakisha, Jemimah. "When Women Bared All." *Nation (Nairobi)*, March 8, 1992, 5.

"Mothers Strip as Riot Police Charge." *Nation (Nairobi)*, March 4, 1992, 1.

Nnaemeka, Obioma. *The Politics of (M)othering: Womanhood, Identity, and Resistance in African Literature.* London: Routledge, 1997.

"Quote of the Day." *Nation (Nairobi)*, March 5, 1992, 7.

Reader, John. *Africa: A Biography of the Continent.* New York: Knopf, 1998.

Sobania, Neal. *Culture and Customs of Kenya.* Westport, CT: Greenwood, 2012.

Spear, Thomas. "Oral Traditions: Whose History?" *History in Africa* 8 (1981): 165–181.

Taking Root: The Vision of Wangari Maathai. Directed by Alan Dater and Lisa Merton. Marlboro Productions, 2008. DVD.

Tibbetts, Alexandra. "Mamas Fighting for Freedom in Kenya." *Africa Today* 41, no. 4 (1994): 27–48.

"US and Germany Riled by Brutality." *Standard (Nairobi)*, March 5, 1992, 3.

Aileen Clarke Hernandez
Advocate for Black Women's Leadership

Carolina Alonso Bejarano and Kim LeMoon

Background

In the mid-1960s, Aileen Clarke Hernandez served as the only woman on the first Equal Employment Opportunity Commission (EEOC). President Lyndon B. Johnson appointed her to the commission in recognition of her work in labor relations and fair employment practices. Created in 1965, the role of the EEOC was to enforce Title VII of the 1964 Civil Rights Act, which prohibited discrimination in the workplace on the basis of race, color, religion, national origin, or sex.

During deliberations in Congress, the sex-discrimination clause had been amended to Title VII at the last hour either as a joke or as an unsuccessful attempt to get the entire bill blocked. Because of this, there were those—including the executive director of the EEOC—who thought that the sex amendment should be disregarded, insisting that the agency's priority was race discrimination. From Hernandez's perspective, race discrimination could not be uncoupled from sex discrimination in the larger struggle for human rights. Employers who tended to discriminate on the basis of race also tended to discriminate on the basis of sex, leaving minority women in the worst economic plight of all.

Hernandez fought aggressively to get the sex-discrimination regulation implemented, but she was outnumbered on the commission. She became increasingly more exasperated at the EEOC's unwillingness to enforce the Title VII sex amendment. Hernandez needed a different strategy if she was to bring about change at the EEOC. During her years as a union organizer, she had come to believe that in order to make lasting change, "you need to challenge the system in terms of getting the barriers down, but you also need to raise the expectations of the group that has been put down for so long."[1] How Hernandez applied this philosophy to the problem of sex discrimination is the leadership story told here.

Early Years

Aileen Clarke Hernandez was born in 1926 to Jamaican immigrants and grew up in the Bay Ridge section of Brooklyn, New York. Both of her parents were employed in the creative arts; her father made artists' brushes, and her mother was a seamstress who sewed costumes for New York theatrical productions. They named their daughter after Aileen Pringle, an American stage and film actress who performed during the silent film era.[2] The Clarkes believed that opportunities in education and employment should not be limited by gender or race. At home, Aileen and her brothers were all taught to sew and cook.[3] She recalled, "I was always told when I was growing up that I had choices, even when really I didn't have a whole lot of them at the time—that it was what I *did* that would make a difference in my life."[4]

From an early age, Aileen was encouraged to speak out against racism. When she was five years old, neighbors petitioned to get her family removed from their all-white neighborhood. Her mother, Ethel, took her by the hand, and they marched down to the house of the man who started the petition. She walked right into his kitchen and said to him, "What made you decide that you should have us not living in this neighborhood? Who are you to make that decision?" She proceeded to give him a lecture about how their family had every right to live there, then she simply turned and left. Hernandez learned then that "if you've got an issue, you'd better start speaking up very early about it."[5]

Precocious and independent, Hernandez envied her older brother, who went to school first. On more than one occasion, she slipped downstairs and followed him to school. After the first time, her mother knew where to find her when she went missing.[6] During her years at P.S. 176, Hernandez frustrated her teachers with her assertiveness and was repeatedly scolded and told to act like a young lady. The attempts to rein in Hernandez continued right up until her graduation from elementary school. She had planned to wear a graduation dress that she had meticulously hand-crafted with the hope of winning the school's Golden Thimble Award. Although she clearly deserved the sewing award, it was given to another girl. Because she had already earned the position of class valedictorian and had also won class medals in French and Latin, the principal told her, "We want you to be a nice young lady and let us spread the prizes around." Hernandez wanted to protest but held her tongue. In her first political decision, she silently resolved never to be submissive again.[7]

Hernandez was fortunate to attend a progressive all-girls high school that shared her parents' belief that girls should be afforded the same opportunities as boys. In the 1940s, girls were expected to marry and be taken care of by men. If they had careers, they were limited to choices such as teachers, nurses, or secretaries. But at Bay Ridge High School, the girls were encouraged to strive for a life and career beyond the gendered constraints of the times. Hernandez remembers, "We did everything. They didn't limit us in any way in terms of our education. We got an opportunity to go all over the state of New York. I met people in those days that were like God to me at that stage. For example, Paul Robeson and his wife would come there periodically. And that gave me an opportunity to broaden the possibilities for a young girl coming from Brooklyn, New York, in those days."[8]

Challenging Perceptions

It was at the very start of Hernandez's college years at the historically Black institution Howard University that she began to forge a lifelong political philosophy that straddled the intersection of race and gender. On full scholarship, an excited Aileen and her father, Charles, traveled by train to Washington, DC, to get her registered for classes. In New York, there was at least the perception that some form of racial equality existed, so it was an immediate affront when Hernandez realized that the nation's capital was completely segregated. As they arrived at Union Station, Aileen watched as Black travelers were required to transfer from the integrated car to the segregated car to travel south. Outside the train station, the Clarkes discovered that the white taxi drivers would not take them up to Howard. They had to wait for a segregated taxi, which was always the last in line.[9]

Chartered as a university by an act of Congress in 1867, Howard University has long played a central role in the African American educational experience. From its inception, it has been committed to graduate and professional education and holds the distinction of establishing the first Black law school in the United States. At Howard, Hernandez thrived in an atmosphere of social activism, community service, and a vital campus life. But first, she had to overcome stereotypes of the time that constrained women's options. On her first day of class in a political science course, the professor came into the room and saw that Hernandez was the only woman among forty-some men. He approached her and said, "If you are not prepared to do all of the work that we're talking about, I would suggest that you leave now and sign up for home economics then."[10] Hernandez remained resolutely in her seat, knowing that her mother would never forgive her if she quit.

The four years at Howard afforded Hernandez the opportunity to become active in the civil rights movement. She was a member of the National Association for the Advancement of Colored People (NAACP) and picketed against segregation at the National Theater, the Eisner Auditorium, and at Thomson restaurants. She described herself as a patriot, believing that people could not afford not to participate in democratic government.[11] During her undergraduate years, Hernandez was influenced by many outstanding women who were active in Washington. But the one she names as her role model is the civil rights activist and lawyer Pauli Murray. Hernandez noted, "She was so different from anybody I had ever met before because she knew exactly what she wanted to do. She had fought discrimination all of her life, both as a woman and as a person who was Black, and Pauli was the one that really got me going."[12] Aileen Hernandez was among a group of undergraduate women that Pauli led in sit-ins at segregated lunch counters throughout Washington, DC. Forerunners to the 1960s lunch-counter sit-ins, these demonstrations were successful in desegregating at least one establishment.[13]

Pauli Murray was a student at Howard Law School in the 1940s when she and Hernandez met on campus. Murray had received national publicity in 1938 after her application to enter the applied social work program at the all-white University of North Carolina was rejected solely on the basis of her race. As one of the few women at Howard Law, Murray encountered endless ridicule and hostility from Black male faculty and classmates. She countered their derision with dogged determination and finished first in her class. Vocal about the discrimination, Murray coined the term "Jane Crow," drawing an analogy between the sexism she experienced and the Jim Crow racial segregation laws.[14] In a 1993 interview in which Hernandez reflected on Murray's influence, she remarked, "I had similar experiences where in one case, I might have been discriminated against because I was a female, and then in another case, because I was Black. So when people ask me, you know, what's more important to you, I can't separate those. It's very hard. It's schizophrenic to try to do that."[15]

After graduating magna cum laude with a degree in sociology and political science, Hernandez went to Oslo, Norway, to study comparative government in the International Student Exchange Program.[16] She then returned to Howard to begin working on a master's degree. She also accepted a position as a research assistant for the same professor who had doubted a woman could handle the rigors of his political science course.[17] Hernandez seemed to have a talent for challenging people's perceptions in a way that allied them to her cause. That facility proved to be valuable years later when, in her leadership roles for the National Organization for Women (NOW), she worked to persuade the overwhelmingly white membership to take seriously the concerns of women of color.

When a bout of tuberculosis interrupted Hernandez's studies, she returned to her parents' home in New York City to get care. After she recovered, she resumed her graduate work at New York University. One day while she was writing a paper at the library, she got tired and decided to skim through a magazine. On the pages, an advertisement jumped out at her that read, "Are you an oddball?

Would you like a job that doesn't pay a lot of money, but gives you lots of positive feelings about what the society ought to be doing?" She thought, "They're talking to me!"[18]

Graduate school was put on hold once again as Hernandez began a year-long internship with the International Ladies' Garment Workers' Union (ILGWU) Institute in California. At the end of her internship she was hired by the union as an organizer. Over the next eleven years in her role as education director and public relations director, she organized social affairs; mobilized strikes, pickets, and legislative bodies; and was responsible for naturalization classes for non-native-born union employees.[19] In 1957, she married the garment cutter Alfonso Hernandez and divorced him only four years later. Aileen blamed their incompatibility on his disappointed expectations, as a man who was raised in a Latin American tradition, that his wife would be subservient.[20]

In 1960, Hernandez left the ILGWU to manage the victorious reelection campaign of the California state comptroller and future US senator Allan Cranston. The following year, she finally completed her master's degree in government at California State University at Los Angeles. In 1962, she was appointed by Governor Edmund G. "Pat" Brown to be assistant chief of the California Division of Fair Employment Practices. With a staff of fifty in four field offices, Hernandez was tasked with enforcing the state's 1959 antidiscrimination law. In that job, she fought for fairer hiring practices for minorities and succeeded in getting employers to revise the discriminatory employment tests widely used at the time.[21] So effective was Hernandez in that role that Governor Brown recommended Hernandez to President Lyndon B. Johnson as an appointee to the newly formed Equal Employment Opportunity Commission. When Hernandez accepted the position, she was the only woman selected to be on the five-member commission and one of two people of color.

Title VII Battle at the EEOC

The EEOC's responsibility entailed enforcing Title VII of the 1964 Civil Rights Act, which prohibited employment discrimination on the basis of race, color, religion, national origin, or sex. When the landmark civil rights legislation was being debated on the House floor, Congressman Howard Worth Smith of Virginia proposed an amendment to the bill that would add sex to the list of criteria that constituted discrimination in the workplace. According to historian Carl Brauer, there are conflicting theories as to whether Smith proposed the amendment as a joke or as a strategy to block the passage of the entire bill, or whether he was sincerely in support of the amendment.[22] In any case, to the surprise and dismay of many people, the bill was passed with the sex amendment attached to Title VII. Having a law in place was merely the first step in challenging sex discrimination by employers. The EEOC would need to develop guidelines that would ultimately define the meaning of the statute. But because the sex amendment was hastily ushered through without much deliberation, the EEOC had little documentation on which to interpret Congress's original intent.[23] It took several years and a substantial amount of pressure exerted by women's groups and legislators on the EEOC before implementation of the law actually protected women workers from discrimination.

There was no shortage of opposition to the sex-discrimination law. The press dubbed it the "bunny law," after an article in the *Wall Street Journal* joked that Title VII might require Playboy Clubs to hire male bunnies.[24] At the EEOC, some of the commissioners and staff denounced it outright. The topic of sex discrimination elicited either boredom or hostility at EEOC meetings, where Executive Director N. Thompson Powers dissuaded discussion, saying that he did not want the EEOC to become known as the sex commission.[25] Hernandez remembers that "the message came through clearly that the Commission's priority was race discrimination—and apparently only as it related to Black men."[26]

Aileen Hernandez found an ally at the EEOC in fellow commissioner Richard Graham, an engineer and business executive who had served as director of the Peace Corps in Tunisia. Though they were both committed to enforcing the anti-sex-bias provisions in the law, they found themselves outnumbered. One of the first battles they lost was the attempt to end the practice of sex-segregated help-wanted advertising. The language of Title VII clearly made it unlawful for employers to publish ads indicating preferences, limitations, specifications, or discriminations based on race, color, religion, sex, or national origin, except in cases where sex was a bona fide occupational qualification for employment. At the end of deliberations, however, the EEOC ruled on September 22, 1965, that sex-segregated advertising was allowable if newspapers included a disclaimer that noted that the "male" and "female" columns were provided simply for the convenience of readers and were not intended to exclude or discourage applications on the basis of sex.[27] Even this minor mandate that the EEOC levied on newspapers was met with harsh criticism. "Why," queried an editorial in the *New Republic*, "should a mischievous joke perpetrated on the floor of the House of Representatives be treated by a responsible administrative body with this kind of seriousness?"[28]

The EEOC was initially unsympathetic to women's issues despite the fact that 37 percent of the complaints filed with the commission in the first year alleged sex discrimination.[29] When the EEOC officially opened its office in the summer of 1965, the very first groups to file grievances were the stewardesses' unions. Two American Airlines stewardesses who came in to register their complaints arrived so early that they ended up helping the staffers unpack the boxed typewriters. Considered at the time one of the most glamorous and desirable jobs available to white women, stewardesses were subject to unreasonable (and what was ultimately proven unlawful) employment standards. They were required by the airlines to be young, single, and slender. There were strict restrictions on how long their hair and skirts could be and how high their heels should be. They were required to wear girdles and could be terminated for gaining weight. Since they were expected to resign when they got married, many of them kept their nuptials a secret. What they could not hide, however, was their age. Women over the age of thirty were no longer considered attractive enough to represent the airlines. When a stewardess reached the age of thirty-two (or in some cases thirty-five), she was fired. Because male employees, such as pilots, had no such age or marital-status restrictions, these policies were in blatant violation of Title VII. Nevertheless, it took nearly a year before the EEOC convened a hearing on their complaints.[30]

In April 1966, the EEOC took a step backward in its enforcement of the sex amendment. Under pressure from newspapers refusing to print the job-advertisement disclaimer, the commission amended its regulations to allow help-wanted ads to be printed in sex-segregated columns without the disclaimer. The only restriction it imposed was that the ad itself could not state a preference of sex. Herman Edelsberg, who had succeeded N. Thompson Powers as EEOC's executive director, justified the commission's decision by arguing that the sex amendment was a "fluke . . . conceived out of wedlock."[31]

That was the final straw for those who had been closely watching the EEOC drag its feet with respect to enforcement of the sex amendment. Michigan US House of Representatives member Martha Griffiths, who had been one of the amendment's principal supporters, condemned the commission's ruling in a June speech that she delivered to Congress. Griffiths charged that the behavior of the EEOC had reached the "peak of contempt" and constituted "nothing more than arbitrary arrogance, disregard of law, and a manifestation of flat hostility to the human rights of women."[32] When the Third National Conference of the State Commissions on Women convened in Washington, DC, later that month, Catherine East, the executive secretary for the Citizen's Advisory Council on the Status of Women, arranged for copies of Griffiths's speech to be distributed to the hundreds of participants who attended the conference.[33]

The purpose of the conference was for the state commission delegates to submit and discuss their carefully prepared reports on the nature and extent of discrimination against women in the United States. In 1961, John F. Kennedy wrote Executive Order 10980 to establish the Presidential Commission on the Status of Women (PCSW), to which he appointed Eleanor Roosevelt chair. The PCSW, in turn, encouraged states to form their own commissions, and in 1964, the Labor Department started convening annual conferences for the state commissions to discuss best practices to combat sex discrimination. At the 1966 conference, the foremost topic on everyone's agenda was how the EEOC was failing women.

Hernandez held the unenviable position of representing the EEOC as an invited speaker for the conference. Though she shared the frustrations of the delegates—certainly she was as enraged as anybody at the battles she and Richard Graham had waged and lost at the EEOC—professional decorum prevented her from speaking publicly about the commission. As an EEOC commissioner, she was also not privy to the private discussions that had gone on in Betty Friedan's hotel room. Friedan, the author of *The Feminine Mystique*, had for some time been in discussions with the EEOC staff lawyer Sonia Pressman Fuentes, Hernandez's former mentor Pauli Murray, and others about the need for an organization that could fight for women like the NAACP fought for African Americans.[34] At the conference, they tried to propose a resolution to press the EEOC to enforce the sex amendment and to call for the reappointment of Richard Graham to the EEOC. The conference organizers refused to accept their resolution, chiefly because criticisms directed at a government agency were being raised at a federally funded conference.[35] At the lunch break, the fifteen fuming women who had caucused in Friedan's hotel room agreed that it was time to launch a new women's organization. On a napkin, Friedan scribbled "NOW, the National Organization for Women to take the actions needed to bring women in the mainstream of American society."[36] By the end of lunch, a total of twenty-seven women had signed on, each contributing five dollars to the fledgling cause. Their first order of business was to send a telegram to the EEOC demanding that it rescind its ruling on sex-segregated help-wanted ads.[37]

Just because Hernandez could not air her grievances at the conference did not mean that she would remain silent. After all, young Aileen had been taught by her mother that if she had issues, she had better speak up about them. Shortly after the conference, she complained to the White House about the delay in replacing the two open commissioner seats and about the high staff turnover. And in September, she wrote a memorandum to the entire EEOC and its staff expressing disappointment in how the EEOC was still failing to enforce the sex amendment more than two years after the Civil Rights Act had been signed into law by President Johnson. She also criticized the EEOC for the unreasonably long lag times that it took to process complaints.[38] Hernandez was unsurprised when her grievances went unanswered: "The majority of both the staff and the Commission, during my tenure on EEOC, had little or no commitment to eliminating sex discrimination."[39]

Aileen Hernandez had been working as diligently as possible to process the deluge of complaints that continued to pile up on her desk. The economic problem of women in the United States was far worse than she had anticipated when she had accepted her position at the EEOC in May 1965. And among those complaints, Hernandez saw evidence of how much more severe the problem of sex discrimination was for women of color.

> There was a remarkable similarity in patterns of discrimination; that those who tended to discriminate on the basis of race or ethnic origin also tended to discriminate on the basis of sex, and vice versa.... Very often minority women had the worst of all possible worlds—exclusion on the basis of race in jobs where white women gained access—clerical, sales, lower level educational positions—and exclusion on the basis of sex where minority men had begun to gain access—blue collar craft jobs, managerial training, law enforcement.... I saw Black women turned down for employment because they had children born out of wedlock while white women were not even asked the question.[40]

Hernandez's frustrations at the EEOC peaked in the fall of 1966. With two seats still vacant, the commission was working at 60 percent capacity. Hernandez was not accustomed to feeling so powerless in a situation. Over the course of her life, her leadership had generally produced positive outcomes. She frequently won the battles she took on. She had proven to a sexist professor that she was more than academically capable to study in a field dominated by men. She and her sisters at Howard had been successful in getting a segregated "white" restaurant to serve them. She had secured workers' rights by mobilizing strikes, pickets, and legislative lobbies as a union organizer for the ILGWU. In her very first foray into election politics, she headed the campaign that won Allan Cranston the position of California state comptroller. And as assistant chief of the California Division of Fair Employment Practices, she made huge strides in enforcing the state's antidiscrimination law fighting for fairer hiring practices for minorities.

But at the EEOC, she was outnumbered and understaffed, and she lacked any real power to enforce Title VII. Years later, when she was testifying before a Senate subcommittee, she was introduced by Senator Evan Bayh as the former chairman of the EEOC. When Hernandez corrected the senator, he remarked that she *should* have been chairman. In her spirited style, Hernandez bantered, "I agree."[41] But because becoming chairman was not an option, Hernandez had to find some other way to bring about change at the EEOC. What could she do to fulfill her commitment to enforce Title VII? How could she bring attention to the unacknowledged problem that women of color face the gravest form of employment discrimination of all? Where would her energies best be directed?

Resolution

The year and a half that Aileen Hernandez had served as commissioner of the EEOC had been an uphill battle to get the agency to enforce the sex amendment. The stewardesses' unions had been the first to file complaints, yet there were still ninety-two of their cases pending, some more than a year old.[42] Hernandez had complained both to the White House and to the commission, but nothing had improved. She was not one to walk away from a problem, but after much deliberation, she finally conceded. On October 10, 1966, with four years left on her term, she turned in her resignation, giving the agency one month's notice. In a 1996 interview, she reflected, "I'd had enough. I'm basically an organizer and wanted to do some things that would get people organized around better enforcement of Title VII."[43]

Leadership in NOW

On the last weekend in October 1966, NOW held its first organizing conference, during which the members issued a press release. They announced the results of their leadership selection, including the decision that Hernandez had been elected executive vice president in absentia. Hernandez declined the position, noting that the nomination was "a charitable, but unauthorized gesture," meant to show support for her resignation from the EEOC.[44] Among the other resolutions mentioned in the press release, the organization announced that NOW was throwing its support behind the stewardesses.

On the second-to-last day of Hernandez's employment at the EEOC, the commission finally ruled that the age-limit policy of the airlines was in violation of Title VII. The airlines fired back just two weeks later with a temporary court order that blocked the ruling, claiming that Hernandez had a conflict of interest. They presumed, based on NOW's press release, that she was a member of the new organization for women. Betty Friedan (NOW's president), Muriel Fox (NOW's public relations person), and Aileen Hernandez were all subpoenaed and ordered to appear in court on Christmas Eve. The attorney for the airlines demanded that the women produce a list of NOW's members, but Friedan refused, as they had all sworn to keep the list secret. In February 1967, a court issued an injunction that rolled back the EEOC's age-discrimination decision because it found Hernandez at fault for having a conflict of interest, even though in actuality she was not a member of NOW. The stewardesses had to begin all over again with their complaints process at the EEOC.

The court ruling refueled Hernandez's commitment to the stewardesses' cause; she reconsidered and agreed to become NOW's western regional vice president in March 1967. NOW eventually was able to help the stewardesses by continuing to lobby the EEOC on their behalf. In June 1968 the EEOC ruled that the marriage restriction violated Title VII, and in August 1968 it published guidelines that disallowed the age restriction.[45] Hernandez remained NOW's regional vice president until March 1970, when she was elected the organization's second president. Under her leadership, NOW continued to pressure the EEOC to enforce Title VII. Concurrently, it fought corporations for the inclusion of women in affirmative action programs and lobbied to get the Equal Rights Amendment passed. In the press, Hernandez frequently drew analogies between racism and sexism, as she considered them equally significant to the greater human rights struggle.[46]

After Hernandez left the EEOC, employers kept inviting her to meet to discuss antidiscrimination legislation: "Having gone to lunch six times in two weeks with the same people, I decided I had enough background and information that I might as well charge them for it."[47] She established her own urban consulting firm, Aileen C. Hernandez Associates, in San Francisco and began to advise clients on issues of transportation, equal opportunity, and housing. Companies that hired her firm included United Parcel Service, Standard Oil of California, the National Catholic Conference on Interracial Justice, the Ford Foundation, Bay Area Rapid Transit District, and the California Department of Health Services.

Black Women and the Difficult Landscape of the Civil Rights Movement

During the civil rights movement, thousands of activists across the United States mobilized politically in a long and tenuous process that sought equality for all before the law.[48] Both Black liberation movements and the women's movement emerged during this era as powerful political groups that fought for the legal equality of African Americans and women, respectively.[49] This does not mean, however, that the women's movement necessarily advocated for racial equality or that Black liberation movements supported the struggle against gender discrimination. Within these organizations, all too often "Black" was equated with Black men, and "woman" was equated with white women.

Black women who participated in the women's movement during the 1960s were often invisible and generally excluded from leadership. Aileen Hernandez was an exception to this norm. Black women were typically not invited to participate on conference panels that were not specifically Black or Third World women;[50] they were not proportionately represented on the faculty of university departments that focused on women's issues,[51] nor were there classes devoted specifically to the study of Black women's literature or history.[52] Furthermore, the few well-known Black women leaders and intellectuals were often treated as tokens—their work accepted as representing the Black experience.[53] Indeed, most women's movement writings from the civil rights era focused on organizing exclusively along the binary gender division and usually excluded women of color. The experiences of white, middle-class women were often described as universal women's experiences, while very few of these women suffered the extreme economic exploitation that most women of color were subjected to day by day.[54] The differences of women's experiences due to race, class, and sexuality were largely overlooked;[55] and the lives, activism, and needs of Black women were rendered invisible by most mainstream feminists.

Reality was not much different for Black women who participated in the Black liberation movements. Similarly, they were often discriminated against by the largely male leadership, but this time they were ignored because they were women. They were rarely allowed to take on leadership roles within the movements, and they were instead expected to care for their men and raise their children "adequately."[56] As a result, several Black women wrote essays and poems discussing the repressive gender relations that characterized male-dominated Black liberation movements in the late 1960s and early 1970s, and denouncing the virulent racial discrimination they were subjected to within the women's movement.[57]

Though often ignored in mainstream media, Black US women like Aileen Hernandez were active participants in the women's movement and the Black liberation movements, but due to subtle and not-so-subtle racism, sexism, and homophobia, Black women decided to form their own organizations, which also included other women of color. The effort to meet the needs of Black women who felt they were being racially oppressed in the women's movement and sexually oppressed in the Black liberation movements—and the need to develop theory that could adequately address the way race, sexuality, gender, and class were interconnected in their lives—prompted the formation of the Black feminist movement, which, though it had been gathering momentum for some time, marks its "birth" with the 1973 founding of the National Black Feminist Organization in New York. This was closely followed by the creation of Black Women Organized for Action (BWOA) in San Francisco, an organization cofounded by Aileen Hernandez.[58]

Cultivating Black Women's Leadership

When Hernandez's term as president of NOW was up in September 1971, she became a committed advocate for women of color in NOW.

She created the Minority Women's Task Force in 1972 and conducted a survey that showed that minorities represented less than 10 percent of NOW's membership. Minority members did not feel as though their concerns were being heard, and they felt isolated in an organization composed of mostly white, middle-class women. In 1973, Hernandez partnered with Patsy Fulcher and Eleanor Spikes, two members of the Task Force, to create BWOA to define and work on Black women's concerns.[59]

In 1973, in BWOA's first public action, the organization addressed the San Francisco Mayor's Committee on the Status of Women, which had held hearings on the status of the city's women yet failed to get any statement from a Black woman. Inspired by this action, the BWOA's founders decided the organization's purpose would be to develop leadership among Black women. The organization would provide education and encouragement to promote Black women's entry into all levels of community operations, such as in government positions and appointments to boards and commissions. In its emphasis on Black women's leadership development, the BWOA was unique for its time.[60] The BWOA appealed to many different women, inside and outside the women's movement, because it recognized the diversity of the women-of-color community in the Bay Area. Members were not required to have a particular political perspective, and they were free to participate in whichever activities they chose. At the end of the day, the imperative for the BWOA was for Black women to be involved in political organizing in any way they considered fit.[61]

Faithful to the organization's mission to develop leadership among as many different Black women as possible, instead of having a top-down structure, the BWOA had rotating leadership: three coordinators served for a three-month period. Hernandez recalled,

> We almost never had an ideological difference because we had agreed that one of the things we had wanted to do was to link African American women from whatever perspective they were in and when people sort of said "that's crazy because some people will do wild things," we said, "How much trouble can you make in three months?" What we said essentially was, "Get the ideas out there.

We don't run from any idea." It certainly made a difference in some cases as to who was participating in the particular event, but it was never an ideological difference in terms of how the organization functioned.[62]

In this way, BWOA was collectively run in a manner that allowed for leadership, work, and community outreach to be shared among those who were willing to participate in the organization. The serving coordinators summoned, prepared, and facilitated the meetings and also served as spokespeople who mediated between BWOA and the media.

After the BWOA meetings ended in 1980, Hernandez continued to work in her urban consulting firm, but her commitment to building and sustaining leadership among Black women never lessened. In 1982, she coordinated a major conference held on the University of California–Berkeley campus titled "Black Women: Toward a Strategy for the Twenty-First Century," and in 1984, along with friend Clara Stanton Jones, she started Black Women Stirring the Waters, a Black women's dialogue group in the San Francisco Bay Area. In 1996, Hernandez renewed the BWOA's status in the Black feminist movement when she signed its name as part of a multipartisan "Contract with Women of the USA" advertisement that appeared in the New York Times. In 1998, she chaired the California Women's Agenda (CAWA), a state action alliance of over six hundred organizations in California that worked together until 2010 to implement the 1995 Beijing Platform at the grassroots. For her relentless work, Hernandez was one of one thousand women from more than 150 countries nominated collectively for the Nobel Peace Prize in 2005. She was an early advocate for bringing together civil rights and women's rights and was applying an intersectional analysis to her own experiences as an African American and a woman before the term intersectionality had even been coined. As a leader in the founding years of both the EEOC and NOW, a feminist in a movement that is often perceived as white, and an advocate of Black women's leadership, Aileen Hernandez has left a rich and unique legacy.

Notes

1 Sojourner Kincaid Rolle, "Interview with Aileen Hernandez," *Outrageous Women*, February 8, 1993, https://archive.org/details/cusb_000085, video.

2 The History Makers, "Aileen Clark Hernandez," n.d., http://www.thehistorymakers.com/biography/aileen-clark-hernandez-41 (accessed March 24, 2015).

3 Emily Teipe, "Aileen Clarke Hernandez," in *The 20th Century Dictionary of World Biography*, vol. 8, *Go–N*, ed. Frank N. Magill (New York: Salem, 1999), 1641.

4 Makers, "Aileen Hernandez," n.d., http://www.makers.com/aileen-hernandez (accessed February 3, 2015), video.

5 KQED News, "Aileen Hernandez: A Pioneer for Women and Civil Rights | KQED This Week," YouTube, March 5, 2013, https://youtu.be/x7hujcEhQuY, video; Makers, "Aileen Hernandez."

6 Makers, "Aileen Hernandez."

7 Joan Oleck, "Hernandez, Aileen Clarke 1926–," Encyclopedia.com, January 1997, http://www.encyclopedia.com/doc/1G2-2871500032.html.

8 Makers, "Aileen Hernandez."

9 Rolle, "Interview with Aileen Hernandez."

10 Makers, "Aileen Hernandez."

11 Otto J. Lindenmeyer, "Aileen C. Hernandez: Commissioner. Equal Opportunity Commission (EEOC) 1965–," in *Negroes in Public Affairs and Government*, ed. Walter Christmas (New York: Educational Heritage, 1966), 330.

12 Jesse B. Clarke, "Through a Gender Lens: Women Re-energize the Movement," *Race, Poverty, & the Environment* 17, no. 2 (2010), http://reimaginerpe.org/node/5634.

13 Blair L. M. Kelley, "Women's History Month: Remembering Pauli Murray—a Heroine Who Fought 'Jane Crow,'" The Grio, March 11, 2014, http://thegrio.com/2014/03/11/womens-history-month-remembering-pauli-murray-a-heroine-who-fought-jane-crow/.

14 Ibid.

15 Rolle, "Interview with Aileen Hernandez."

16 Teipe, "Aileen Clarke Hernandez," 1641.

17 Oleck, "Hernandez, Aileen Clarke 1926–."

18 Clarke, "Through a Gender Lens."

19 Teipe, "Aileen Clarke Hernandez," 1641.

20 Oleck, "Hernandez, Aileen Clarke 1926–."

21 Teipe, "Aileen Clarke Hernandez," 1641.

22 Carl M. Brauer, "Women Activists, Southern Conservatives, and the Prohibition of Sex Discrimination in Title VII of the 1964 Civil Rights Act," *Journal of Southern History* 49, no. 1 (1983): 37–56.

23 Flora Davis, *Moving the Mountain: The Women's Movement in America since 1960* (New York: Simon and Schuster, 1991), 45–46.

24 Cynthia Harrison, *On Account of Sex: The Politics of Women's Issues, 1945–1968* (Berkeley: University of California Press, 1988), 189.

25 Ibid., 187.

26 Aileen Hernandez, "The Women's Movement: 1965–1975, for the Symposium on the Tenth Anniversary of the EEOC," sponsored by Rutgers University Law School, November 28–29, 1975, quoted in Serena Mayeri, *Reasoning from Race: Feminism, Law, and the Civil Rights Revolution* (Cambridge, MA: Harvard University Press, 2011), 45.

27 Feminist Majority Foundation, "The Feminist Chronicles, 1953–1993. Part I—No Women Need Apply," 2014, http://www.feminist.org/research/chronicles/part1b.html.

28 *New Republic*, September 4, 1965, in folder "General 1964–1966," box "Title VII," Catherine East Papers, Arlington, VA, quoted in Harrison, *On Account of Sex*, 188.

29 Sonia Pressman Fuentes, "Representing Women," *Frontiers* 18, no. 3 (1997): 97.

30 Davis, *Moving the Mountain*, 16, 17, 22.

31 Herman Edelsberg, quoted by Martha Griffiths in her speech to the House, June 20, 1966: "Congresswoman Griffiths on the EEOC," *Congressional Record* 112:13689–13694, quoted in Harrison, *On Account of Sex*, 190.

32 Martha Griffiths in her speech to the House, June 20, 1966, quoted in Harrison, *On Account of Sex*, 191.

33 Harrison, *On Account of Sex*, 191.

34 Fuentes, "Representing Women," 102; Feminist Majority Foundation, "Feminist Chronicles."

35 Harrison, *On Account of Sex*, 194.

36 Betty Friedan, *It Changed My Life: Writings on the Women's Movement* (New York: Norton, 1985): 83, quoted in Davis, *Moving the Mountain*, 54.

37 Feminist Majority Foundation, "Feminist Chronicles."

38 Harrison, *On Account of Sex*, 195–196.

39 Aileen Hernandez, "Statement of Aileen C. Hernandez, Former Member, Equal Employment Opportunity Commission," in *Economic Problems of Women: Hearings before the Joint Economic Committee, Congress of the United States, Ninety-Third Congress, First Session, Part 1, July 10, 11, and 12, 1973* (Washington, DC: US Government Printing Office, 1973), 130–131, https://ia600402.us.archive.org/3/items/economicproblems00unit/economicproblems00unit.pdf.

40 Ibid., 129.

41 Aileen Hernandez, "Statement of Mrs. Aileen Hernandez, President, National Organization for Women," in *Women and the "Equal Rights" Amendment: Senate Subcommittee Hearings on the Constitutional Amendment, 91st Congress*, ed. Catharine Stimpson (New York: R. R. Bowker, 1972), 38.

42 Davis, *Moving the Mountain*, 22–23.

43 Oleck, "Hernandez, Aileen Clarke 1926–."

44 Hernandez, "Women's Movement," quoted in Davis, *Moving the Mountain*, 23.

45 Davis, *Moving the Mountain*, 22–24.

46 Mayeri, *Reasoning from Race*, 46.

47 Oleck, "Hernandez, Aileen Clarke 1926–."

48 For more on the Civil Rights Movement and its relation to the demand of equality before the law, see Sara Evans, *Personal Politics: The Roots of Women's*

Liberation in the Civil Rights Movement and the New Left (New York: Vintage Books, 1980).

49 There were several different movements for Black liberation, including the Civil Rights Movement, Black nationalism, the Black Panthers, and the Student Nonviolent Coordinating Committee; and there were similarly various movements for the emancipation of women during the civil rights era, including, e.g., the League of Women Voters and the National Organization for Women.

50 Audre Lorde, "The Master's Tools Will Never Dismantle the Master's House," in *Sister Outsider* (New York: Crossing Press, 1984), 110.

51 V. P. Franklin, "Hidden in Plain View: African American Women, Radical Feminism, and the Origins of Women's Studies Programs, 1967–1974," *Journal of African American History* 87 (2002): 433–445.

52 Armstead L. Robinson, "A Concluding Statement," in *Black Studies in the University: A Symposium*, ed. Armstead L. Robinson, Craig C. Foster, and Donald H. Ogilvie (New Haven, CT: Yale University Press, 1969), 216–217.

53 Gloria T. Hull and Barbara Smith, "Introduction: The Politics of Black Women's Studies," in *All the Women Are White, All the Blacks Are Men, but Some of Us Are Brave: Black Women's Studies*, ed. Gloria T. Hull, Patricia Bell Scott, and Barbara Smith (New York: Feminist Press, 1982), xxvi.

54 Frances M. Beal, "Double Jeopardy: To Be Black and Female," in *The Black Woman*, ed. Toni Cade Bambara (New York: Washington Square, 1970), 109–122.

55 See, for example, Patricia H. Collins, *Black Feminist Thought: Knowledge, Consciousness and the Politics of Empowerment* (New York: Routledge, 1999); Paula Giddings, *When and Where I Enter: The Impact of Black Women on Race and Sex in America* (New York: William Morrow, 1984); Robin Morgan, ed., *Sisterhood Is Powerful: An Anthology of Writings from the Women's Liberation Movement* (New York: Vintage Books, 1970).

56 Angela Davis, *An Autobiography* (New York: Random House, 1974), 161, 181, 187.

57 See, for example, Angela D. Le Blanc-Ernest, "The Most Qualified Person to Handle the Job: Black Panther Women 1966–1982," in *The Black Panther Party Reconsidered*, ed. Charles E. Jones (Baltimore: Black Classic Press, 1998); Frances E. White, "Africa on My Mind: Gender, Counter Discourse and African American Nationalism," *Journal of Women's History* 2 (1990): 73–97.

58 Beverly Davis, "To Seize the Moment: A Retrospective on the National Black Feminist Organization," *SAGE* 5 (1988): 46–49.

59 Kimberly Springer, *Living for the Revolution: Black Feminist Organizations, 1968–1980*, Kindle Edition (Durham, NC: Duke University Press, 2005), 846–854.

60 Ibid., 870.

61 Ibid., 1017–1019.

62 Kimberly Springer, "Aileen Hernandez, BWOA Founder," audio recording, Black Feminism Archives, September 14, 1997, http://blackfeminism.omeka.net/items/show/2.

Bibliography

Beal, Frances M. "Double Jeopardy: To Be Black and Female." In *The Black Woman*, edited by Toni Cade Bambara, 109–122. New York: Washington Square, 1970.

Brauer, Carl M. "Women Activists, Southern Conservatives, and the Prohibition of Sex Discrimination in Title VII of the 1964 Civil Rights Act." *Journal of Southern History* 49, no. 1 (1983): 37–56.

Clarke, Jesse B. "Through a Gender Lens: Women Re-energize the Movement." *Race, Poverty, & the Environment* 17, no. 2 (2010). http://reimaginerpe.org/node/5634.

Collins, Patricia H. *Black Feminist Thought: Knowledge, Consciousness and the Politics of Empowerment*. New York: Routledge, 1999.

Davis, Angela. *An Autobiography*. New York: Random House, 1974.

Davis, Beverly. "To Seize the Moment: A Retrospective on the National Black Feminist Organization." *SAGE* 5 (1988): 43–60.

Davis, Flora. *Moving the Mountain: The Women's Movement in America since 1960*. New York: Simon and Schuster, 1991.

Evans, Sara. *Personal Politics: The Roots of Women's Liberation in the Civil Rights Movement and the New Left*. New York: Vintage Books, 1980.

Feminist Majority Foundation. "The Feminist Chronicles, 1953–1993. Part I—No Women Need Apply." 2014. http://www.feminist.org/research/chronicles/part1b.html.

Franklin, V. P. "Hidden in Plain View: African American Women, Radical Feminism, and the Origins of Women's Studies Programs, 1967–1974." *Journal of African American History* 87 (2002): 433–445.

Friedan, Betty. *It Changed My Life: Writings on the Women's Movement*. New York: Norton, 1985.

Fuentes, Sonia Pressman. "Representing Women." *Frontiers* 18, no. 3 (1997): 92–109.

Giddings, Paula. *When and Where I Enter: The Impact of Black Women on Race and Sex in America*. New York: William Morrow, 1984.

Griffiths, Martha. "Congresswoman Griffiths on the EEOC." *Congressional Record* 112 (June 20, 1966): 13689–13694.

Harrison, Cynthia. *On Account of Sex: The Politics of Women's Issues, 1945–1968*. Berkeley: University of California Press, 1988.

Hernandez, Aileen. "Statement of Aileen C. Hernandez, Former Member, Equal Employment Opportunity Commission." In *Economic Problems of Women: Hearings before the Joint Economic Committee, Congress of the United States, Ninety-Third Congress, First Session, Part 1, July 10, 11, and 12, 1973*, 128–150. Washington, DC: US Government Printing Office, 1973. https://ia600402.us .archive.org/3/items/economicproblems00unit/economicproblems00unit.pdf.

———. "Statement of Mrs. Aileen Hernandez, President, National Organization for Women." In *Women and the "Equal Rights" Amendment: Senate Subcommittee Hearings on the Constitutional Amendment, 91st Congress*, edited by Catharine Stimpson. New York: R. R. Bowker, 1972.

———. "The Women's Movement: 1965–1975, for the Symposium on the Tenth Anniversary of the EEOC." Sponsored by Rutgers University Law School, November 28–29, 1975.

History Makers, The. "Aileen Clark Hernandez." n.d. http://www.thehistorymakers
.com/biography/aileen-clark-hernandez-41 (accessed March 24, 2015).

Hull, Gloria T. and Barbara Smith. "Introduction: The Politics of Black Women's
Studies." In *All the Women Are White, All the Blacks Are Men, but Some of Us Are
Brave: Black Women's Studies*, edited by Gloria T. Hull, Patricia Bell Scott, and
Barbara Smith, xvii–xxxii. New York: Feminist Press, 1982.

Kelley, Blair L. M. "Women's History Month: Remembering Pauli Murray—a Heroine Who Fought 'Jane Crow.'" The Grio, March 11, 2014. http://thegrio.com/
2014/03/11/womens-history-month-remembering-pauli-murray-a-heroine-who
-fought-jane-crow/.

KQED News. "Aileen Hernandez: A Pioneer for Women and Civil Rights | KQED
This Week." YouTube, March 5, 2013. https://youtu.be/x7hujcEhQuY. Video.

Le Blanc-Ernest, Angela D. "The Most Qualified Person to Handle the Job: Black
Panther Women 1966–1982." In *The Black Panther Party Reconsidered*, edited by
Charles E. Jones, 305–335. Baltimore: Black Classic Press, 1998.

Lindenmeyer, Otto J. "Aileen C. Hernandez: Commissioner. Equal Opportunity
Commission (EEOC) 1965–." In *Negroes in Public Affairs and Government*, edited
by Walter Christmas, 330–331. New York: Educational Heritage, 1966.

Lorde, Audre. "The Master's Tools Will Never Dismantle the Master's House." In
Sister Outsider. New York: Crossing Press, 1984.

Makers. "Aileen Hernandez." n.d. http://www.makers.com/aileen-hernandez
(accessed February 3, 2015). Video.

Mayeri, Serena. *Reasoning from Race: Feminism, Law, and the Civil Rights Revolution*.
Cambridge, MA: Harvard University Press, 2011.

Morgan, Robin, ed. *Sisterhood Is Powerful: An Anthology of Writings from the Women's
Liberation Movement*. New York: Vintage Books, 1970.

New Republic, September 4, 1965. In folder "General 1964–1966," box "Title VII,"
Catherine East Papers, Arlington, VA.

Oleck, Joan. "Hernandez, Aileen Clarke 1926–." Encyclopedia.com, January 1997.
http://www.encyclopedia.com/doc/1G2-2871500032.html.

Robinson, Armstead L. "A Concluding Statement." In *Black Studies in the University:
A Symposium*, edited by Armstead L. Robinson, Craig C. Foster, and Donald H.
Ogilvie, 216–217. New Haven, CT: Yale University Press, 1969.

Rolle, Sojourner Kincaid. "Interview with Aileen Hernandez." *Outrageous Women*.
February 8, 1993. https://archive.org/details/cusb_000085. Video.

Springer, Kimberly. "Aileen Hernandez, BWOA Founder." Audio recording. Black
Feminism Archives, September 14, 1997. http://blackfeminism.omeka.net/
items/show/2.

———. *Living for the Revolution: Black Feminist Organizations, 1968–1980*, Kindle
Edition. Durham, NC: Duke University Press, 2005.

Teipe, Emily. "Aileen Clarke Hernandez." In *The 20th Century Dictionary of World
Biography*, vol. 8, *Go–N*, edited by Frank N. Magill, 1641–1643. New York: Salem,
1999.

White, Frances E. "Africa on My Mind: Gender, Counter Discourse and African
American Nationalism." *Journal of Women's History* 2 (1990): 73–97.

Mirna Cunningham

Indigenous Women and Revolutionary Change in Nicaragua

Miriam Tola and Alison R. Bernstein

Background

A Miskitu Indian from the Atlantic Coast region of Nicaragua, Mirna Cunningham is a leading voice for Indigenous rights in a variety of international forums, including the United Nations. She has been an important figure in Nicaragua's political landscape since the early 1980s, the turbulent years of the Sandinista revolution. This is the period when she faced a complex host of issues related to ethnicity, national liberation, and gender.

On the one hand, as representative of the Sandinista Front for National Liberation (FSLN) in her native area on the Coco River, she had to address the hostility of the Indigenous population toward the Sandinista government. On the other hand, she confronted the distrust of the same Sandinista party leadership toward Indigenous peoples and rural women. In that difficult context, marked by violence and poverty, her skills as a mediator proved crucial for creating the legal platform for the autonomy of Indigenous peoples and ethnic communities in coastal Nicaragua. During key years in the 1980s, Cunningham became increasingly identified with Indigenous struggles. In particular, she became an outspoken advocate for Indigenous women, working relentlessly to advance their demands. The experience gained at the local level enabled her to become an internationally recognized activist for Indigenous rights to land, health, education, and self-government.

What strategies did she use to implement her vision of creating a bridge between the Sandinista nationalist project and Indigenous autonomy? How did she use her skills as a mediator and negotiator to strengthen Indigenous political participation? What has been her contribution to the development of Indigenous women's leadership?

Born in 1947, Cunningham was raised in a mother-centered extended Miskitu family on the Coco River. She experienced discrimination as a child when a Catholic school refused to accept her and a group of Miskitu children because they subscribed to the Moravian religion and did not speak Spanish. Eventually, the school granted them admission. In high school, she developed a keen sense of the hierarchy separating white kids whose families worked for US multinationals from the Spanish-speaking Mestizos and the black and Indigenous kids who were at the bottom of the pyramid. Later in her life, she described her situation in terms of "triple oppression" to indicate the situation of women who were poor and ethnically different from the dominant Nicaraguan class. Marked by differences of ethnicity, gender, and class, Cunningham went on to become the first Miskitu Indian to graduate with a degree in medicine. She was one of the few women from the coast studying in Léon, a conservative city on the Pacific side of Nicaragua.

In 1979, Cunningham, then a young thirty-two-year-old doctor, witnessed the overthrow by the FSLN of Anastasio Somoza, the last ruler of a family dictatorship that had been in power in Nicaragua since 1936. Founded by a group of university students including Carlos Fonseca, Tomás Borge, and Silvio Mayorga in 1961, the FSLN was a vanguard organization with heterogeneous ideological inspirations. The Cuban socialist revolution was an important source of influence, as was the anti-imperialist and nationalist example of Augusto Cesar Sandino, the Nicaraguan general who had challenged US interventionism in the 1920s. The organization also had ties with the emerging theology of liberation that advocated on behalf of the poor. The FSLN enjoyed vast support among students, peasants, and workers, but even sectors of the bourgeoisie funded the organization in the hope of getting rid of the Somoza family's regime.

Opposition to the regime grew dramatically after Somoza diverted parts of the international aid that poured into the country in the aftermath of the devastating Managua earthquake of 1972. Somoza's failure to repress a generalized insurrection, an urban strike, and the FSLN military offensive in 1979 led the junta to seize power, and Sandinistas took over. During the insurrection, fifty thousand Nicaraguans, or 2 percent of the population, lost their lives.

In Leon, Cunningham became involved with the FSLN. She not only joined other students in mass demonstrations but also conducted various clandestine activities. She said, "I think we were all of two women from the coast studying in Léon at the time, . . . and on top of being black we were poor. The discrimination we suffered certainly pushed us toward the FSLN, and our sense of what the FSLN was about was much more emotional than political back then."[1] The Sandinista movement, however, had its own problems of discrimination. As Cunningham explained, "The Sandinista National Liberation Front, besides being sexist, is an ethnocentric organization. At a certain political level, politically, I believe that the comrades have tried to understand and deal with the problems of the Atlantic Coast. But in more subtle ways there's still a lot of sexism, a lot of ethnocentricity, and this puts Sandinista women at a disadvantage."[2] These comments resonate with the experience of many other women militants. For example, the popular writer Gioconda Belli, an upper-class Nicaraguan who took part in the guerrilla movement and later occupied various government posts, observed, "We'd led troops into battle, we'd done all sorts of things, and then as soon as the Sandinistas took office we were displaced from the important posts. We'd had to content ourselves with intermediate-level positions for the most part."[3]

At the peak of the revolution, however, Cunningham was determined to contribute to the Sandinista project. She went back to work as a doctor in the hospital of Bilwaskarma, the village on the Coco River where she was born. She was appointed delegate of the Ministry of Health. Here, the Indigenous population had grown increasingly hostile to the Sandinista government and its supporters.

In 1980, the powerful, autonomist Indian organization MIS-URASATA, until then allied with the Sandinistas, challenged the central government with demands for the autonomy of the Atlantic Coast that included bilingual education and, most importantly, the claim to 30 percent of the national territory. Initially, the Sandinista government maintained that the revolutionary state had the exclusive right to decide on questions of land ownership. Indigenous demands for territorial rights were viewed as a threat to national unity. Tensions exploded when the revolutionary authorities ordered the arrest of MISURASATA leaders, accusing them of fomenting a separatist uprising. They were all released within a week except for the popular Steadman Fagoth, who eventually became the leader of a Miskitu guerrilla group supported by the CIA. The conflict between the Sandinista army and the Miskitu insurgency, sometimes allied with the contras, deepened until the Sandinistas decided to negotiate a political settlement to the conflict.

The Sandinistas faced a strained economy, with only $3 million in the treasury and a foreign debt of $1.6 billion, and the new government promised to promote a mixed economic policy. Among its first acts after assuming control was the confiscation of land owned by the Somozas and other wealthy families. Approximately 20 percent of the country's agricultural land was redistributed among poor and landless farmers. Next, the Sandinistas launched massive campaigns to address illiteracy and improve the health of the Nicaraguan people. In the course of a five-month "literacy crusade," one hundred thousand volunteer teachers reached about forty thousand people. As a result, the rate of illiteracy dropped from 50 to 13 percent. In 1981, a public health campaign mobilized about twenty-five thousand volunteers to implement a program including mass immunization, sanitation measures, and breast-feeding support. The effort reduced infant mortality and contributed to a rapid demographic increase. These achievements received international recognition. The literacy crusade was awarded a prize by the United Nations Educational, Scientific and Cultural Organization (UNESCO), and the World Health Organization praised Nicaragua's health care model as an example for the developing world.

Despite the machismo of the FSLN's leaders, the organization promoted a largely progressive gender policy. The Sandinista government instituted equal pay for equal work, provided health care for mothers and children, built day-care centers, and banned advertising that exploited women's bodies.[4] Women played an important role in the revolutionary process. In 1979, they constituted between 25 and 30 percent of the insurrectional forces engaged in combat.[5] Women constituted 60 percent of the literacy brigades, and over 70 percent of the workers engaged in the health campaign were women. The massive involvement in the literacy and health campaigns was largely the result of the recruitment strategy pursued by the Luisa Amanda Espinosa Association of Nicaraguan Women (AMNLAE), the Sandinista organization that worked to integrate women in the construction of the Sandinista state and to advance reproductive rights and gender equality. However, as the counterrevolutionary threats and attacks increased, the AMNLAE was asked to prioritize the defense of the Sandinista nation over the struggle for gender rights. Members of the organization were mobilized to provide support to the families of the soldiers wounded in the civil war against the counterrevolutionary forces, to sew military uniforms, and to raise money for community projects.

Ultimately, the FSLN had mixed success with regard to gender policies and women's struggles in revolutionary Nicaragua. A striking example of the difficulties in the transformation of gender roles in the country was women's underrepresentation in the key decision-making bodies of the FSLN. Until 1994, women were excluded from the National Directorate, the executive organ of the party.

The ousting of the Somozas had taken place in a favorable geopolitical situation. The social democracies in Europe and Latin America supported the removal of the corrupt regime. After a long tradition of US interference in Nicaraguan economy and politics, the Carter administration was oriented toward nonintervention. This scenario, however, changed quickly in 1981 with the election of Ronald Reagan as president of the United States. Nicaragua became a top foreign-policy issue that generated heated debate in and outside Washington. Soon after the deposition of Somoza, members of his

National Guard formed counterrevolutionary forces, known as the "contras," that operated from bases in Nicaragua, Honduras, and Costa Rica. The contras attacked rural villages; kidnapped, raped, and killed civilians who supported the FSLN, boycotted infrastructures; and disrupted social and economic services. During the Reagan administration, the United States spent over $19 million to provide financial aid, arms, and training to the counterrevolutionary militias. The CIA was authorized to undertake a series of covert operations that included the mining of Nicaraguan harbors in 1984. As a result of congressional opposition to secret CIA missions, the aid to the contras was officially cut off. However, as the Iran-Contra scandal later revealed, the White House continued to transfer weapons and money to the counterrevolutionary groups illegally.

To make things more complicated for the Sandinista government, on the Atlantic Coast of Nicaragua, the contras forged an alliance with some leaders of the Indigenous autonomist movement in an attempt to undermine the central government. The history and culture of the region differs profoundly from the rest of the country. While Pacific Nicaragua was colonized by Spain, the Atlantic region was under the influence of British colonial power and represented a strong Indigenous and Afro-Caribbean tradition. Among several Indigenous communities living on the coast, the Miskitu are the most populous and had enjoyed a privileged status because of their close relationship with the English crown. In the nineteenth century, however, with the establishment of US economic enclaves on the coast, the balance of power shifted in favor of the Creole population.

In December 1981, a squad of twenty men kidnapped Cunningham and the Miskitu nurse Regina Lewis outside the hospital of Bilwaskarma. They were taken to a house on the Coco River, beaten, and raped. Cunningham recalled, "They had us there for seven hours. During those hours we were raped for the first time."[6] Then, the two prisoners were transferred across the river to a training camp in Honduras, where their kidnappers, Miskitu Indians from MISURASATA and former members of Somoza's army, offered them American cigarettes and boasted of the support they received from the United States. They were released a few hours later.

According to Cunningham, the Indigenous community of Bilwas-karma asked the kidnappers to set them free. This happened because, in addition to being from the area, Cunningham had gained the trust of the Indigenous community through her medical practice. As she put it, "I was born in Bilwaskarma. And by the time of this incident, I'd worked as a doctor there for eight years. The ordinary people in the village were very upset over what had happened: the women, the old people. They were anguished about the kidnapping. . . . They also put an enormous pressure on MISURASATA for a public trial: they wanted to set us free. And at 5:00 in the morning, with the entire community assembled, they made the decision to let us go."[7] In the days following the kidnapping, amid rumors of Indigenous uprisings in the region, contras' attacks, and Sandinista reprisals, almost the entire community fled in terror.

At the national level, despite conflicts within the FSLN about the merits of democratic elections, the people of Nicaragua went to vote in 1984. The FSLN won with 67 percent of the popular vote. In order to further increase the pressure on the Sandinista government, the United States imposed an economic embargo that weighed heavily on the Nicaraguan economy. In the United States, the policies of the Reagan administration were countered by a strong grassroots movement that denounced the US aid to the contras, demanded the end of the embargo, and created a network of solidarity with the people of Nicaragua. The civil war took a devastating toll on Nicaragua: 30,000 people were killed and 350,000 were displaced.[8] In the 1990 elections, the Unión Nacional Opositora (UNO) defeated the FSLN with 55 percent of the popular vote. Violeta Barrios de Chamorro, an outspoken foe of the Sandinistas and the widow of a prominent newspaper editor killed by the Somoza regime, became president. Her government immediately shifted from the Sandinista redistributive model to structural adjustment policies devised in conjunction with the International Monetary Fund (IMF). Chamorro's economic measures included privatization of state agencies and cuts of social services.

Looking back, throughout the late 1980s, Cunningham found herself in the eye of a never-ending storm. A victim of war, violence, and rape, how was she to find the strength to address the challenge to represent the Sandinista movement in an area where large segments of the population were joining the contras forces? How was she to mediate between the project of economic redistribution pursued by the Sandinistas and the demands for autonomy of her Indigenous community? Further, she was immersed in a geopolitical scenario in which a foreign superpower, the United States, was waging a low-intensity war against the FSLN. How was she to contribute to a political process influenced by actors and forces operating outside Nicaragua's borders?

Resolution

When the American writer Margaret Randall asked Mirna Cunningham to recount what she did in the days following the contras attack, she glossed over the personal trauma and simply said, "I returned to the community. But of course the community no longer existed; everyone had gone."[9] Yet, looking retrospectively, it is clear that her response was multifaceted and articulated on different levels. Not only did she decide to stay in an area that was fraught with dangers for her, but her work as a mediator was crucial for integrating the demands of autonomy and rights of Indigenous peoples into the Sandinista national project. In the process, however, she became increasingly interested in the development of a political agenda for Indigenous groups, with particular focus on health, education, and gender. Importantly, she also contributed to building the Indigenous rights solidarity movement at the international level.

The kidnapping of Mirna Cunningham was followed by the destabilization of the entire area of the Coco River. The Nicaragua government reacted to the guerrilla attacks in the Atlantic Coast with a move that provoked much criticism. An estimated eighty-five hundred to ten thousand Miskitus and Sumu people were relocated fifty miles from the Rio Coco region into resettlement camps called Tasba Pri (Free Land). Another ten thousand people crossed the river into Honduras. The Sandinistas destroyed houses and livestock in the evacuated areas to prevent the contras from establishing their camps there. The government's official motivation for the resettlement was that the Indigenous communities had to be protected from attack by contras. Many among the Miskitus, however, viewed the relocation as an imposition by the "Spanish" central government. The United States condemned the resettlement as an act of genocide and disseminated information about mass killings that was later rejected as a fabrication by international human rights organizations. In a 1984 speech, Reagan reiterated these charges: "There has been an attempt to wipe out an entire culture, the Miskito Indians, thousands of whom have been slaughtered or herded into detention camps where they have been starved and abused."[10]

What was Cunningham's role in the resettlement? Despite the controversies, she expressed support for it and argued that the government "began evacuating people for their own safety."[11] As a doctor, she was charged with supervising the health condition of the evacuated Miskitus. Under intense international scrutiny for the forced evacuation, the Sandinista authorities invested considerable human and economic resources to improve the living conditions at Tasba Pri and invited international observers to visit the camps. Cunningham's responsibilities, however, extended beyond her medical practice. Although she was considered a traitor by some members of the Miskitu exile organizations, Cunningham was among a handful of Sandinista militants who put pressure on the FSLN to shift from a merely military approach to the Atlantic Coast to a political one.

Cunningham's effort to combine the nationalist, revolutionary project and the Indigenous project of autonomy in the same framework proved fruitful. In 1984, after intense internal debate, the FSLN announced measures leading to an autonomy law for the Atlantic Coast, a region representing over one-third of Nicaragua territory with a population of about three hundred thousand Indigenous people. Acting as a bridge between Sandinistas and Indigenous leaders and well regarded by both parties, Cunningham was a key participant in the difficult negotiations leading to the agreement. Because of her work of mediation, she has been described as an "insider-partial," an essential figure in conflict resolution "whose acceptability to the conflictants is rooted not in distance from the conflict or objectivity regarding the issues, but rather in connectedness and trusted relationship with the conflict parties. The trust comes partly from the fact that the mediators do not leave the postnegotiation situation. They are part of it and must live with the consequences of their work. They must continue to relate to conflictants who have trusted their commitment to a just and durable settlement."[12]

The Nicaraguan autonomy reform acknowledges the right of Indigenous peoples, Afro-descendants, and ethnic communities that live within Nicaraguan territory to preserve and develop their culture and languages. It guarantees the right, use, and control of communal lands and resources according to customs and stipulates the structure of local governments, whose composition reflects the multiethnic character of the region. In 1984, Mirna Cunningham was appointed the first governor of the North Atlantic Coast. A multiethnic assembly ratified the proposal that became national law in 1987 when it was approved by the National Assembly.

Cunningham was also active at the international level as the plaintiff in two lawsuits in US courts against the Reagan administration. The first case, *Sanchez Espinoza v. Reagan*, was filed by the New York–based Center for Constitutional Rights in 1982. In this case, Cunningham was joined by other Nicaraguan victims of contras' violence. According to the Center for Constitutional Rights (CCR) attorney Jules Lobel, the complaint was the first "to portray the contras as terrorists who were attacking the civilian population" and to request "broad relief—an injunction against US aid to the contras, as well as damages—that a court was unlikely to grant."[13] Cunningham's motivation for suing the United States was straightforward: "Because I was kidnapped, beaten, raped, because I have seen so many Nicaraguan mothers crying because they lost their children, because I have seen and I have heard about hundreds of Nicaraguans who have been kidnapped, I have joined the lawsuit against the Reagan Administration, hoping this would help stop the attack against Nicaragua and protect other Nicaraguans from these brutalities."[14]

The second lawsuit, *Dellums and Cunningham v. Smith*, was filed by Cunningham, Congressman Ron Dellums of California, and the

Florida ACLU president Eleanor Ginsberg, who lived in the area where the CIA was running contras training camps. The goal of the suit was to force Attorney General William French Smith to initiate an investigation to verify whether the Reagan administration had violated the US Neutrality Act through its policies in Central America. Enacted in 1794, the Neutrality Act states that it is illegal for the United States to support, organize, and finance paramilitary actions against a country with which the United States is not officially at war.

Eventually, both lawsuits were dismissed by the courts. Yet the publicity they generated was instrumental for the growth of a solidarity movement in the United States. In order to spread information about the role of the United States in the conflict in Nicaragua, Cunningham, assisted by the Center for Constitutional Rights, traveled to New York and Washington to meet with Senator Ted Kennedy and other members of Congress. She effectively used the media by participating in the launch of *Talking Nicaragua*, a dramatization and video involving testimony of Nicaraguans affected by contras' violence. *Talking Nicaragua* was produced by the activist and poet Kathy Engel and narrated by, among others, the actress Susan Sarandon. Soon after, Engel and Sarandon established the women's rights organization MADRE, which today considers Cunningham as a "founding partner." Executive Director Kathy Engel explained that the purpose of the organization was "to get women here to connect the issues they face in their own communities with the effect of our policies in Central America."[15] In 1984, members of MADRE traveled to Nicaragua for a trip that generated considerable media attention. According to Sarandon's biography, "They walked through bombed-out daycare centers, witnessed children playing in abandoned tanks, and saw young children begging for pencils rather than money."[16]

Meanwhile, in Nicaragua, the autonomy-building process for Indigenous communities living on the Atlantic Coast proved long and complex. It was not until 1990 that the people of this coast were able to elect their first regional authorities. The FSLN, which at the national level lost the elections to UNO, the coalition headed by Violeta Chamorro, was excluded by the Junta Directive of the regional council. Cunningham, in a shift in her primary allegiances, commented on the defeat and the transition of the Sandinista party from government to opposition, as a member of the first regional autonomous council of the North Atlantic Autonomous Region and also as a member of the National Assembly: "I think the future of the Atlantic Coast depends upon our ability to articulate the people's needs and put Party interests in second place. For us, those interests may be less relevant than in the rest of the country; it's time we prioritize the specific interests of the region."[17]

Through her political work in coastal Nicaragua, Cunningham had become more involved with indigenous issues and grassroots organizing. Her break with the FSLN occurred in the mid-1990s. By 1994, women had achieved some victories at the FSLN Congress. The delegates voted to institute a "quota of power" of 30 percent women at all leadership levels. The number of the National Directorate was increased to fifteen members, and for the first time, one-third of them, including Cunningham, were women. Yet the party seemed unable to make substantial progress on questions of gender and Indigenous autonomy. Because of these and other political factors, Cunningham left the ranks of the party. Building on the remarkable experience of multiethnic autonomy developed in Nicaragua and on the acute awareness of the importance of creating alliances among Indigenous groups, Cunningham continued to pursue the advancement of Indigenous self-government in a variety of local and international forums.

Since the mid-1990s, Cunningham has focused particularly on Indigenous women's struggles for land, education, and health, thus contributing to the development of Indigenous feminism. She worked to make gender an integral part of the struggle of Indigenous peoples in Nicaragua and beyond. At home, on the Atlantic Coast, while men traditionally worked for multinational companies, women were in charge of managing the life in the communities. Their considerable power was reflected in the large number of women in public office. And yet they also had to deal with widespread domestic violence. One way in which Cunningham addressed these issues was through the promotion of educational paradigms that integrate Indigenous traditional knowledge and gender perspectives.

To accomplish this, Cunningham became the driving force behind the creation of the University of the Autonomous Region of the Caribbean Coast of Nicaragua (URACCAN), and she served as the first chancellor of the institution. A multiethnic, intercultural community university, URACCAN offers affordable access to higher education to people from the coast. Its main goal is to provide local youth with the knowledge and the skills necessary to exercise their autonomous rights. "We literally started in the streets," recalled Cunningham. "Little by little, we've built our own buildings."[18] Currently, over ten thousand students distributed in four Atlantic Coast campuses attend the university, with over two hundred professors teaching courses. The curriculum includes courses in natural resources management, nursing, multicultural education, traditional medicine, and regional autonomy administration.

URACCAN was one of the first Latin American institutions of Indigenous higher education to introduce a gender perspective in the curriculum with the opening of the Center for Studies and Information on the Multiethnic Woman (CEIMM). The goal of such an innovative approach is to strengthen the visibility and demands of Indigenous women within Indigenous communities. For Cunningham, "Indigenous women face a different type of oppression. Although we are all Indigenous people facing external oppression, sometimes the internal oppression that women face makes it much more difficult for women to participate. Usually the mixed organizations, men and women, are struggling together to advance the rights of the community as a whole, but sometimes women's rights are invisible in that context."[19]

Given Cunningham's background, it is not surprising that she was one of the organizers of the first Indigenous Women's Summit in Oaxaca, Mexico, in 2002. This was followed by the International Indigenous Women's Forum in New York in 2005 and the 2013 World Conference of Indigenous Women in Lima, Peru. Cunningham played a prominent role in each of these important gatherings. The meetings offered the participants the opportunity to discuss local realities and global processes affecting them, to identify common goals, and to strategize about how to achieve them. In addition, from 2011 to 2013, Cunningham was named chair of the United Nations Permanent Forum on Indigenous Issues. Today, in Bilwi, on the north coast of Nicaragua, Cunningham runs Casa Museo Judith Kain and the Center for Indigenous People's Autonomy and Development (CADPI), a non governmental organization working on intercultural communication, cultural revitalization, climate change and its impact on Indigenous communities, and of course, indigenous women's rights. Cunningham's evolution from committed community-based physician to Sandinista revolutionary, government official, and finally, internationally recognized Indigenous women's rights advocate demonstrates the ability of a woman leader to remain true to core values within shifting political and social movements.

Notes

1 Margaret Randall, *Sandino's Daughter Revisited: Feminism in Nicaragua* (New Brunswick, NJ: Rutgers University Press, 1994), 4.
2 Ibid., 75.
3 Ibid., 179.
4 Lorraine Bayard de Volo, *Mothers of Heroes and Martyrs: Gender Identity Politics in Nicaragua 1979–1999* (Baltimore: John Hopkins University Press, 2001), 35.
5 Randall, *Sandino's Daughter Revisited*, 26.
6 Holly Sklar, *Washington's War on Nicaragua* (Boston: South End, 1988), 103.
7 Randall, *Sandino's Daughter Revisited*, 73.
8 Roger Peace, *A Call to Conscience: The Anti-contra War Campaign* (Amherst: University of Massachusetts Press, 2012), 24.
9 Randall, *Sandino's Daughter Revisited*, 73.
10 Ronald Reagan, "Address to the Nation on United States Policy in Central America," May 9, 1984, Ronald Reagan Presidential Library and Museum, http://www.reagan.utexas.edu/archives/speeches/1984/50984h.htm, quoted in Sklar, *Washington's War on Nicaragua*, 105.
11 Randall, *Sandino's Daughter Revisited*, 74.
12 Paul Wehr and John Paul Lederrach, "Mediating Conflict in Central America," in *Resolving International Conflicts: The Theory and Practice of Mediation*, ed. Jacob Bercovitch (Boulder, CO: Lynne Rienner, 1996), 58.
13 Jules Lobel, *Success without Victory: Lost Legal Battles and the Long Road to Justice in America* (New York: NYU Press, 2004), 197.
14 Ibid., 195.

15 Marc Shapiro, *Susan Sarandon: Actress-Activist* (New York: Prometheus Books, 2001), 104.
16 Ibid., 106.
17 Randall, *Sandino's Daughter Revisited*, 82.
18 Peter Bate, "A College for Real Life," *IDB América: Magazine of the Inter-American Development Bank*, May 1, 2000, http://www.iadb.org/en/news/webstories/2000–05–01/a-college-for-real-life,8485.html.
19 Sarah Cadorette, "The Prescription for Indigenous Rights," *Cultural Survival*, Summer 2009, https://www.culturalsurvival.org/publications/cultural-survival-quarterly/prescription-indigenous-rights.

Bibliography

Bate, Peter. "A College for Real Life." *IDB América: Magazine of the Inter-American Development Bank*, May 1, 2000. http://www.iadb.org/en/news/webstories/2000–05–01/a-college-for-real-life,8485.html.

Bayard de Volo, Lorraine. *Mothers of Heroes and Martyrs: Gender Identity Politics in Nicaragua 1979–1999*. Baltimore: John Hopkins University Press, 2001.

Cadorette, Sarah. "The Prescription for Indigenous Rights." *Cultural Survival*, Summer 2009. https://www.culturalsurvival.org/publications/cultural-survival-quarterly/prescription-indigenous-rights.

Lobel, Jules. *Success without Victory: Lost Legal Battles and the Long Road to Justice in America*. New York: NYU Press, 2004.

Peace, Roger. *A Call to Conscience: The Anti-contra War Campaign*. Amherst: University of Massachusetts Press, 2012.

Randall, Margaret. *Sandino's Daughter Revisited: Feminism in Nicaragua*. New Brunswick, NJ: Rutgers University Press, 1994.

Reagan, Ronald. "Address to the Nation on United States Policy in Central America." May 9, 1984. Ronald Reagan Presidential Library and Museum. http://www.reagan.utexas.edu/archives/speeches/1984/50984h.htm.

Shapiro, Marc. *Susan Sarandon: Actress-Activist*. New York: Prometheus Books, 2001.

Sklar, Holly. *Washington's War on Nicaragua*. Boston: South End, 1988.

Wehr, Paul, and John Paul Lederrach. "Mediating Conflict in Central America." In *Resolving International Conflicts: The Theory and Practice of Mediation*, edited by Jacob Bercovitch, 55–74. Boulder, CO: Lynne Rienner, 1996.

Gloria Steinem
Getting the Message Out

Jeremy LaMaster and Mary K. Trigg

In 2013, the renowned American feminist icon Gloria Steinem received the Presidential Medal of Freedom in recognition of her enduring advocacy that sparked social and political change around issues of gender and race. Upon receiving her medal from President Barack Obama, Steinem remarked, "I'd be crazy if I didn't understand that this was a medal for the entire women's movement." Steinem has been a recognizable face of US feminism—and a frequent traveler in the service of global feminism—from the 1970s until today. A feminist writer, activist, lecturer, and media spokeswoman, she is one of the movement's most familiar and celebrated organizers. Although there are a number of prominent women's rights activists, when it comes to visual representations of 1960s and 1970s US feminism, Gloria Steinem's image surfaces, complete with long, brown hair, a slender build, and iconic aviator glasses. Steinem's life experiences and class consciousness lent her an ability to export a relatable image of the women's movement and provided her with tools to be able to authentically reach across differences. Although Steinem holds a legendary status within the women's rights movement, her journey to feminist leadership was not without challenges.

Roots: Packing a Toolbox of Experiences

Steinem's experiences as a child and young adult provide clues to how her ability to manage and negotiate a strategic public life developed. Throughout her career, Steinem has been relatively open about her early life and her family. Born in 1934, Steinem was ten when her parents separated. They later divorced. Her father, Leo, who, she wrote, "loved and honored" her "as a unique person," was a resort operator in summer and, in winter, put the family in a house trailer and earned a living buying and selling antiques along the way.[1] Her mother, Ruth, was college educated and had been a newspaper reporter years before Gloria was born but had given up this work that she loved to care for Gloria's nine-years-older sister and to follow her husband in his dream of creating a resort in rural Michigan.[2]

Ruth had her first breakdown before Gloria was born and struggled with anxiety and addiction to an early prescription tranquilizer for many years. Gloria and her mother lived mostly in Toledo, Ohio, from 1944 to 1951, which were difficult years of financial worries and poverty and of Gloria acting as a caretaker for her mother. Steinem's biographer Carolyn Heilbrun writes that her "experience of poverty permanently shaped her outlook on life." "Something in her childhood," Heilbrun notes, "made her wary of the middle class. . . . That wariness would never vanish."[3]

Steinem has drawn on her personal experiences to inform her politics and activism. She often uses stories of her mother's battle with anxiety and depression to highlight the intersections of sexism, classism, and ableism as well as the lack of social support for unmarried women (including divorced women and single mothers). Being forced to take on many of the tasks and duties of an adult prematurely taught Steinem how to project a calm exterior. Despite her difficult childhood, Heilbrun concludes that it served to produce "a passionately engaged and loving human being."[4]

In addition to Steinem's taking care of her mother, her early life experiences with traversing communities of varying socioeconomic status gave her intimate and lasting knowledge of classism and racism within the United States. Steinem went from living in a poor community in Toledo, Ohio, to finishing high school in the rapidly gentrifying Georgetown neighborhood of Washington, DC. Her mother sold their house in Toledo—which was torn down to build a parking lot—and used that money to send Gloria to college at Smith in rural Northampton, Massachusetts, then a recent mill town with some "town/gown" tensions. A "womblike, protected place" after her peripatetic childhood, Smith College was a refuge. Her Smith classmates later remembered Steinem as not only a fine storyteller but a great listener, one who focused on the speaker even amid distractions. "When you spoke to her, she looked at you," they recalled.[5] After graduating magna cum laude with a degree in government from Smith in 1956, she spent a pivotal nearly two years studying at the University of Delhi in New Delhi and traveling in India, where Steinem found herself at home. She walked through villages for a time with a team of Gandhi's followers and decades later recalled several critical pieces of organizing advice she learned from them: "If you want people to listen to you, you have to listen to them" and "If you want people to see you, you have to sit down with them eye-to-eye."[6] India affected Steinem profoundly, in part because "she let India take her over and she learned what it could offer."[7] This geographic shifting gave Steinem further insight into class differences, poverty, caste as a parallel to race (especially in restricting female bodies as the means of reproduction), and the importance that the simple act of listening can have to leadership and to social change movements.

Socioeconomic class in the United States is not only about income but also about sets of skills, appearances, mannerisms, behaviors, and values. Steinem recognized ways in which her life experiences allowed her to think differently about issues compared to her peers in secondary school and college. Steinem learned the value of speaking and writing understandably, of not giving into the code words of professions, whether academic or other, in order to effectively connect with people as well as to provide connection for herself. She never misrepresented who she was. She later wrote, "[At Smith] I discovered that my experience could be put to use because it did not duplicate the experiences of the others. . . . This . . . was the beginning of an important lesson: Don't worry about your background; whether it's odd or ordinary, use it, build on it."[8] Steinem's experience with class mobility allowed her later to identify with the multiple populations with whom she was working, especially working-class women and women of color who suffered from a caste system here. As she moved into her feminist work, these experiences and insights would serve her well.

A Bunny's Tale

After returning from India in 1958, Steinem moved to New York, drawn to its freedom, diversity, excitement, and choice.[9] The rest of the country was less liberal and vibrant at the time. Dwight Eisenhower was president; Richard Nixon was vice president. It was the era that Betty Friedan later famously described as "the feminine mystique." Feminism was in a quiescent phase, and the civil rights movement was just dawning. Carolyn Heilbrun has written that "the 1960s—Steinem's 1960s—can be grasped under three headings: the articles she wrote, the men in her life, and the causes she gave her time and money to but was unable to publicize through the press as she would have wished." The celebrity journalist Liz Smith recalled that knowing Steinem in those days was like knowing Mother Teresa or Gandhi: she was a living rebuke to those who did not have her dedication.[10]

Professional roles in journalism, the field Steinem set her sights on, were not easy for women to come by in these years. Heilbrun notes that not until the founding of *Ms.* magazine in 1972 did Steinem's struggle to find meaningful work in the world end.[11] Journalism was difficult for women to break into, and routinely, men without writing experience were privileged over skilled female writers. Additionally, the gendering of assignments made it challenging for women to write credibly on anything that was not related to fashion or domesticity. "When it came to assignments as a freelance writer," Steinem later recalled, "I was assigned things about fashion and food and makeup and babies."[12] Through hard work and determination, Steinem began to establish herself as a capable freelance writer, working for magazines like *Help! A Magazine of Political Satire*, the *New York Times*, *Ladies' Home Journal*, *Glamour*, *Esquire*, and *Show*. Eventually, Steinem stumbled, accidently, into one of her first major assignments: an undercover exposé of the working conditions at Hugh Hefner's Playboy Club of New York.

While at a *Show* editorial meeting, a discussion on the newly opened New York City Playboy Club and how to cover it led to

Steinem jokingly suggesting a fly-on-the-wall piece similar to articles found in the *New Yorker*. She was thirty years old at the time, already too old to be a Bunny, and was not thinking of doing this assignment herself. The editors took her suggestion seriously, and Steinem was pegged as the undercover agent.

The editor wanted her to write an amusing piece about the Playboy Club, but after spending a few weeks as a Bunny, Steinem decided that the piece could not be humorous; she needed to deliver a message. She had discovered dozens of abuses occurring at the club. Wage theft and sexual harassment were both commonplace. Prospective Bunnies were even forced to submit to a gynecological exam to determine if they had venereal disease, on the grounds that this was routine for food servers in New York State. (In fact, it was because at least some of the servers were expected to be sexually available.) Above all, Steinem wanted to "show the public that the Playboy Bunnies were real people."[13] She concluded later, "all women are Bunnies."[14] The article, "A Bunny's Tale: *Show*'s First Exposé for Intelligent People," ran in the May 1963 issue of *Show*.[15] With the publication of the Bunny article, Steinem leapt into immediate fame.[16]

Faced with the opportunity to turn this experience into a book, Steinem later commented, "Though I returned an advance payment for its expansion into a book, thus avoiding drugstore racks full of paperbacks emblazoned with my name, 'I was a Playboy Bunny,' and god-knows-what illustration, that article quickly became the only way I was publicly identified."[17] Through her experiences with the article and the response it elicited, Steinem began to develop a consciousness about what some people call "lookism," the systemic or individual privileges assigned to physically attractive individuals. As a slender, beautiful white woman, Steinem contended with the public consumption of her body and physical appearance throughout her career, despite actively working to end the very objectification she was experiencing. Steinem began to realize the ways in which her appearance kept her from being taken seriously. For instance, when her literary agent sent her for an assignment at *Life* magazine, the editor looked up from his desk and said, "We don't want a pretty girl, we want a writer, go home."[18]

After "A Bunny's Tale," and despite a desire to pursue more political journalism assignments, Steinem found herself with a variety of freelance projects. She was often stuck with fluff pieces like "How a Single Girl Spends Her Money," "How to Put Up With / Put Down a Difficult Man," "So You Want to Be a Spy," and even an article on textured stockings for the *New York Times Magazine*, which she later described as "the low point of [her] life."[19] Throughout the 1960s, Steinem was able to hone her skills and land magazine profile pieces on people like Margo Fonteyn, Paul Newman, James Baldwin, Barbra Streisand, Julie Andrews, and Rudi Gernreich. Though only some of these celebrity profiles represented Steinem's true ambitions to cover political causes—for instance, her profile of the African American novelist, essayist, and social critic James Baldwin—they did give her an opportunity to continue to expand her repertoire as a journalist.

Steinem was integral to the fund-raising and development of a new magazine, *New York*, in 1968. Steinem's first article was about the time the Vietnamese Communist revolutionary leader and president Ho Chi Minh had spent in New York as a young man, a controversial subject in the midst of the Vietnam War. She subsequently wrote a regular political column and named it "The City Politic," an offering she continued for two years. Through this assignment, Steinem was able to garner more hands-on experience working on a variety of causes, from writing about her experiences as a volunteer for Senator George McGovern at the 1968 Democratic National Convention to working in New York and California for Cesar Chavez's and Dolores Huertes's United Farm Workers movements. Her political work translated to her column, where she was writing on increasingly more diverse groups like the National Welfare Rights Organization, the Black Panthers, and the Young Lords, a mainly Puerto Rican parallel to the Black Panthers in New York.

The feminist movement that was reborn in the 1960s revolutionized and radicalized women's position in US society. Although Friedan's *The Feminine Mystique* jolted upper-middle-class suburban, educated women who lived lives of domesticity, being a wife and mother was not Steinem's world, nor was what Friedan dubbed "the problem that has no name."[20] At the same time that Friedan's book was causing a stir among white, middle-class suburban wives, younger radical women were joining student movements and the civil rights movement. Women of color also created their own organizations, often in response to the sexism of their male peers.[21] Steinem was by then a successful journalist, unmarried, glamorous, and identified with people suffering unfairness, but in the mid-1960s, she did not yet understand that this was because females as a caste suffered unfairness, too, and that one name for fighting unfairness was feminism.[22]

As Steinem's venture into politics deepened, she began to encounter more issues related specifically to women's rights. Her increasing visibility garnered an invitation to participate on a panel with Jean Faust, the national legislative chairperson of the recently formed National Organization for Women (NOW). A more moderate, centrist group than radical organizations like Students for a Democratic Society (SDS) or the Redstockings, NOW was established in 1966. Betty Friedan was one of its founders. A largely upper-middle-class organization of women and men, it aimed to bring women into US society as equal players with men.[23] Faust, impressed with Steinem's contribution to the panel discussion, attempted to coax her into joining NOW. Steinem dodged the invitation by claiming that she was not a feminist but, rather, a humanist. In addition, she supported but could not identify with the situation of suburban women striving to get into the labor force. She was already in the labor force and being treated unequally. However, Steinem's interest was piqued.

Three years later, Steinem experienced a feminist awakening. In 1969, she attended a consciousness-raising hearing held by the Redstockings that focused on women's experiences with abortion. The Redstockings were a radical feminist group, mostly active in New York City and noted for their "speakouts" and street theater, especially on abortion rights. Although Steinem attended the meeting for purely journalistic purposes, as she herself had had an abortion a decade earlier, she found memories of her own experience returning. She later recalled, "I had had an abortion when I first graduated from college, and I had never told anyone. And I listened to women testify about all that they had had to go through . . . to get an illegal abortion. . . . And I began to understand my experience was not just mine but an almost universal female experience, and that meant only if you got together with other women was it going to be affected in any way."[24] What was a deeply personal experience was at the same time a women's issue calling for political action and reform. Steinem wrote, "Suddenly, I was no longer learning intellectually about what was wrong. I knew. Why should each of us [who had an abortion] be made to feel criminal and alone?"[25] Heilbrun writes, "In 1969 Steinem attended the abortion hearing organized by the Redstockings and underwent her conversion to feminism, recognizing at last the explanation for all the attitudes toward women she had endured and witnessed."[26] Steinem has described her conversion at the abortion speak-out as "the great blinding lightbulb" that suddenly illuminated a previously dark room.[27]

After this incident, Steinem began wanting to write more about women's issues and the women's liberation movement. She began to read every feminist essay she could find and joined small consciousness-raising groups that were meeting to talk and explore. Her first explicitly feminist article, "After Black Power, Women's Liberation," premiered in her New York column and marked her formal foray into the politics of the expanding movement.[28] The article also established Steinem's policy of inclusivity, depicting poor women and women of color as central agents in the women's movement. She was not yet able to write in her own authentic voice. She later remarked, "[The article] contained none of the emotions I had felt in that church basement, and certainly not the fact that I, too, had an abortion. . . . But I did predict that if these younger, more radical women from the peace and civil rights movements could affect what were then the middle-class reformists of the National Organization for Women, and join with poor women already organizing around welfare and child care, a long-lasting and important mass movement would result."[29]

In those early years, Steinem notably tried to highlight the participation and leadership of African American women in the movement. In a 1972 article, "Women Voters Can't Be Trusted: The Birth of the Gender Gap," Steinem drew on results of the 1971

Harris-Setlaw poll, a survey of women's opinions commissioned by Philip Morris, creator of the woman-directed cigarette, Virginia Slims. She reported Black women being about 60 percent favorably disposed to the terms and issues of women's liberation and white women being only about half that, "in spite of the white or middle-class connotations often given it by the press." The poll also revealed, Steinem noted, that Black women more often put white feminist leaders on their list of "greatly respected" women than their white counterparts did. She described Black women coming out stronger on just about every feminist issue, "whether it's voting for a woman candidate, ending violence and militarism, or believing that women are just as rational as men, and have more human values."[30]

Steinem was intent on promoting women's issues, but she faced significant roadblocks within the male-dominated journalism industry. Most publishers insisted that there was no need for articles focusing on women's rights or that they were too controversial or that if they published an article saying women were equal, they would have to publish another article saying women were not equal, in order to be objective. She was frustrated with her inability to publish as a freelance writer on the topic that was now at the center of her interests—the women's movement. However, she was beginning to receive invitations to speak on campuses and to activist groups because of her writing. Yet Steinem was a reluctant public speaker. In fact, she was terrified of public speaking. How could she most effectively get the message out?

Resolution

Gloria Steinem's attendance at the 1969 Redstockings' speakout on abortion sparked her awakening and marked her emergence as a feminist. The kindling was already in place: Steinem's childhood in a single-parent family exposed her to the many ways in which society marginalizes women who do not participate fully in marriage. Feminism provided her a more comprehensive view of how her and her mother's experiences were in part systemic and not entirely individual: how the personal was political. Additionally, Steinem's experiences pushed her to include race and class in her thinking about gender-based oppression.

Before the Redstockings' meeting on abortion and before Steinem's feminist awakening, she interviewed Dorothy Pitman Hughes for an article in *New York* magazine. Hughes, an African American, was a pioneer in establishing support services for women and children. She founded the West 80th Street Day Care Center. At the time, Hughes was the creator of a nonsexist, multiracial community day-care center in an empty storefront on the West Side of Manhattan. During the interview, a young man who worked closely with Hughes expressed his concern about his fiancée and the prospect of her having a job outside the home. She would not marry him because he did not want her to continue her work. Hughes and Steinem paused their interview to explore the values and beliefs he held and to point out to him the double standards he was expressing. They explained that his understanding of race and class could and should be extended to sex. Their arguments sunk in, and the young man left the conversation with a completely different viewpoint. Steinem and Hughes found this a revelation: if they were able to change this young man's mind simply through interpersonal communication, they could likely change the minds of entire groups of people through a similar method.[31]

Months later, Steinem was invited to give a speech at New York University (NYU). She reached out to Hughes to join her for a number of reasons. First, Steinem wanted to continue writing about gender and race discrimination and knew it was important that Black women's voices be in this conversation. Additionally, Hughes's visual presence would help challenge stereotypes of feminism as solely a white, middle-class, antifamily movement made up of childless women. Perhaps most of all, Steinem was terrified of public speaking and knew that Dorothy was fearless.

Before Steinem could dive more seriously into lecturing, she needed to conquer her fears. She had always been comfortable with interpersonal interactions. Her childhood experiences of moving from poverty to upper-class education provided her the ability to adapt to the diverse individuals and varied environments in which she found herself. This adaptability was honed through years of working in male-dominated journalism. Steinem describes how her positioning and identity as a woman of a lower socioeconomic class combined with her experience in journalism to contribute to these chameleon-like qualities:

> Well, I think that's what makes you a journalist. The ability to become, to enter into a different life, is kind of what a journalist needs. And it's something that women are especially trained to do, because we're supposed to fit into society: to acquire the persona of our husbands or the men we're with, even for the evening. . . . And class, I must say, gives you a terrific ability to learn quickly—you know, that desperate feeling of not knowing what's right or what fork or what social mores. It is amazing how fast you can learn because you're scared—so you absorb this knowledge very quickly. It's a great lesson in the power of socialization actually.[32]

However, despite this ability, she had neither the experience nor the self-confidence for the podium. By deciding to share the platform for that event, Steinem and Hughes tapped into an effective formula. After their speech at NYU, Steinem was asked by a speakers' bureau to tour and talk on other college campuses. Steinem agreed on the condition that she and Hughes would be an equal team. As a white and Black woman speaking together, they soon discovered that they attracted more diverse audiences than either one would have on her own.

Hughes, through her work as a community organizer and civil rights activist, contributed years of public-speaking experience to their duo. Her oration style was reminiscent of other civil rights leaders of the time, and her tone and articulation instilled a call to action. Hughes offered Steinem not only comfort and confidence by sharing the podium; her speaking style perfectly complemented Steinem's. Steinem's calm tone provided a sense of order and matter-of-factness that helped quell visceral responses to controversial topics around gender, race, and class. Steinem would speak first and provide a broad, general overview of the movement's guiding theories and principles, and Hughes would continue by carrying these into the family and child care as well as the parallels between sex and race.

Steinem recognized the benefit and effect that these lectures had on audiences—it was very different from print journalism. Through her public speaking, Steinem was able to develop an emotional connection with an audience, to learn from them, and to create a community meeting that could continue after Steinem and Hughes were gone. Both women's concern for their audience was evidenced by their insistence on waiting after lectures until every individual question was answered and every woman's story had been heard. The lessons Steinem had learned in India about the important role of listening in building social movements served her well.

Steinem often used her own personal experiences and narratives to help illustrate how the personal was political, why the women's movement was necessary, and to find common ground with the men and women she met during her lectures. Steinem and Hughes resonated with audiences and were striking a nerve. Steinem commented, "In our lectures, where only hundreds were expected, thousands began to turn out. You realized there was a great hunger for anything that took the women's experiences seriously."[33] As she continued on the lecture circuit throughout the 1970s, Steinem routinely relied on the support of leaders and mentors throughout her travels. Eventually Flo Kennedy, a Black feminist activist, stepped in for Hughes to provide Hughes time to take care of her new child. Kennedy taught Steinem even more public-speaking tools, specifically the role of humor and passion. Steinem would also work with other Black feminists, including Margaret Sloan and Jane Galvin-Lewis. Whenever Steinem spoke, she made a point to partner with Black women leaders. She became not just a writer but a traveling organizer, with other women or on her own, in this and other countries.

Through her writing and speaking engagements, Steinem gathered more tools and greater confidence. She had catalogued a repertoire of aphorisms and comebacks to the frequent questions, not just about the women's movement but about her own personal life, including her appearance and sexuality. Steinem learned how to deal with difficult situations and hostile audiences with grace and humor.

Although Steinem did share personal experiences with her audiences, she carefully selected the narratives that would be most fruitful in delivering her message. Steinem consistently downplayed her life as a heterosexual woman, in part because she saw the need to counteract stereotypes of feminists as man-hating lesbians without slighting lesbian women.[34] If asked directly about being a lesbian, Steinem often replied, "Not yet" or sometimes, borrowing from Flo Kennedy's answer to men in the audience, "Are you my alternative?"[35] These quips were a method to answer the question not only strategically but humorously and in a way that Steinem did not desert lesbians or reaffirm heterosexuality as the only acceptable path, unlike some antilesbian feminist activists at that time.

As the 1970s progressed, Steinem was ready for the next step. As her speaking tours proceeded, her writing continued. Through her lectures, she learned how to effectively disseminate and acquire feminist knowledge through talking and listening. As Steinem's notoriety spread beyond New York City, she was quickly adopted as a face of the movement.[36] She began fielding invitations for interviews, not just for print journalism but for television, for which she had occasionally been an off-camera writer.

Television as a technology could only handle feminism in a very specific way. Although the 1970s were a different landscape for television broadcasting, by the end of the decade, there was already a push for shorter sound bites and digestible messages. Additionally, televisions were a central technology of the family and of commercialism. As a result, hypervigilance surrounded the content that television delivered to American living rooms and that advertisers supported. Steinem seemed cognizant of this and worked to apply the tools she gathered from journalism and public speaking to continue an "uncomplicated narrative" of women's life stories and needs, both visually and contextually.[37] Steinem's appearance, humor, tranquility, tone, and personal background fit nicely into an image that a mass audience could consume, though she found speaking to a camera even more difficult than speaking to a live audience had been and was clear that she did not want a job in television.

Steinem used her communication skills and gifts to utilize mass media for the strategic purpose of advancing feminist causes. She was always cognizant of including others and not forefronting only herself as a messenger or advancing her own status but building a connection with her audience (even through a television). She continued to consider the content of her messages and their delivery. According to the media scholar Patricia Bradley, Steinem's "ability to use the medium on its own terms gave profound strength to her message."[38] Steinem quickly became an icon of women's liberation but continued to be a reluctant spokesperson.

Steinem's role as the public face of feminism increasingly left her vulnerable to efforts to tarnish her character and reputation, whether in magazine articles or interviews. Her consistent response was to maintain a cool, calculated image, even though she reveals that this did not come without significant personal and psychological cost. Steinem's appearance combined with her rapidly growing popularity made her the target of criticism and provocation, within both liberal and conservative circles. She endured criticism from other feminist leaders while facing sexual harassment and misogyny from the political Right.

After Steinem and others established *Ms.* magazine in 1972 (which they created because of a need for a place to publish the articles women wanted to write), *Esquire* magazine published a particularly vilifying article that attributed Steinem's success to her appearance and her "seduction" of powerful men. Despite these roadblocks that continued to be thrown Steinem's way, *Ms.*—which was a group effort with Suzanne Braun Levine as the new magazine's managing editor—was a success. Its first spring issue in 1972 sold out in eight days. "It just walked off newsstands," Steinem later remarked. "We were shocked. . . . It was heady, and exciting, and naïve. Because we thought these injustices are so great, surely if we just explain them to people, they will want to fix them."[39]

But it was not so simple. Steinem, like feminist leaders before her, found herself hurt by personal attacks. In 1973, she wrote, "I'm tired of all that people write about me; I can't take it any longer unless I grow another skin." She cut back her public appearances from fifteen a month to five and noted, "My current rule, is don't do anything that another feminist could do instead."[40] She was consistently an advocate of working to get more women into visible, leadership positions. "It's the practice of the media to set up leaders and knock them down, which is very damaging to movements," she wrote at forty. "We need to have enough women in the public eye so that we can't all get knocked down."[41]

Steinem's natural optimism, graciousness, and strength could not let her remain discouraged for long, however. Her use of humor—in both her speeches and writing—made her radical message more palatable and challenged the stereotype that feminists lacked a sense of humor. Her now-famous one-page essay "If Men Could Menstruate," published in *Ms.* in 1978, demonstrated her tongue-in-cheek sassiness along with her serious underlying message. "What would happen," she asked, "if suddenly, magically, men could menstruate and women could not?" Her witty answers included Congress funding a National Institute of Dysmenorrhea to help stamp out monthly discomforts; boys marking the onset of menses with religious ritual and stag parties; and the government offering federally funded, free sanitary supplies. Steinem wrote, "Street guys would brag ("I'm a three-pad man") or answer praise from a buddy, 'Man, you lookin' *good*' by giving five and saying, 'Yeah, man, I'm on the rag!'"[42]

Throughout the rest of the 1970s, 1980s, and 1990s, Steinem continued her work in advancing feminism through the various platforms she found. She remained an editor at *Ms.* for fifteen years and was instrumental in the magazine's move to join and be published by the Feminist Majority Foundation. *Ms.* editors also established the Ms. Foundation for Women, which is devoted to helping the lives of women and girls in economic security, leadership, and health and safety.[43] Steinem became a highly profiled activist and was interviewed by Larry King, Oprah Winfrey, and Barbara Walters—about whom Steinem had written an article years before when Walters become the first woman reporter on the *Today* show. Steinem went on to publish books on her work, including

Outrageous Acts and Everyday Rebellions (1983) and *Revolution from Within: A Book of Self-Esteem* (1992). In *Revolution from Within*, part memoir, cultural critique, and self-help book, Steinem aimed to connect internal change with external change in the world. She wrote it because she could not find a high-quality book on self-esteem to recommend to the many women she believed would benefit from one. "Wherever I traveled," she wrote, "I saw women who were smart, courageous, and valuable, who didn't *think* they were smart, courageous, or valuable—it was as if the female spirit were a garden that had grown beneath the shadows of barriers for so long that it kept growing in the same pattern, even after some of the barriers were gone."[44] The book shot to number one on the best-seller list, and despite the critics' dismissal of it as "an exercise in squishy new-age thumb-sucking," Steinem was mobbed by crowds at the bookstores on her book tour.[45] In March 1992, *Time* magazine put Gloria Steinem and Susan Faludi, the author of *Backlash: The Undeclared War against American Feminism* (1991), on its cover under the headline, "Fighting the Backlash against Feminism."[46] The cover was, in Steinem's estimation, "by way of apologizing for panning *Backlash* and *Revolution from Within*, then discovering they both were successful."[47]

Steinem's beauty has both fostered her public visibility and sharpened her feminist rapier. The focus on her physical appearance has dogged her throughout her career. Writing in *Ms.* in 1990, she stated, "Even as I write this, I get a call from a writer for *Elle*, who is doing a whole article on where women part their hair. Why, she wants to know, do I part mine in the middle?"[48] Steinem took this overemphasis on the female body, beauty culture, and corporate profit to wage a ten-year campaign against the link between advertisements and editorial content in magazines. She described the campaign in her well-known essay "Sex, Lies, and Advertising." Her beauty also, however, made the photogenic, stylish, eternally youthful Steinem a magnet for the media and an inspiration to other women. When, on her fiftieth birthday, someone told her she looked good for her age, Steinem's now oft-quoted response was, "This is what fifty looks like. We've been lying so long, who would know?" "The miracle about Gloria," as a friend and former editor of the *Columbia Journalism Review* noted, "is that she's stayed so beautiful while talking so tough."[49] Heilbrun describes her as "simultaneously the epitome of female beauty and the quintessence of female revolution."[50] Steinem herself modestly noted in 2015, "I was 'a pretty girl' before feminism and only after feminism was I 'beautiful.' It was the contrast with what people *thought* feminists looked like."[51]

Steinem's writing, public-speaking skills, and ability to communicate, charm, and captivate are key to her leadership. Although a surface assessment of her leadership approach might highlight individualized notions of leadership, complemented by the narrative of a self-made, bootstrap woman, a closer analysis shows that Steinem's savvy use of mass media and her authentic interactions with a growing public audience were central to her success. Her openness to learning from others, including her audiences, also sets her apart. She wrote, "As an itinerant organizer, my own two biggest rewards are still a sense of making a difference and the birth of ideas. The first would be enough in itself, for that is how we know we are alive, but the second is magic. On a good night, a roomful of people can set off a chain of ideas that leads us all to a new place—a sudden explosion of understanding, a spontaneous invention. We hear ourselves saying things we had felt but never named. It will take a lifetime to write them all down."[52]

Steinem displays feminist leadership in a number of ways: through editorial decision, reclamation of women's agency and voice, and the distillation of feminist theoretical concepts into a practical women's rights movement. What sets Steinem apart from other feminist activists and women leaders is that she was what would have been called in the 1930s "a media worker." The media was her field of work as a freelance writer, a magazine editor, and a sometime interviewee. If she had been the same person and, say, a scientist, the result would have been different. In addition, as Heilbrun notes, "there is a completeness, a steadfastness of purpose, a willingness to work for chosen goals, and a firmness in maintaining her principles that can be discerned throughout her life."[53]

Steinem was able to invoke notions of a universal woman's experience through her use of "I," "us," and "we," while simultaneously contextualizing these experiences along lines of race, class, and sexuality. As she stated at seventy-nine, in accepting the Presidential Medal of Freedom, she always rejected "the false idea that we are ranked as human beings, rather than linked." Her ideal is "to have a paradigm in life that is a circle, not a pyramid."[54] Steinem was also always cognizant of including men in her discussions on gender. Heilbrun notes that when Steinem described Gandhi in *Revolution from Within*, she described her own philosophy: "His hope and his heart were with average people and ordinary actions."[55] Steinem recognized that leadership meant, as she has said numerous times, "sharing the torch." "If I could have one wish for the women's movement internationally," she stated in 2013, "it would be a kind of Alcoholics Anonymous–like structure, a whole lacework of little groups, meeting in church basements, in school gyms, and around the well in a village . . . that meet once a week. . . . They're leaderless, they're free, they have as their goal supporting each other's self-authority. That's really what we need."[56] As a writer, speaker, and occasional media interviewer, Steinem aimed at the heart and brought to her leadership an ethic of care, humility, and the ability to listen. She is currently at work on a book about her more than forty years on the road as a feminist organizer. Fittingly, it is titled *Nomad: My Life on the Road Listening—As If Everyone Mattered*.

Notes

1 Quoted in Carolyn G. Heilbrun, *The Education of a Woman: The Life of Gloria Steinem* (New York: Dial, 1995), 20–21.
2 Ibid., 6.
3 Ibid., 23.
4 Ibid., 39.
5 Quoted in ibid., 48.
6 Quoted in ibid., 76.
7 Ibid., 81.
8 Quoted in ibid., 51–52.
9 Ibid., 84.
10 Ibid., 101–102.
11 Ibid., 82.
12 Makers, "Makers Profile: Gloria Steinem," n.d., http://www.makers.com/gloria-steinem (accessed February 4, 2015).
13 Sondra Henry and Emily Taitz, *One Woman's Power: A Biography of Gloria Steinem* (Minneapolis: Dillon, 1987), 56.

14 Gloria Steinem, *Outrageous Acts and Everyday Rebellions* (1983; repr., New York: Holt, 1995).

15 Gloria Steinem, "A Bunny's Tale: *Show*'s First Exposé for Intelligent People," *Show*, May 1, 1963, available at http://dlib.nyu.edu/undercover/sites/dlib.nyu.edu.undercover/files/documents/uploads/editors/Show-A%20Bunny%27s%20Tale-Part%20One-May%201963.pdf.

16 Heilbrun, *Education of a Woman*, 106.

17 Mark Hoff, *Gloria Steinem: The Women's Movement* (Brookfield, CT: Millbrook, 1991), 35.

18 Gloria Steinem, email to Mary Trigg, November 1, 2014.

19 Makers, "Makers Profile."

20 Betty Friedan, *The Feminine Mystique* (1963; repr., New York: Norton, 2010).

21 Benita Roth, *Separate Roads to Feminism: Black, Chicana, and White Feminist Movements in America's Second Wave* (Cambridge: Cambridge University Press, 2004).

22 Heilbrun, *Education of a Woman*, 103.

23 Ibid., 162.

24 Makers, "Makers Profile."

25 Steinem, *Outrageous Acts*, 21.

26 Heilbrun, *Education of a Woman*, 169.

27 Quoted in ibid., 170.

28 Gloria Steinem, "The City Politic: After Black Power, Women's Liberation," *New York*, April 7, 1969.

29 Quoted in Heilbrun, *Education of a Woman*, 172.

30 Gloria Steinem, "Women Voters Can't Be Trusted: The Birth of the Gender Gap," *Ms.*, July 1972, reprinted in "The Best of 30 Years: Reporting, Rebelling, and Truth-Telling," *Ms.*, Spring 2002, 11.

31 Heilbrun, *Education of a Woman*, 70–71.

32 *Gloria: In Her Own Words*, dir. Peter Kunhardt (Home Box Office Network, 2011), DVD.

33 Quoted in Tom Brokaw, *Boom! Voices of the Sixties* (New York: Random House, 2007), 206.

34 Patricia Bradley, *Mass Media and the Shaping of American Feminism, 1963–1975* (Jackson: University Press of Mississippi, 2003), 162.

35 Quoted in Heilbrun, *Education of a Woman*, 255.

36 Bradley, *Mass Media*.

37 Ibid., 161.

38 Ibid., 142.

39 Makers, "Makers Profile."

40 "Gloria Steinem Tries to Lower Her Famed Profile," *People*, September 23, 1974, 8.

41 "Gloria Steinem Tries to Lower Her Famed Profile."

42 Gloria Steinem, "If Men Could Menstruate," *Ms.*, October 1972, reprinted in "Best of 30 Years," 41.

43 Ms. Foundation for Women, http://forwomen.org/.

44 Gloria Steinem, *Revolution from Within* (Boston: Little, Brown, 1992), 3.

45 Quoted in Nancy Gibbs, "The War against Feminism," *Time*, March 9, 1992.
46 "Fighting the Backlash against Feminism," *Time*, March 9, 1992.
47 Gloria Steinem, written comment to Mary Trigg, April 2015.
48 Gloria Steinem, "Sex, Lies, and Advertising," *Ms.*, July–August 1990, reprinted in "Best of 30 Years," 60–64.
49 "Gloria Steinem," *People*, May 8, 1995.
50 Heilbrun, *Education of a Woman*, xviii.
51 Gloria Steinem, written comment to Mary Trigg, April 2015.
52 Steinem, *Outrageous Acts*, 14.
53 Heilbrun, *Education of a Woman*, 413.
54 White House, "The Presidential Medal of Freedom," n.d., http://www.whitehouse.gov/medal-of-freedom (accessed April 5, 2015).
55 Heilbrun, *Education of a Woman*, 79.
56 Ibid.; Makers, "Makers Profile."

Bibliography

"Best of 30 Years, The: Reporting, Rebelling, and Truth-Telling." *Ms.*, Spring 2002.
Bradley, Patricia. *Mass Media and the Shaping of American Feminism, 1963–1975*. Jackson: University Press of Mississippi, 2003.
Brokaw, Tom. *Boom! Voices of the Sixties*. New York: Random House, 2007.
"Fighting the Backlash against Feminism." *Time*, March 9, 1992.
Friedan, Betty. *The Feminine Mystique*. 1963. Reprint, New York: Norton, 2010.
Gibbs, Nancy. "The War against Feminism." *Time*, March 9, 1992.
Gloria: In Her Own Words. Directed by Peter Kunhardt. Home Box Office Network, 2011. DVD.
"Gloria Steinem." *People*, May 8, 1995.
"Gloria Steinem Tries to Lower Her Famed Profile." *People*, September 23, 1974, 8.
Heilbrun, Carolyn G. *The Education of a Woman: The Life of Gloria Steinem*. New York: Dial, 1995.
Henry, Sondra, and Emily Taitz. *One Woman's Power: A Biography of Gloria Steinem*. Minneapolis: Dillon, 1987.
Hoff, Mark. *Gloria Steinem: The Women's Movement*. Brookfield, CT: Millbrook, 1991.
Makers. "Makers Profile: Gloria Steinem." n.d. http://www.makers.com/gloria-steinem (accessed February 4, 2015).
Roth, Benita. *Separate Roads to Feminism: Black, Chicana, and White Feminist Movements in America's Second Wave*. Cambridge: Cambridge University Press, 2004.
Steinem, Gloria. "A Bunny's Tale: Show's First Exposé for Intelligent People." *Show*, May 1, 1963. Available at http://dlib.nyu.edu/undercover/sites/dlib.nyu.edu.undercover/files/documents/uploads/editors/Show-A%20Bunny%27s%20Tale-Part%20One-May%201963.pdf.
———. "The City Politic: After Black Power, Women's Liberation." *New York*, April 7, 1969.
———. "If Men Could Menstruate." *Ms.*, October 1972. Reprinted in "The Best of 30 Years: Reporting, Rebelling, and Truth-Telling," *Ms.*, Spring 2002, 41.

————. *Outrageous Acts and Everyday Rebellions.* 1983. Reprint, New York: Holt, 1995.

————. *Revolution from Within: A Book of Self-Esteem.* Boston: Little, Brown, 1992.

————. "Sex, Lies, and Advertising." *Ms.,* July–August 1990. Reprinted in "The Best of 30 Years: Reporting, Rebelling, and Truth-Telling," *Ms.,* Spring 2002, 60–64.

————. "Women Voters Can't Be Trusted: The Birth of the Gender Gap." *Ms.,* July 1972. Reprinted in "The Best of 30 Years: Reporting, Rebelling, and Truth-Telling," *Ms.,* Spring 2002, 11.

White House. "The Presidential Medal of Freedom." n.d. http://www.whitehouse.gov/medal-of-freedom (accessed April 5, 2015).

Audre Lorde

Black, Lesbian, Feminist, Mother, Poet Warrior

Kathe Sandler and Beverly Guy-Sheftall

Background

About to turn fifty years old in February 1984, Audre Lorde—the self-described "Black, lesbian, feminist, mother, poet warrior"—inspired a near rock-star following in several social, political, and cultural movements in the United States and abroad. A celebrated writer, activist, and educator, Lorde was among the most revered and visible "out" Black lesbian feminists of her generation. She claimed and affirmed the multiplicity of her identities, arguing that the recognition of differences among all kinds of women and people was central to building progressive communities. Lorde stated, "It is not our differences that divide us. It is our inability to recognize, accept and celebrate those differences."[1]

As a participant in many radical social justice movements, Lorde developed cutting-edge theory about racial, gender, sexual, and class differences. She maintained that the future of the planet depended on the ability of women throughout the world to work with one another. One of the few Black women actively engaged in socialist lesbian feminist circles, she was also among the very few out lesbians amid a cadre of increasingly acclaimed African American women writers whose writings helped catalyze the modern Black feminist movement.

Lorde transitioned into prose writing after publishing many critically acclaimed books of poetry. Her cutting-edge essays articulated poetic and highly accessible feminist and social justice theory.

As a breast-cancer survivor, Lorde published *The Cancer Journals* in 1980, a groundbreaking memoir in which she documented her battle with breast cancer, her struggle to take charge of her own medical care, and her decision not to wear a prosthesis. She broke the culture of silence and erasure about women and breast cancer by openly acknowledging the loss of her right breast and urged other survivors to do the same. She argued that masking her mastectomy with a prosthesis would be detrimental to her well-being, and she encouraged breast-cancer survivors to come together and recognize one another.[2]

Lorde taught and worked with students, activists, writers, and artists across the country and around the world. She advocated for the erotic in women's lives and promoted lesbian parenting and motherhood.[3] Lorde confronted classism and racism in the academic feminist community and called on white feminists to examine their racial privilege.[4] She also critiqued masculinist nationalism in Black communities. Arguing that "unity" was often a call for patriarchy, heterosexism, and homophobia, Lorde urged Black heterosexual women to resist being baited into antifeminist and antilesbian stances.[5] She affirmed the efficacy of anger as a useful tool for battling oppression, championed radical self-care and self-mothering, and spoke of the necessity of Black women bonding across sexualities.[6]

Lorde also pioneered a new literary genre—the "biomythography" in *Zami: A New Spelling of My Name* (1982)—a weave of poetry, memoir, and biography in which she described her erotic and political coming of age as a Black gay girl in New York City. In 1983, she was selected amid controversy and dissention on the part of some traditional African American leadership to speak on behalf of gay and lesbian rights at the twentieth anniversary of the March on Washington. She delivered an address on August 27, 1983, in which she linked her multiple identities with a collective quest for social justice.[7]

However, less than one year later and weeks before turning fifty years old on February 18, 1984, Lorde received alarming news from her doctor—that the breast cancer for which she had undergone a mastectomy six years earlier had metastasized in her liver. She was urged by doctors to immediately undergo a liver biopsy to determine the extent of the damage and chart a course of treatment. Lorde, who spent years educating herself about cancer treatments, felt that undergoing such a procedure would greatly weaken her and diminish her quality of life, without offering her much more time. She began researching every option that existed. Lorde believed that the US medical approach to cancer treatment was fundamentally flawed, in its centering of treating illness, as opposed to centering wellness.[8] Her research revealed that there were alternatives— holistic ones being pioneered in Europe.

Lorde also strongly believed that she had a great deal more to do in her time on earth. She wanted to spend some of it in the service of transnational organizing with Black people around the world. She had projects to complete and more books to write. Yet with the return and spread of cancer, how would she proceed medically, personally, and professionally? She surrounded herself with friends and loved ones, called on the goddess for courage, and looked back on her life for a sign.

Early Years

Audre Lorde pursued a life of radical self-invention, experimentation, and creativity in which she questioned and resisted social hierarchies and conventions at an early age. Later she wrote, "If I didn't define myself for myself, I would be crunched into other people's fantasies for me and eaten alive."[9] She was born Audrey Geraldine Lorde on February 18, 1934, to Caribbean parents in New York City. Raised in Harlem, her childhood and early adult experiences were informed by a blend of distinct New York City cultures shaped by urban racial apartheid, massive population migrations and social movements, the impact of the Great Depression, World War II, and the rise of McCarthyism. Lorde was tongue-tied and born so near-sighted that she was considered legally blind as a child. Inspired by her mother's "special and secret relationship with words," she gravitated to poetry at an early age. She dropped the y from her name and changed the spelling to *Audre* because she preferred the symmetry of seeing her first and last name ending in *e*. A crucial theme in Lorde's future writing would emerge around self-naming and self-definition.

She noted that because her mother, Linda, was from Grenada and her father, Byron, was a native of Barbados, there was a magical "home" invoked in their household that was always somewhere else. Lorde reflected "No matter how bad it got here, . . . if we really did right, someday we'd go back."[10] As a first-generation American, Lorde was greatly influenced by her parents' Caribbean culture, language, and transnational perspective.[11]

Audre Lorde came to see herself as an outsider in her family of outsiders. She was the chubbiest of her sisters, often tongue-tied, and considered unruly and "wildish" in relation to her well-behaved sisters. Though relatively light skinned, Lorde was the darkest of her siblings. She internalized disparaging things that her very light-skinned mother said about dark-skinned people. She wrote years later, "Growing up Fat Black Female and almost blind in America requires so much surviving that you have to learn from it or die."[12]

Acceptance into Hunter High School, a public all-girls school for high academic achievers, in 1947 provided Lorde with a formal immersion into poetry. She joined a group of young poets who skipped school, wandered the streets and bookstores, held séances for departed poets, and read one another's poems. As the only Black girl in the group, she often felt alone—an outsider within an outsider group of high school girls. Notwithstanding this isolation, Lorde became the literary editor of the school arts magazine. Her first love poem, though rejected by a faculty adviser as "a bad sonnet," was accepted and published in *Seventeen* magazine. She noted that she earned more money from that poem than she earned from any poetry she published for the next ten years.[13]

Lorde began to openly date white males, to her parents' displeasure, but she also had secret crushes on other girls and on a female teacher.[14] She was influenced by an active left-wing movement in Harlem and Greenwich Village and by pan-Africanist thinkers who encouraged her to study and embrace African history and culture. The teenaged Lorde joined a small group of Black women freethinkers who rejected the "hot comb" and compulsory hair straightening fully two decades before the "Black is beautiful" movement gained prominence. She experienced resistance and downright hostility from other Black women, her own mother included, to her "nappy" and "unruly" natural hairstyle and would write about natural hair politics in the years to come.

Lorde attended weekly workshops as a teenager at the Harlem Writer's Guild, a pan-Africanist group that nurtured progressive Black writers and promoted political activism. Cofounder John Clarke, a self-taught Africanist scholar, mentored Lorde, encouraged her as a poet, and briefly became a father figure. Through Clarke, she learned "wonderful things about Africa." Yet she ultimately left the group, feeling "tolerated but never accepted" as a bisexual young woman involved with white women downtown.[15]

Her experiences with left-leaning Blacks and whites led her to believe that the Left had its share of homophobia. Though she was active in civil rights and social justice movements, it was years before she integrally claimed and lived her many identities—as a Black woman lesbian feminist socialist—out loud. How would Audre Lorde live and write her way toward that future?

"Learn[ing] to Hold On to All the Parts of Me"

In Lorde's early adult years through her midthirties, she continued to transgress racial, sexual, gender, and political boundaries. She worked and studied part-time. She experimented with her sexuality, with men and women of different races. She married, had children, and became increasingly involved in the civil rights movement. She developed as a writer and began teaching, which became her passionate vocation for nearly two decades.

While working and pursuing a college degree part-time, Lorde frequented the gay-girl bar scene in New York City's East and West Villages. Lorde rejected monogamy, as well as the "butch and femme" gender binaries popular in lesbian circles. However, she found her racial identity submerged in these nearly all-white circles. Lorde completed her bachelor's degree in library sciences from Hunter College in 1959. She earned a master's degree from Columbia University two years later, while working as a librarian.

Lorde surprised many of her lesbian friends when she married Edwin Rollins, an attorney and a bisexual white man. Her close friend Blanche Wiesen Cook declared that Lorde's marriage became a model of sorts for her lesbian circle of friends—many of whom would marry men, have children, and continue to love women.[16] Lorde maintained her work as a librarian and gave birth to a daughter, Elizabeth, in 1963 and, less than two years later, to a son, Jonathan.

During the 1960s, Lorde became active in the civil rights movement. She participated in the 1963 March on Washington, noting that she made coffee in the tents for the marshals along with the legendary actress, singer, and activist Lena Horne, "because that is what most Black women did in the 1963 March on Washington."[17] Riveted by the many speeches, especially Martin Luther King, Jr.'s "I Have a Dream," Lorde wondered if she might see an end to racism in her lifetime. However, two weeks later, she was shocked by news of the 16th Street Baptist Church bombing in Birmingham, Alabama—a blast in which four little Black girls were killed by local white supremacists.

The news and images rocked the world and made international headlines. The church served as a gathering place for civil rights leadership including Revs. Martin Luther King, Jr., Ralph Abernathy, and Fred Shuttlesworth. While this act of racial terrorism was intended to deter the movement against racial segregation, it instead had an opposite effect. Many more people were inspired to join the struggle. Viscerally affected, Lorde penned a poem about the bombing, "Suffer the Children," which was published in *Negro Digest*, framed by smiling snapshots of the slain girls.

In 1968, as the civil rights movement transformed into the Black Power movement, Lorde accepted a poet-in-residency position at Tougaloo College, a historically Black college in Mississippi. It was her first prolonged experience in the South. This semester-long appointment, teaching young undergraduates, stirred profound feelings in her. She later recalled, "When I taught a poetry workshop at Tougaloo, a small Black college in Mississippi, where white rowdies shot up the edge of campus every night, . . . I felt the joy of seeing young Black poets find their voices and power through words in our mutual growth."[18]

The experience set her on a path as a poet-educator over the next two decades. While at Tougaloo, she met Frances Clayton, a white psychology professor on exchange from Brown University. She and Clayton would fall in love and build a life together in a few short years.

Erasures, silences, and tensions in the Black freedom movement propelled Lorde to write some years later, "Over and over again in the 60s I was asked to justify my existence and my work, because I was a woman, because I was a Lesbian, because I was not a separatist, because some part of me was not acceptable. I had to learn to hold on to all the parts of me that served me, in spite of the pressure to express only one to the exclusion of others."[19] Lorde spent her youth through her midthirties exploring ways to embrace consciously her multiple and often stigmatized identities. How would her future words and deeds help forge new spaces in which she could live them?

Black, Lesbian, Feminist, Mother, Poet . . . Teacher

In the early 1970s, Audre Lorde became a college professor and began to publish prolifically. She participated in several critical movements that shaped the political and cultural landscape—the Black women writers' literary movement, the lesbian socialist feminist movement of which she was one of the few Black women, and the Black Arts / Black Consciousness movement—which Black feminists increasingly challenged for its masculinist and homophobic turn. She separated from her husband, lived openly as an out lesbian mother, and also emerged as a powerful mentor to a generation of Black lesbian feminists.

While working as a poet/instructor in the SEEK program at the City University of New York, Lorde encountered a handful of extraordinary writers with whom she bonded. They included Adrienne Rich, Barbara Christian, June Jordan, and Toni Cade—later known as Toni Cade Bambara. Bambara published two of Lorde's poems in the ground-breaking 1970 anthology *The Black Woman*, a hugely popular publication of writings by and for Black women. Several of the writers included in the anthology—Alice Walker, Bambara, Frances Beal, and Lorde herself—became architects of an emerging radical Black feminist movement.

Lorde's second book of poetry, *Cables to Rage*, was also released in 1970, a year in which more Black women writers were published than in the prior decade. Included in this literary outpouring was Toni Morrison's *The Bluest Eye;* Louise Meriwether's *Daddy Was a Number Runner;* Shirley Chisholm's autobiography, *Unbought and Unbossed;* and Alice Walker's first novel, *The Third Life of Grange Copeland*. By the mid- to late 1970s, a full-scale Black women's literary revolution was in full swing, in which Lorde played a key role. But unlike many other prominently recognized Black women writers, she was distinguished as the out lesbian within that group.

In 1971, Lorde separated from Ed Rollins, moved to Staten Island, and lived as an out lesbian with Frances Clayton. They remained a couple until 1988. The two women coparented Lorde's children, Elizabeth and Jonathan. Lorde "officially" came out in 1973 at a women's book store and published a lesbian love poem in 1974 in *Ms.* magazine titled "Love Poem."

Lorde was also nominated for a National Book Award for her third book of poetry, *From a Land Where Other People Live*, along with Adrienne Rich and Alice Walker. Rich, who cowon the award with Allen Ginsberg, shared her award with Lorde and Walker. Lorde's friendship with Rich grew, and they significantly influenced each other.

Lorde began writing feminist theory, fostered in part by her complex experiences—both positive and negative—in the mainstream feminist movement and in the Black literary and arts movements. In her 1976 essay "Poetry Is Not a Luxury," she defined poetry as a vital source of power for women and "the skeleton architecture of our lives." She argued against the separation of the intellect from feeling, insisting on the wholeness of the two. "The white fathers told us: I think, therefore I am. The Black mother within us—the poet—whispers in our dreams: I feel, therefore I can be free."[20] By 1977, Lorde's seventh volume of poetry, *The Black Unicorn*, was on its way to publication. The title poem redefined the Eurocentric phallic symbol of the unicorn through a Black lesbian feminist erotica. In

"Litany for Survival," she urged Black lesbians and others "who love in doorways / coming and going in the hours between dawns . . . / to speak / remembering / we were never meant to survive."[21] As in her life, her writing increasingly transgressed national boundaries. She envisioned Black women loving one another in spaces across time, and in *The Black Unicorn*, she claimed three matrilineal ancestral and spiritual homes: Harlem, the African continent, and the Caribbean.[22]

Lorde's fame as a writer grew alongside a more clearly articulated Black feminist movement, which was fueled in part by Black women writers. By the mid-1970s, a full-blown "gender war" had erupted in African American political and intellectual circles around critical mainstream acclaim for the poet Ntozake Shange's stage-adapted choreopoem *For Colored Girls Who Have Considered Suicide / When the Rainbow Is Enuf*. The play, which opened on Broadway, critiqued gender violence and sexism in Black communities and contained many Black feminist themes. However, Shange became demonized as "a Black female traitor to the race" and was said to be "against the Black man" and in "cahoots with" or "under the thumb of White feminists." Over the years, other Black feminist writers, notably Michelle Wallace and Alice Walker—whose *Black Macho and the Myth of the Superwoman* and *The Color Purple*, respectively, received mainstream acclaim—found themselves similarly attacked.[23] Although Lorde herself critiqued Black sexism and patriarchy and argued against those who attacked Shange, Wallace, and Walker, her own Black-lesbian-centered writing escaped direct attacks from the Black male intelligentsia.[24] Instead, her writing became a touchstone for a younger generation of Black lesbian feminists.

At the invitation of the writer and activist Barbara Smith, Lorde participated in a series of Black feminist retreats throughout the Northeast between 1977 and 1979. Smith and others, including Cheryl Clarke and Demita Frazier, called on Lorde to help them galvanize a Black lesbian feminist movement. In the years to come, these women published Lorde and one another, formed independent presses, and edited lesbian journals and women-of-color feminist anthologies.

One of the most canonic texts of the emerging Black lesbian feminism movement was the 1977 "Black Feminist Statement," authored by the Combahee River Collective (CRC).[25] Drafted by Barbara Smith, Smith's twin sister, Beverly, and Demita Frazier, the CRC members described themselves as Black lesbian feminist socialists whose mission was to institutionalize Black feminism as a distinct body of thought. The CRC critiqued the limitations of mainstream white feminists' tendency to organize solely around the centrality of gender as an oppression. They furthermore advocated for solidarity with progressive Black men, rejected the separatism of their white lesbian feminist colleagues, and affirmed, "We struggle with Black men against racism, while we also struggle with Black men around sexism."[26]

Lorde contributed philosophical insights, guidance, and support to the CRC and was mutually influenced by this younger generation. The CRC's "Statement of Purpose" helped lay the groundwork for the popular Black feminist theory of difference known today as "intersectionality."[27] Lorde herself wrote a few short years later, "Among those of us who share the goals of liberation and a workable future for our children, there can be no hierarchies of oppression."[28]

Warrior Woman

In the late 1970s, Audre Lorde became a breast-cancer survivor and health advocate. She challenged conventional medical practices and encouraged all women to take charge of their own treatment. Lorde increasingly transitioned into prose writing and began to write at a feverish pace. Her stunning literary output was often delivered in public addresses and lectures. Her writing helped transform critical thinking about race, gender, sex, and women's health for generations to come. She also increasingly worked to build transnational antiracist and feminist movements of color. Lorde, at the age of forty-three, underwent a biopsy on her right breast in New York City. Though the procedure revealed her to be cancer-free, she was informed that she was at high risk for breast cancer. The experience had so shaken her that she wrote about it in essay form. Lorde delivered her "Transformation of Silence into Language and

Action" at the Modern Language Association conference in Chicago on December 28, 1977.

The essay became widely circulated in activist circles for years to come. Lorde spoke of the profound fear she experienced as she awaited the news of her status with cancer and of how she had been forced to confront the reality of death. She entreated her audience that there were no silences worth keeping, and she called on the women to consider what silences they too lived with and pronounced, "Your silence will not protect you."[29] Lorde also argued that racism in the women's movement perpetuated Black women's invisibility and made it difficult to bridge differences between women in spite of aspirations to sisterhood.[30]

While a sense of urgency and fear fueled Lorde's life, she transformed that fear into action and activism. Convinced that writing prose would propel her writing onto a broader stage, she began work on several essays. She delivered one of the most anthologized essays of her career, "Uses of the Erotic: The Erotic as Power," at the Berkshire Conference on the History of Women at Mount Holyoke College in August 1978. She highlighted the ways that women had been warned away from their deepest sexual energies, as a means of keeping women in the service of men. Lorde argued that women were trained to fear the *yes* within themselves and that recognizing the power of the erotic within women's lives gave women the energy to pursue genuine social change within a racist, patriarchal, and antierotic society.

By early September 1978, however, Lorde had received a diagnosis of breast cancer in her right breast and underwent a radical mastectomy. Lorde wrote about her experiences and her battle with cancer in her 1980 book *The Cancer Journals*. The publication was a first of its kind. Lorde documented the challenges she faced, emotionally within herself as well as in her experiences with the medical community.

When Lorde returned to her doctor's office to have her stiches removed, she was confronted by a nurse who informed her that appearing without a prosthesis was bad for the morale of the office. Lorde saw this as an assault on her right to define and claim her own body. Lorde compared the scenario to that of the then prime minister of Israel, Moishe Dayan, who wore an eye patch over his empty socket. She contended that the world saw him as a warrior with an honorable wound, which he had marked and mourned. Lorde wrote, "Well women with breast cancers are warriors, also. I have been to war and still am." She refused to hide her body, "simply because it might make a woman-phobic world more comfortable." Lorde identified the prosthesis as a lie. She instead wished to affirm the difference and "share that strength with other women. If we are to translate the silence surrounding breast cancer into language and action . . . the first step is that women with mastectomies must become visible to each other."[31]

The Cancer Journals marked a turning point in breast-cancer awareness that served to engender public discussions among large groups of American women. Lorde linked her healing to African-based spirituality and mythologies that she had long pioneered in her poetry. How would Lorde's spirituality, healing, and truth telling about her mastectomy broaden her influence as a leader and shape her future decisions with respect to her health?

Poet, Philosopher, Mentor, and Activist

Lorde's reputation and international celebrity grew following the release of *The Cancer Journals*. From her base as a sought-after professor at Hunter College, Lorde mentored aspiring writers, emerging poets, and activists. The noted writers Jewel Gomez, Sapphire, Cheryl Clarke, and Sarah Schulman counted her as a mentor who deeply influenced their development.[32] She also grew close to a young cohort of gay Black male writer/activists—notably, Essex Hemphill and Joseph Beam—who credited her work as inspiring their own.[33] Lorde traveled throughout the country and world, delivering addresses and participating in international literary and feminist conferences. She became increasingly committed to organizing transnationally as she encountered Black activists and writers throughout Europe, the Caribbean, and Africa.

Lorde also cofounded along with Barbara Smith and the Chicana feminist Cherríe Moraga the first women-of-color press in the United States, Kitchen Table: Women of Color Press, in 1980. Lorde contributed essays and poetry to Moraga and Gloria Anzaldúa's landmark anthology *This Bridge Called My Back: Radical Writings by Women of Color* (1981). Furthermore, she penned many more critical essays—a number of which were anthologized in *Sister Outsider*, published by Crossing Press (1984). Many of the essays, along with *Zami*, *The Cancer Journals*, and her poetry, are widely read and taught today in literary, women's, queer, Black, and ethnic studies courses—and in a myriad of combinations therein.

She published and presented other ground-breaking essays about transcending homophobia, patriarchy, and sexism in African American communities. At her address at Medgar Evers College in Brooklyn, "I Am Your Sister: Black Women Organizing across Sexualities," Lorde noted that homophobia and heterosexism robbed many Black women of the strengths and gifts of Black lesbians.[34] She likened stereotypes about Black lesbians to racist stereotypes and contended that these stereotypes were indeed the problems of those who believed them and not of Black lesbians.[35] She further contended that she had no desire to be either tolerated or misnamed but instead wanted to be recognized, concluding, "I am a Black Lesbian, and I *am* your sister."[36]

Lorde's growing public stature as a Black lesbian feminist writer and activist led to her invitation to address the 1983 March on Washington. Twenty years after being electrified by Dr. King's "I Have a Dream" speech, Lorde's personal experiences convinced her that racism, homophobia, heterosexism, and patriarchy were inextricably linked. She reminded the crowd, "We marched in 1963 with Dr. Martin Luther King, and dared to dream that freedom would include us, because not one of us is free to choose the terms of our living until all of us are free."[37]

Yet nine months later, Lorde received demoralizing news that her cancer had returned after six years and had probably metastasized in her liver. Despite her strong team of loved ones and friends, she felt alone and vulnerable. Her New York City oncologist aggressively urged her to undergo a liver biopsy to assess the extent of the damage. Lorde's research, however, convinced her that this dangerous procedure might be detrimental to her wellness and that rather than aid in her recovery, the procedure might in fact shorten her life or even kill her.

While Lorde was en route to St. Croix to visit her friend Gloria Joseph, she wrote, "I wish I knew a doctor I could really trust to talk it all over with. . . . If there's one thing I learned from all the work I've done since my mastectomy, it's that I must listen keenly to the messages my body sends. But sometimes they are contradictory."[38] At the same time, Lorde received an invitation from Dagmar Schultz, a German feminist who had translated Lorde's work into German, to conduct a special workshop in Berlin at the Free University in spring 1984. The teaching opportunity would enable her to work with a community of Black German women who were in the early stages of political and cultural mobilization.[39] Lorde, who considered herself a cultural traveler, was increasingly interested in building transnational Black feminist communities throughout the world. She believed that her battle against racism, sexism, patriarchy, and homophobia would fortify her in her battle against cancer. She visualized battling malignant cancer cells within her body as a battle against racial apartheid.

As an activist artist, Lorde struggled for years to create spaces where she could openly embrace her multiple identities. She was anxious to share her knowledge internationally and intergenerationally, to encourage new generations to find their voices. She wanted more time to write and engage in community building, and she sought to reduce her teaching load in New York City. She wished to pursue alternative and holistic ways of living that would enhance the quality and longevity of her remaining years. Given her health crisis and her desires, how would she, Audre Lorde—the Black, lesbian, feminist, mother, poet warrior—proceed?

Resolution

Audre Lorde refused to have a liver biopsy. While American doctors predicted that without her adherence to their medical advice, she would only survive at best a few short years, Lorde actually lived eight more years. In Berlin and at the Lukas Clinik in Switzerland, she began holistic experimental treatments of Iscador injections, which prolonged her life. Though considered highly experimental in the 1980s, Iscador, an extract of mistletoe, is now commonly used in leading cancer treatments in the United States.[40] Lorde wished to accelerate her writing projects and her international work. She accepted Dagmar Schultz's invitation to teach at the Free University in Berlin in June 1984. While in Germany, she identified a Black community that could benefit from her experiences and social and political work. She became deeply engaged in the nascent antiracist movement in Berlin and throughout Germany, which buoyed her and helped keep her spirits up.

Lorde helped coin the term "Afro-German" and inspired Afro-German women in particular to recognize one another. Lorde created a writing workshop out of which she developed close friendships with May Ayim, Katharina Oguntoye, Helga Emde, and Ilka Hugel-Marshall, who became leading Afro-German women writers. This led to the publication *Showing Our Colors*, for which Lorde wrote the foreword.[41] She stressed the importance of women of the African diaspora listening to each other's stories and learning from one another. Lorde's engagement with Black communities in Germany led to the founding in 1986 in Berlin of the Initiative Schwarze Deutsche, which spread to Frankfurt, Munich, and Stuttgart.[42] She is remembered as a galvanizing figure in an emergent national consciousness movement among Black Germans in the fight against racial discrimination and state repression.

Lorde continued to travel, teach, and write and to seek experimental treatment for her cancer in Berlin. She wrote of these developments and her quest for health in *A Burst of Light* (1988), which won an American Book Award in 1989. Central to her wellness was her naturopathic treatments in Berlin with Dr. Manfred Kuno, who prioritized her wellness over the constricted mission of "fighting cancer." Lorde's experiences and her influences in Germany became the subject of a documentary film directed by her friend Dagmar Schultz, titled *Audre Lorde: The Berlin Years, 1984–1992*.[43]

By 1986, Lorde's relationship with her long-term romantic partner, Frances Clayton, was in decline. Lorde spent more and more time in St. Croix with Gloria Joseph, a Black feminist scholar, writer, and activist. The two women shared a common cultural and political background as children of Caribbean immigrants who came of age in New York City in the postwar era. Lorde delighted in the warmth, sun, and sea in St. Croix. Together with Joseph and another noted Black feminist, Johnnetta Cole, Lorde cofounded the Sisterhood for Sisters in South Africa and other successful movements in coalition with women of color throughout the world.

By 1988, Lorde and Clayton entirely separated, and Lorde relocated to St. Croix. She traveled extensively throughout Europe and the world with Joseph by her side. Together, the two women founded several organizations in St. Croix, including the Che Lumumba School for Truth and the Women's Coalition of St. Croix. They also compiled *Hell under God's Orders*, a range of personal accounts of Hurricane Hugo, which devastated St. Croix in 1989.[44] Lorde's essay "Of Generators and Survival: A Hugo Letter" concerned the disastrous geopolitics of Hugo.

Lorde continued to write and publish poetry, including *Undersong: Chosen Poems Old and New* (1992) and *The Marvelous Arithmetics of Distance: Poems 1987–1992* (1993). She was named the state poet of New York from 1991 to 1992 by Governor Mario Cuomo and was the first woman and African American to achieve that honor. Lorde succumbed to cancer in St. Croix on November 17, 1992. She had been surrounded by loved ones and friends most of the week, including her children, Gloria Joseph, Maya Ayim, Dagmar Schultz, Ilka Huegel, and the filmmaker Ada Griffith Gay, who was chronicling Lorde's life. Memorial services were held in New York City's Cathedral of St. John the Divine, in St. Croix, and in Berlin. Shortly before her death, Lorde took the name Gamba Adisa, meaning "warrior" and "she who makes her meaning known." At her memorial in New York City, attended by more than four thousand people, a sizable contingent of Afro-German women traveled there to praise Lorde as a catalyst to their movement.

Audre Lorde's critically acclaimed body of writing, her cultural fluidity, her transnational activism, and her "out and proud" life are celebrated by generations of activists, students, writers, and artists throughout the world. Lorde drew from her experiences of being othered as a Black woman lesbian poet socialist and mother of two to forge her own bold and integrally laced self-definition of herself. She staked out the urgency of recognizing difference and worked to create inclusive radical movements among women and people of color. Lorde authored highly accessible essays that are crucial to feminist theory. Her writing on her experiences with cancer is critical to contemporary discourse about women's health advocacy, particularly among Black women. She is one of the most known and cited Black feminist theorists in the world.[45]

In Lorde's widely taught essay "Age, Race, Class, and Sex: Women Redefining Difference," she writes, "My fullest concentration of energy is available to me only when I integrate all the parts of who I am, openly allowing power from particular sources of my living to flow back and forth freely through all my different selves, without the restrictions of externally imposed definitions. Only then can I bring myself and all my energies which I embrace as part of my living."[46]

Notes

1   Audre Lorde, *Our Dead behind Us: Poems* (New York: Norton, 1986).
2   Audre Lorde, *The Cancer Journals* (San Francisco: Aunt Lute Books, 1980), 58–61.
3   Audre Lorde, "Uses of the Erotic: The Erotic as Power," in *Sister Outsider: Essays and Speeches* (Berkeley, CA: Crossing Press, 1984), 53–59; Lorde, "Man Child: A Black Lesbian Feminist's Response," in *Sister Outsider*, 72–80.
4   Audre Lorde, "The Transformation of Silence into Language and Action," in *Sister Outsider*, 40–44; Lorde, "An Open Letter to Mary Daly," in *Sister Outsider*, 66–71.
5   Audre Lorde, "Age, Race, Class, and Sex: Women Redefining Difference," in *Sister Outsider*, 114–123.
6   Audre Lorde, "The Uses of Anger: Women Responding to Racism," in *Sister Outsider*, 124–133; Lorde, "Eye to Eye: Black Women, Hatred, and Anger," in *Sister Outsider*, 145–175.
7   Audre Lorde, "An Address Delivered as Part of the 'Litany of Commitment' at the March on Washington, August 27, 1983," in *I Am Your Sister: Collected and Unpublished Writings of Audre Lorde*, ed. Rudolph R. Byrd, Johnnetta Betsch Cole, and Beverly Guy-Sheftall (New York: Oxford University Press, 2009), 212.
8   Audre Lorde, *A Burst of Light* (Ithaca, NY: Firebrand Books, 1988), 55.
9   Audre Lorde, "Learning from the Sixties," in *Sister Outsider*, 137.
10 *A Litany for Survival: The Life and Work of Audre Lorde*, dir. Ada Gay Griffin and Michelle Parkerson (New York: Third World Newsreel Film Collective, 1995), DVD.
11 Ibid.

12 Lorde, *Cancer Journals,* 40.
13 *Litany for Survival.*
14 De Veaux, *Warrior Poet,* 39.
15 Audre Lorde, "An Interview: Audre Lorde and Adrienne Rich," in *Sister Outsider,* 91.
16 *Litany for Survival.*
17 Audre Lorde, "I Am Your Sister: Black Women Organizing across Sexualities," in *I Am Your Sister,* 60.
18 Ibid.
19 Lorde, "Learning from the Sixties," 143.
20 Audre Lorde, "Poetry Is Not a Luxury," in *Sister Outsider,* 37–38.
21 Audre Lorde, *The Black Unicorn* (New York: Norton, 1978), 3 ("The Black Unicorn"), 31–32 ("Litany for Survival").
22 Cheryl Clarke, *After Mecca: Women Poets and the Black Arts Movement* (New Brunswick, NJ: Rutgers University Press, 2006), 131–161. We are indebted to Clarke's thorough analysis of *The Black Unicorn* in *After Mecca.*
23 Nikol Alexander-Floyd, *Gender, Race, and Nationalism in Contemporary Black Politics* (New York: Palgrave Macmillan, 2007), 115–117, 126–132, 165–168.
24 Audre Lorde, "Sexism: An American Disease in Blackface," in *Sister Outsider,* 72–80.
25 Beverly Guy-Sheftall, introduction to *Words of Fire: An Anthology of African American Feminist Thought,* ed. Guy-Sheftall (New York: New Press, 1995), 14–16; Combahee River Collective, "A Black Feminist Statement," in ibid., 231–240.
26 Combahee River Collective, "A Black Feminist Statement," 235. For a review of several key Black feminist writings that influenced the Combahee River Collective's "Statement of Purpose," see Frances Beale, "Double Jeopardy: To Be a Black Woman," 146–155; Linda LaRue, "The Black Movement and Women's Liberation," 164–173; Pauli Murray, "The Liberation of Black Women," 186–197; and Michele Wallace, "Anger in Isolation: A Black Feminist's Search for Sisterhood," 220–227, all in *Words of Fire.*
27 For more information on the theory of "intersectionality," see Kimberlé Williams Crenshaw, "Demarginalizing the Intersection of Race and Sex: A Black Feminist Critique of Antidiscrimination Doctrine, Feminist Theory and Antiracist Politics," *University of Chicago Legal Forum* 140 (1989): 139–167.
28 Audre Lorde, "There Is No Hierarchy of Oppression," in *I Am Your Sister,* 219–220.
29 Ibid., 41.
30 Ibid., 42–44.
31 Lorde, *Cancer Journals,* 61.
32 *Litany for Survival.*
33 De Veaux, *Warrior Poet,* 255–256.
34 Lorde, "I Am Your Sister," 61.
35 Ibid., 62.
36 Ibid., 63.

37   Lorde, *I Am Your Sister*, 212.

38   Lorde, *Burst of Light*, 55.

39   Ibid., 56.

40   AfroLez Productions, "Feminists We Love: Elizabeth Lorde-Rollins, M.D., M.Sc.," Vimeo, February 25, 2014, http://vimeo.com/87539969, video, from the Feminist Wire's Global Forum on Audre Lorde; see http://www.thefeministwire.com/2014/02/feminists-love-elizabeth-lorde-rollins-m-d/.

41   May Ayim, Katharina Oguntoye, and Dagmar Schultz, eds., *Showing Our Colors: Afro-German Women Speak Out* (Amherst: University of Massachusetts Press, 1992).

42   Jennifer Michaels, "The Impact of Audre Lorde's Politics and Poetics on Afro-German Women Writers," *German Studies Review* 29 (2006): 21–40.

43   *Audre Lorde: The Berlin Years, 1984–1992*, dir. Dagmar Schultz (Germany: Third World Newsreel Film Collective, 2012), DVD.

44   Gloria I. Joseph, Hortense M. Rowe, and Audre Lorde, *Hell under God's Orders: Hurricane Hugo in St. Croix—Disaster and Survival* (St. Croix, VI: Winds of Change, 1990).

45   This study was enriched by the many essays, poems, and videos posted on the Feminist Wire's Global Forum on Audre Lorde, curated by Aishah Shahidah Simmons. The Global Forum on Audre Lorde launched on February 18, 2014—the eightieth anniversary of Lorde's birth. For more information, see the index: http://www.thefeministwire.com/2014/03/afterword-standing-lordean-shoreline/.

46   Audre Lorde, "Age, Race, Class, and Sex: Women Redefining Difference," in *Sister Outsider*, 120.

Bibliography

AfroLez Productions. "The Feminist Wire's Feminists We Love: Elizabeth Lorde-Rollins, M.D., M.Sc." Vimeo, February 25, 2014. http://vimeo.com/87539969. Video. From the Feminist Wire's Global Forum on Audre Lorde; see http://www.thefeministwire.com/2014/02/feminists-love-elizabeth-lorde-rollins-m-d/.

Alexander-Floyd, Nikol. *Gender, Race, and Nationalism in Contemporary Black Politics.* New York: Palgrave Macmillan, 2007.

Audre Lorde: The Berlin Years, 1984–1992. Directed by Dagmar Schultz. Germany: Third World Newsreel Film Collective, 2012. DVD.

Ayim, May, Katharina Oguntoye, and Dagmar Schultz, eds. *Showing Our Colors: Afro-German Women Speak Out.* Amherst: University of Massachusetts, 1992.

Bambara, Toni Cade, ed. *The Black Woman: An Anthology.* New York: New American Library, 1970.

Chisholm, Shirley. *Unbought and Unbossed.* Boston: Houghton Mifflin, 1970.

Clarke, Cheryl. *After Mecca: Women Poets and the Black Arts Movement.* New Brunswick, NJ: Rutgers University Press, 2006.

Combahee River Collective. "A Black Feminist Statement." In *Words of Fire: An Anthology of African American Feminist Thought*, edited by Beverly Guy-Sheftall, 231–240. New York: New Press, 1995.

Crenshaw, Kimberlé Williams. "Demarginalizing the Intersection of Race and Sex: A Black Feminist Critique of Antidiscrimination Doctrine, Feminist Theory and Antiracist Politics." *University of Chicago Legal Forum* 140 (1989): 139–167.

De Veaux, Alexis. *Warrior Poet: A Biography of Audre Lorde.* New York: Norton, 2004.

Guy-Sheftall, Beverly. Introduction to *Words of Fire: An Anthology of African American Feminist Thought,* edited by Guy-Sheftall, 1–22. New York: New Press, 1995.

———, ed. *Words of Fire: An Anthology of African American Feminist Thought.* New York: New Press, 1995.

Joseph, Gloria I., Hortense M. Rowe, and Audre Lorde. *Hell under God's Orders: Hurricane Hugo in St. Croix—Disaster and Survival.* St. Croix, VI: Winds of Change, 1990.

Litany for Survival, A: The Life and Work of Audre Lorde. Directed by Ada Gay Griffin and Michelle Parkerson. New York: Third World Newsreel Film Collective, 1995. DVD.

Lorde, Audre. "An Address Delivered as Part of the 'Litany of Commitment' at the March on Washington, August 27, 1983." In *I Am Your Sister,* 212.

———. "Age, Race, Class, and Sex: Women Redefining Difference." In *Sister Outsider,* 114–123.

———. *The Black Unicorn.* New York: Norton, 1978.

———. *A Burst of Light.* Ithaca, NY: Firebrand Books, 1988.

———. *Cables to Rage.* London: Paul Breman, 1970.

———. *The Cancer Journals.* San Francisco: Aunt Lute Books, 1980.

———. "Eye to Eye: Black Women, Hatred, and Anger." In *Sister Outsider,* 145–175.

———. *From a Land Where Other People Live.* Detroit: Broadside, 1973.

———. "I Am Your Sister: Black Women Organizing across Sexualities." In *I Am Your Sister,* 57–63.

———. *I Am Your Sister: Collected and Unpublished Writings of Audre Lorde.* Edited by Rudolph R. Byrd, Johnnetta Betsch Cole, and Beverly Guy-Sheftall. New York: Oxford University Press, 2009.

———. "An Interview: Audre Lorde and Adrienne Rich." In *Sister Outsider,* 81–109.

———. "Learning from the Sixties." In *Sister Outsider,* 134–144.

———. *The Marvelous Arithmetics of Distance: Poems 1987–1992.* New York: Norton, 1993.

———. "An Open Letter to Mary Daly." In *Sister Outsider,* 66–71.

———. *Our Dead behind Us: Poems.* New York: Norton, 1986.

———. "Poetry Is Not a Luxury." In *Sister Outsider,* 36–39.

———. "Sexism: An American Disease in Blackface." In *Sister Outsider,* 72–80.

———. *Sister Outsider: Essays and Speeches.* Berkeley, CA: Crossing Press, 1984.

———. "There Is No Hierarchy of Oppression." In *I Am Your Sister,* 219–220.

———. "The Transformation of Silence into Language and Action." In *Sister Outsider,* 40–44.

———. *Undersong: Chosen Poems, Old and New.* New York: Norton, 1992.

———. "The Uses of Anger: Women Responding to Racism." In *Sister Outsider.* 124–133.

———. "Uses of the Erotic: The Erotic as Power." In *Sister Outsider,* 53–59.

————. *Zami: A New Spelling of My Name*. New York: Crossing Press, 1982.

Meriwether, Louise. *Daddy Was a Number Runner*. Englewood Cliffs, NJ: Prentice Hall, 1970.

Michaels, Jennifer. "The Impact of Audre Lorde's Politics and Poetics on Afro-German Women Writers." *German Studies Review* 29 (2006): 21–40.

Moraga, Cherríe, and Gloria Anzaldúa, eds. *This Bridge Called My Back: Writings by Radical Women of Color*. New York: Kitchen Table, Women of Color, 1983.

Morrison, Toni. *The Bluest Eye*. New York: Plume Books, 1994.

Shange, Ntozake. *For Colored Girls Who Have Considered Suicide, When the Rainbow Is Enuf*. San Lorenzo, CA: Shameless Hussy, 1975.

Walker, Alice. *The Color Purple: A Novel*. New York: Harcourt Brace Jovanovich, 1982.

————. *The Third Life of Grange Copeland*. New York: Harcourt, 1970.

Wallace, Michele. *Black Macho and the Myth of the Superwoman*. New York: Dial, 1979.

This chapter's title comes from Alexis De Veaux, *Warrior Poet: A Biography of Audre Lorde* (New York: Norton, 2004), 179. This study benefited from indispensable information found in *Warrior Poet*.

Charlotte Bunch

Leading from the Margins as a Global Activist for Women's Rights

Mary K. Trigg and Stina Soderling

Background

Charlotte Bunch is a prominent and well-regarded leader in the global women's movement. Over the past four decades, she has led numerous campaigns as well as educated new generations of women leaders. She describes her leadership style as "collaborative" and as being "about everyone having a voice."[1] In her leadership, Bunch serves as a bridge between groups that might otherwise not connect to each other. She describes this as her "tendency to try to be radical but still to interact with mainstream institutions."[2] Her feminist leadership journey has led her from social justice movements and radical organizations to become a coalition and idea builder who brings together disparate groups with powerful decision makers to create change. In a 2014 interview, she remarked, "If I look back now, fifty years later, I have constantly, in different ways, worked on the margins of the mainstream to be able to be inside some institutions and try to influence that power and, at the same time, not being really completely of that and being connected to the movements outside that I think are the source of change. But that change has to get translated in the institutions, or it becomes ephemeral."[3] Bunch's activist leadership has forced her to grapple with the ambivalence, and feminist challenge, of speaking up and taking credit for her work, while at the same time giving credit to others also and providing a public voice to those who have little access or visibility.

Early Years of Social Justice Work

Charlotte Bunch was born in North Carolina in 1944, the third of four siblings. Because of her father's asthma and work as a family doctor, the family moved to Artesia, New Mexico, when Charlotte was six weeks old. Her parents were active Methodists and considered a social conscience to be part of their religious conviction. This social conscience was handed down to Charlotte, who has carried it with her throughout her life's work. Bunch credits her mother's involvement as the only woman, and often a lone dissenting voice, on the local school board as an early activist influence, teaching her daughter that one must speak up for what one believes in.

After graduating from high school, Bunch attended the Women's College at Duke University in Durham, North Carolina, where she studied history and political science and graduated magna cum laude in 1966. Bunch credits this time with leading to her entry into social justice work. It was the time of the Black civil rights movement, and North Carolina, located in the US South, was a key site for racial justice activism. She was involved in the Methodist student movement (MSM), and her first overtly political act was a pray-in protesting racial segregation at a local church in Durham. At the time that Bunch entered college, Duke University's undergraduate colleges were still all white.[4] As desegregation was approaching, the next year, the MSM at Duke and nearby North Carolina Negro College (NCNC) instituted an exchange program for white and Black students to get to know each other. Bunch participated in this program and became acquainted with some of the students from NCNC. Soon after, she saw a picture of one of these students getting arrested and beaten at a sit-in. This personal connection became a motivating point for Bunch's participation in the civil rights movement.

Through involvement with the Methodist student movement, Bunch was also introduced to liberation theology, a Latin American theory and practice grounded in the experiences of poor people. Liberation theology considers involvement in social justice work as a key component of Christian faith. During Bunch's time in college, she was an organizer of the University Christian Movement (UCM), an early ecumenical experiment, and served as its first national president. She was also part of the World Student Christian Federation (WSCF), an international organization using Christian faith as a basis for social justice work. Her participation in UCM and WSCF gave her organizing experience at the national and international levels. Later, from 1968 to 1972, Bunch served on the executive committee of the WSCF, one of many examples of her assuming leadership roles at an early age.

Bunch also became active in the peace movement, joining a picket line against the war at the Durham Post Office in 1965. In the 1960s, the US war in Vietnam was at the forefront of national awareness. College campuses were among the most active sites in the antiwar movement, and thus Bunch had many chances to interact with this movement.

Bunch's involvement in the antiwar and civil rights movements in college and then in Washington, DC, showed her that even within movements that were struggling for equality and a decent life for all, there was widespread sexism. Women were not listened to or treated as the equals of men. This complaint was common among women in the social movements of the 1960s, and it was one of the catalysts of the women's liberation movement. Many of those who were involved in women's liberation had previous organizing experience in other social movements but did not feel fully appreciated within these male-dominated spaces.

Already, part of Bunch's strategy as a leader was to change institutions from the inside. She was involved in Duke University's Young Women's Christian Association (YWCA). When she and her close friend Sara Evans were both seen as potential candidates for the presidency of the Duke YWCA, they decided to run as copresidents, so as not to compete against each other.[5] Though this was not a model that the organization had previously utilized, the two women were elected as a team.

After college, Bunch moved to Washington, DC. She lived in a communal setting and organized nationally as president of the University Christian Movement. Over time, she started to doubt her Christian convictions and decided to work outside faith-based organizations. She became a fellow at the Institute for Policy Studies (IPS), a progressive think tank devoted to issues such as peace, antiracism, economic justice, and the environment. Bunch was the first woman to be appointed as a permanent fellow with tenure at IPS. Bunch enjoyed her work at IPS; but she and the other women there found they were not taken as seriously as the men were, and their ideas were not fully considered. Bunch recalled, "I'd make a comment at a meeting and nobody would even acknowledge me. Then some man would say virtually the same thing and they'd all nod and say, 'Good idea.'"[6] This was a key feminist consciousness-raising moment for Bunch, one that reinforced her experiences in the antiwar and civil rights movements. In 1968, together with other women at IPS, Bunch started the Radical Women's Discussion Group, which became one of the starting points for the women's liberation movement in Washington, DC.

Through involvement in the women's liberation movement, Bunch came in contact for the first time with women who were out as lesbians. At the time, Bunch was married to Jim Weeks, a social activist whom she had met at a national student Christian conference, and the thought that she might be a lesbian had not crossed her mind. Her interactions in the women's liberation movement eventually led her to realize that she was a lesbian, and this became a key aspect of her activism. In 1971, she came out publicly as a founding member of the feminist collective the Furies, a separatist group. Through its newspaper *The Furies* (1972–1973), the group shared its theories about why heterosexism was part of upholding patriarchy within the larger feminist movement. But the kind of "outrageous" statements and acts that the Furies represented was not Bunch's natural approach to leadership. "I think what's brave about me," she stated in 2014, "is that I was willing to try it. And that I've been able to work back from it [the Furies' separatist model]—back into a collaborative model."

Charlotte Bunch considered coming out to be part of her involvement in the feminist movement. This was not a popular stance among all feminists: many in the mainstream movement saw bringing up lesbian issues as divisive. Some were worried that if lesbians in the women's movement came out, all feminists would be labeled as lesbians. The prominent feminist Betty Friedan derogatorily referred to the lesbian presence within the women's liberation movement as "the lavender menace"—lavender and purple were colors associated with the lesbian, gay, bisexual, and transgender population. These negative attitudes had tangible consequences for lesbian women in the feminist movement: some lesbians were even expelled from feminist groups when they shared their sexual identity. Bunch, on the other hand, argued that lesbian rights are central to feminism, as homophobia is one example of how women's—and other people's—sexuality is controlled.

But soon, Bunch found separatism too narrow and confining. Her next step in working in the women's liberation movement was to found *Quest: A Feminist Quarterly* in 1974; the journal was published until 1982. Originally, *Quest* was housed at IPS, but over time, it became an independent entity. "To me, if you ultimately think about the work I did," Bunch said in 2014, "the Furies could be a sentence, and *Quest* would be a chapter." Bunch spent six years building *Quest* and developing feminist community through the journal. It came to symbolize the feminist movement building she would focus on over her long activist career. "I actually think what we did in *Quest*," Bunch stated, "was much more this kind of [collaborative] work and also linked theory to activism. It had a huge impact." Bunch became one of the leading voices of the feminist movement. The Argentinian sexual rights activist Alejandra Sarda recalled, "When we started reading feminism, we read [Charlotte Bunch]. And everybody was reading her."[7] During these years, Bunch wrote an important article, "The Reform Tool Kit" (1974), in which she struggled with finding the balance between reform and revolution.[8] She was grappling with a question that would be key to her leadership: "How do you try to make some impact, some effective reform, when what you believe is needed is more revolutionary?"

The Global Women's Rights Movement, 1980 to 1993

Charlotte Bunch brought her vision of transformative change with her into the global women's rights movement. Though less prominent than her activism in the local feminist community, Bunch also had a long-standing commitment to international solidarity and global justice. Much of her work brought her into contact with the United Nations, the multilateral organization of governments headquartered in New York City that works to promote peace, security, human rights, and development cooperation among its member states. Created in the aftermath of World War II, the UN had 51 member states at its founding, a number that has now grown to 193. Women's rights have been on the agenda of the United Nations since its founding, as they had been on the agenda of the organization that preceded it, the League of Nations. Between 1975 and 2014, the Commission on the Status of Women, one of several thematic policy bodies of the United Nations, organized four world conferences on women: in Mexico City (1975), Copenhagen (1980), Nairobi (1985), and Beijing (1995). In addition, the 2000 Beijing Plus Five meeting, the Ten Year Review held in 2005, and the Fifteen Year Review and Appraisal (2010) all assessed the implementation of the Beijing Declaration and Platform for Action as well as the achievement of the Millennium Development Goals.[9] These important conferences coincided with the years of Bunch's global activism on behalf of women's rights.

Bunch's initial work around the United Nations began in the late 1970s. She recalled,

> I had met people and done some organizing around the International Women's Year Conference in Mexico City. I did not go, but helped organize to get Frances Doughty from the National Gay Task Force there to make some lesbian connections. Also a friend of mine from Australia became the deputy director for the UN Women's Conference in 1980 in Copenhagen, and she hired me to do some consulting for it. I met Peggy Antrobus in Bangkok in 1979, and she then hired me to organize a feminist strategy meeting in preparation for the UN conference.[10]

Antrobus—who was a leader in women's empowerment organizations in the Caribbean and later a founder of DAWN (Development Alternatives with Women for a New Era)—explained Bunch's influence by pointing to her modesty and generosity in sharing her own experiences with others in the movement. Antrobus stated, "She was never imposing anything on anybody. She was just another woman sharing her experience, and something in her experience that she shared resonated with me."[11]

At the 1980 Copenhagen conference, Bunch organized a section of workshops on international feminist networking. She grew increasingly interested in the work on trafficking and female sexual slavery. Her next step was to organize an international workshop on that topic in 1983; there she began to develop a real curiosity about why these women's issues were not understood as human rights concerns. "Why are these people not getting the benefits of being treated as victims of human rights, rather than as criminals or outlaws or pariahs?" Bunch asked.[12] The notion of women's rights as human rights acknowledges that violations of women's bodies and minds are just as serious as violations against men are. At the same time, violations of human rights have gendered dimensions and can only be properly addressed when gender is taken into account. For example, in many war situations, the rape of women is used as a weapon. This issue can only be adequately addressed by engaging with both gender and militarism.

After Bunch worked as a feminist consultant for a decade, a turning point for her was getting a position at Rutgers University. She lived in New York City by then and first went to Rutgers on a two-year contract in 1987 as the Blanche, Edith and Irving Laurie New Jersey Chair in Women's Studies at Douglass College. During this time, she ran a seminar on global feminism and human rights. The seminar became a place to think through the connection between human rights and feminism, which became the central focus of Bunch's work from that time forward. After her initial two years were up, Bunch was invited to stay on at Rutgers, to create the Center for Women's Global Leadership (CWGL), which she launched in 1990. The CWGL's work is based in the idea of "women's rights as human rights" and aims to bring women who are leaders on a local level to engagement at the global level, into work connected to the United Nations. Bunch emphasizes that this endeavor is largely about convincing women that what they have to say is important.[13]

To Bunch, nurturing women's leadership is not just about getting as many women as possible into power but rather about making sure that women (and men) in power are accountable to women at the grassroots level. Women leaders are not by definition feminist, and it is important that they listen to their constituents. Otherwise, the interests of women in power can overshadow the needs of the majority of women. On the other hand, without power or without the ability to influence those who have power, women's organizations have no real teeth. Bunch was increasingly recognizing this quandary.

Bunch has argued that women have been leading in their families and communities for many years, but they have not been allowed to lead in the public arenas where decisions are made that affect their lives. "We need to look at how to move women leaders into a position of more power and impact on the world," she wrote. "[We need to consider] how to move the leadership that women take, the ideas and experiences that women have into the public sphere in a more forceful way; and how to give women more recognition, more power, and more opportunity to influence the public sphere."[14]

In the 1980s, Bunch was part of an international network of feminists who were united by shared concerns and prepared by education and training for leadership and activism. Through her speeches and organizing at international conferences, she served as a key catalyst for action on women's issues, especially around the idea that women's rights are human rights. According to Bunch, the idea had been in circulation as early as the 1970s, but mostly in private conversations that did not lead to public dialogues. She explained, "The time had not come for this to take root yet. The work had to be done, and the movement had to come."[15]

A growing global feminist movement emerged in the 1980s and 1990s. In Bunch's words, it was "a social movement that crossed Global South and North lines and saw the UN as an important international space for advancing women's rights."[16] As global feminists sought to bring a feminist analysis and women's presence to bear on global issues including peace, security, development, environment, and human rights, they aimed to influence the UN World Conferences held on all these topics.[17]

When the United Nations adopted the Universal Declaration of Human Rights, a document promoted by Eleanor Roosevelt in 1948, that text did include the need to end discrimination based on sex but did not spell out women's rights further. The First World Conference on Women in Mexico City in 1975 began to spell out in more detail what it means to end discrimination based on gender.[18] After the Second (1980) and Third (1985) UN Conferences on Women, activists kicked off the Global Campaign for Women's Human Rights[19] in 1991 with a petition to those who were preparing for the UN-sponsored World Conference on Human Rights to be held in Vienna, Austria, in 1993. This petition asserted, "Violence against women violates human rights," and requested that the conference "comprehensively address women's human rights at every level of its proceedings."[20] The petition—which touched a nerve with women—was translated at the grassroots level into twenty-five languages and, pre-Internet, quickly circulated in 124 countries, in Bunch's words, "sparking widespread debate over why women's rights were not already considered human rights."[21] Petitions were gathered and delivered over the next two years; some were signed with thumbprints by illiterate women.[22]

Most mainstream human rights groups and governments were reluctant to formally include women's rights in the category of human rights. Although the Cold War had ended and dictatorships had fallen in Latin America, parts of Asia, and much of eastern Europe, the meaning of human rights was still contested. The 1993 World Conference on Human Rights brought together seven thousand participants from 171 nations to consider the current state of human rights in the world. In four regional preparation meetings over the two years preceding the conference, participants raised many contentious issues regarding national sovereignty, universality, the role of nongovernmental organizations,[23] and the effectiveness of new human rights instruments.[24] The search for common ground involved intense dialogue among governments and dozens of UN bodies, intergovernmental organizations, and thousands of human rights and development NGOs from around the world. Women's rights had not initially been on the agenda, but feminists in each region organized to bring visibility to it and especially to violence against women. The ground was shifting.

The Global Campaign for Women's Human Rights worked to draw attention to the ways that women face distinct human rights challenges, and the approach they took in Vienna was to focus on acts of violence against women as the principal human rights concern.[25]

Because much violence against women and girls takes place in the home, gender-based violence is often considered a matter to be handled in the family, rather than a question of human rights. For example, it can be difficult, or even impossible, for a woman to leave an abusive relationship if she is dependent on her abuser for financial support. Another issue addressed was how women and girls face specific risks in wartime, most notably through the use of rape as a weapon. The brutal rapes in the Bosnian War—in the months leading up to Vienna—drew media attention and made such gendered violations difficult for governments to ignore. Forced prostitution is also very common in areas under military occupation or near military bases; examples include so-called South Korean comfort women used by the Japanese military during World War II.

One of the most controversial issues in women's human rights is reproductive justice. Because of the strongly held beliefs that many people have on questions such as when life begins, demanding full reproductive freedom is often very difficult. The Women's Campaign did not shy away from this issue but rather highlighted how women's reproductive rights are violated by issues such as forced sterilization and lack of access to prenatal care, as well as by unsafe abortions.

The key event the Women's Campaign organized was a daylong Global Tribunal on Violations of Women's Human Rights, held in Vienna on June 15, 1993. The tribunal was part of the larger landscape of work on women's human rights issues at the time and was one of many activities that the Women's Campaign conducted to influence the larger conference. It provided a forum for female survivors of violence—and their advocates—to tell their own stories.[26] The one-day tribunal ran simultaneously with the World Conference on Human Rights, which had begun the day before (June 14) and continued through June 25, 1993. In considering the legacy of Vienna, Bunch wrote, "The Campaign did not take an 'add women and stir' approach but aimed at transforming human rights to be more inclusive by bringing women's experiences and feminist gender analysis to bear on all issues. We sought to demonstrate what violations of human rights such as torture, denial of the freedom of expression and movement as well as of the right to food and security look like in the lives of women."[27]

Women's groups in each region selected the testimonies and issues they wanted to highlight from their region. Thirty-three women from twenty-five countries across the globe eventually testified at the tribunal. Bunch moderated the tribunal overall and introduced the sections, which were moderated by feminists from differing regions.[28] The tribunal sought to put women's human rights in a larger perspective of social and economic rights, as well as civil and political rights. As long as women are financially and socially dependent on men, they cannot fully exercise their human rights. The women's testimony was dramatic and riveting. This pivotal event made women's demands concrete, graphically demonstrating that being female can be life threatening and often includes degrading, inhuman treatment as well as torture, terrorism, and slavery.[29] At the end of the tribunal, the four judges who heard the testimonials made a list of recommendations, including installing a UN Special Rapporteur on the issue of violence against women and the implementation of a gender lens in all groups working on human rights issues.

The entire two-year campaign, and the vital day of women's public statements about the horrific violations they had faced in many countries, led to a personal decision point for Bunch. The decision she had to make was about how—as a leader—she could best honor and publicize the violations of women's human rights around the world. Bunch had been working on these issues and in activist leadership for a long time. Yet both her family background and her feminist philosophy made her reluctant to step forward as the media spokesperson. How, at this important moment, could she advocate on behalf of global women's causes in a way that would balance her own public recognition with her feminist belief in a collective movement where leadership was shared by many people?

This decision point was one that had reverberated for many feminists who came before Bunch, as well as for those in her generational cohort who equated public recognition with seeking the spotlight and advancing the hierarchical leadership that men often represented. But the quandary, as Bunch saw it, was whether at this moment to step forward and claim credit publicly for the organizing work she had been doing for the past twenty years. Was she going to allow herself to become more visible? Would she commit to a more visible media strategy? How could she accept and take credit for her own role in a way that would not deny the importance of others and that would not set her up for a traditional leadership dynamic? How could she make the greatest impact at Vienna and beyond?

Resolution

Up until the work on Vienna, Charlotte Bunch had managed to maintain a low profile as a leader. Although she was certainly well-known by people within the movements, she was neither a media darling nor a celebrity. "It's not that I ever denied leadership," she remarked, "but I was not trying to be, or being in a big way, a public leader. And that was partly because of my feeling that, in the women's movement, if you want to keep working with people, you have to be careful how much you put yourself forward." Feminists who rallied to the cause in the late 1960s and 1970s in the United States had a frank distrust of the singular "leader" who represented the movement. This was not a new phenomenon in the history of US feminism. Early twentieth-century feminists in the postsuffrage years in the United States were divided by jealousy, irreconcilable differences over strategy, and occasional infighting over media attention and publicity.[30] This was at times detrimental to the movement.

Charlotte Bunch was aware that this was a key juncture in a movement she had been working on for much of her career. According to Bunch, the United Nations World Conference on Human Rights held in Vienna in 1993 is now widely recognized as the watershed in the effort to gain international acceptance that "women's rights are human rights," and the Vienna tribunal played a key role in establishing the platform for that.[31] As Bunch remarked, "As we got into the final stages of the Vienna process, . . . I don't know that we knew it would be what we call now the tipping point. But we did begin to sense that this was the moment when something important could happen on this issue." Bunch had been thinking for a decade about the intersection of women's rights with human rights:

this had been a central component of the work she had done at Rutgers since 1987. But she was reluctant to take too much credit: "I'm trained—both by my family and by feminist culture—not to boast and put yourself forward, and I know that ideas can be more powerful coming from many sources," she noted.

Further complicating her decision was the fact that a media team was involved. The Communications Consortium, a Washington, DC–based group, had initially approached the Ford Foundation for funding to do media work and publicity at the Vienna World Conference. The Ford program officers were familiar with Bunch's work at CWGL and told the Communications Consortium that if it wanted to cover women testifying at the tribunal, it would have to work with CWGL staff and Bunch, because they were the people who had done this work. Bunch described "a kind of recognition" in this, which forced on her a realization: "If I wasn't going to put myself forward in the media at this point, when was I ever going to do that?"

Bunch understood the delicacy of the situation. She knew that in a global movement, especially being a white American lesbian and being sensitive to race and class issues, she had to be careful how much she was seen as the face of the movement. But Bunch also recognized and observed that if she did not allow herself to be out front, someone else would take that platform. She stated, "And so any effort I was making not to be too visible wasn't necessarily going to lead to a better situation as the media was looking to women in the US. At least if I had that media attention, I could try to share it with other women, to keep bringing in the fact that this was a multidimensional movement, not just a white, Western one. Whether I succeeded or not, I trusted myself to try that better than the other people that were also in the limelight—who also were white, Western women." Bunch acknowledged that she was not the only person doing this work, but she had indeed played an important leadership role. "It was very definitely my work," she reflected in 2014. "I had led the strategy in many, many ways, . . . even ways that I only understood years later, how much I was leading it." In addition, she knew from her years in the women's movement that if she did not step forward, others would, or the media would select those whom they wanted to be spokespeople. Over the past thirty years, Bunch had watched this happen in the feminist movement: "There were many feminist leaders in addition to Bella [Abzug] and Betty Friedan. But they're the ones that the media chose to focus on," she remarked. Some feminist stars like Gloria Steinem used their celebrity to bring other people into the limelight; others were less gracious and generous. "I watched people be invisibilized by others," Bunch observed, and she understood at that moment that if you want power in order to help direct where a movement goes, you have to step into that visible media role at some points. And at age forty-eight, she did. She later reflected, "You have to choose, and that's part of the juncture in my mind, whether you're going to just keep saying it out there in the wilderness or whether you're going to try to make it happen. And when you try to make it happen, you have to engage with institutions—and you have to deal with the consequences of making compromises and going to the media, which was this particular juncture."

At the same time, Bunch understood the delicate balance that claiming credit involves. "It can be counterproductive if, by being too visible, it takes away from other people's sense of agency of what they made happen."[32] To lessen this potential risk, she continued organizing with the Women's Campaign to build momentum from many directions. There were five discussion sections at the preconference NGO Forum in Vienna in June 1993, which brought together twenty-seven hundred NGOs with the objective of submitting recommendations to the UN World Conference on Human Rights. Women from the Women's Campaign placed themselves in each section of the NGO Forum to ensure that gender issues would be addressed. Bunch had been selected to prepare the background paper, which introduced women's human rights and included the Women's Caucus paper from the final international Preparatory Committee meeting. The Ugandan activist Florence Butegwa was reporter for the session and presented the conclusions at the NGO Forum Plenary, receiving a standing ovation.[33]

Bunch and her fellow women activists also negotiated with the conference secretariat to gain time on the agenda for a report from the tribunal. Working within organizations and their protocol, they realized that by reporting on the tribunal, its recommendations would then officially become part of the documentation of the World Conference on Human Rights. They also exerted external pressure by arranging with the secretariat and security officials for delivery of the third round of 270,000 petition signatures to the conference floor immediately before the report on the tribunal was given. According to Bunch and Niamh Reilly, "On June 17, 1993, tens of thousands of signed petitions demanding human rights for women were delivered to the podium of the plenary hall, bringing the total of signatures received by the UN to almost half a million."[34] Bunch and Florence Butegwa stood at the back of the hall with NGO representatives and presented a statement on behalf of the tribunal. The statement endorsed many of the demands that the women's NGOs had made and added a call from the tribunal judges for the "establishment of an International Criminal Court for Women to protect and enforce women's human rights." It concluded with a warning to governments to recognize that the demands that women were making at the conference were not "an appeal on behalf of a special interest group, but rather, a demand to restore the birthright of half of humanity."[35]

In addition, Bunch worked with the Communications Consortium, which linked her to the press. Although the consortium put together a list of a dozen spokespeople from other parts of the world to be interviewed, the media began to see Bunch as the key person. This had certain repercussions for her. "There were negative consequences," she recalled two decades later. "There were women who thought that I shouldn't be so visible. And I knew there would be. . . . I knew enough about the dynamics of leadership, whether out of jealousy or whether out of their political perspective, that it shouldn't be a white American no matter what. I knew there would be some women who wouldn't like it." But there were important positive consequences as well. Bunch's newfound visibility led her to play a larger role in the next several years of discussions about women's rights as human rights at the UN and with governments. "It meant that I got invited to meetings and places that I had never been before," Bunch stated. "Because I was identified as a visible person at the moment that the human rights community was starting to realize it needed to deal with women—I wasn't the only woman; there were others too—but it meant that I had a seat at the table that I didn't have before."

Having a seat at the table, and being a media presence, gave Bunch legitimacy to have her voice heard. At that point in her activist and leadership career, she made a conscious decision to play a more public leadership role and decided that the social change she sought was worth that compromise. While she enjoyed increased access to decision-making places, at the same time, her new prominence had consequences for how people viewed and related to her. Bunch's relationships with some of her colleagues became more complicated, because some saw her as having stepped out and taken more power. She became a minor celebrity, which changed the way new colleagues often approached her. Bunch understood the risk she was taking. "I had lived through decades of watching the women's movement not deal very well with its leaders. And so I had been very careful about how I was viewed and not being seen as too much ahead of the pack."

Yet, at the same time, Bunch understood the importance of power and access to power. While women's issues are now recognized as critically linked to human rights issues, Bunch believes that one of the downsides of coalitional leadership is that she and her colleagues did not spend enough time building the power base of feminist groups. "I was not an institution builder," she explained in 2014. "I was an idea and coalition builder. And I think not enough has been done about strengthening feminist institutions, in order that women are listened to more in the UN. Women don't have enough effective organizational power. Our organizations are vital but yet weak and vulnerable." She concluded, "I do think that we were afraid—in the feminist movement—of power and leadership and organization, and probably still are, so that it's hard to build really long-range, powerful, effective institutions." While Bunch supports women like Hillary Clinton who (in Bunch's words) "play male power" while still caring about women in the process, she believes that most people from her generation who are deeply feminist still have considerable ambivalence about that kind of power. They have seen it abused and believe it is connected to patriarchal domination. "We want a way to use power for the good," Bunch explained, "in a world where power is not wielded that way. And there's a lot you can do from outside, but I don't know that you can change it all from that place. And to me, that's a big dilemma that we just constantly face."

It was not easy for Bunch to decide to use power, and her own public visibility, to create the social change she believed in. Two decades earlier, she might not even have wanted the opportunity to sit at these kinds of tables. This moment had a new urgency for her, because she recognized the potential, as well as the decades of work and preparation she had put in to be ready for it. "Women were trying to have influence at the UN," she said, "and not just at a women's conference in the UN but in the center of human rights in the UN. And that meant that I got to know people—men and women—who had real power in these institutions." She used these valuable connections to build coalitions that brought women's groups together with human rights and development groups, with groups that have much more authority than feminist groups, for what Bunch considered a feminist goal. The kind of coalitional leadership that this example demonstrates is, in Bunch's words, "about how you bring more established power to support a feminist purpose."

Yet, for Bunch, claiming her own credit and right to be heard—which harked back to her days being spoken over by men in IPS and in the civil rights and antiwar movements of the 1960s—was a challenging thing to do. It involved soul-searching and weighing the balance of what mattered most to her. Ultimately, what mattered most to her was making change and gaining the authority and recognition to bring others along with her. Looking back, she remarked, "If you want to influence the world, you're always struggling with, how much do you play in that world? Idealistically, from a pure point of view, you just do your work. My father used to say, 'So many things could happen in the world, if it didn't matter who got the credit.' And that's the way I was raised. But you know, it does sometimes matter who gets the credit—because the ones who get the credit get the power and resources and opportunities to go on and do other things."

Bunch is not always credited with the work that led to a historic speech by Hillary Clinton in 1995 at the Beijing UN Women's

Conference. That year, Clinton stated, "If there is one message that echoes forth from this conference, let it be that human rights are women's rights and women's rights are human rights once and for all."[36] This idea came from many people and from many places—from feminist social movements in particular, as Bunch is quick to point out. But it also came from Bunch, who played an important role in moving this idea into the international arena, a role that is now often overlooked. Clinton took the idea into the mainstream world and, because of her fame, is often therefore credited with the work done by Bunch and others in the movement. Bunch remarked,

> I want credit for what I did. It was a big chunk of my life work. I want to be credited for really moving this idea into the public and being one of the key people who came up with the strategies to do that. But I also don't want to say that nobody else had the idea. I got it out of the global women's movement, . . . out of the ground of the women's movement. I began to see this, and I began to see what it could mean; and so did some other people. And I worked with many of them. And that's the ambivalence about how much credit you take. But if I don't take credit, it will all go to someone else, like Hillary.

Collaboration has been a key component of Bunch's work for social change. She explained, "Working in a social movement is really about collaboration and about everyone having a voice. I didn't start this work with power in the UN. I started this work as a person who jumped up and grabbed the mic from those who had power to say something that wasn't being said. Part of my job now is to find ways to help give the mic to people who don't have the access, because we won't find the answers if we don't hear from a wider range of people."[37] Through her NGO work, Bunch creates an opportunity for smaller organizations to have the "microphone" and share in the work and achievements. Bunch characterizes her own leadership over her lifetime as a collective, coalitional leadership. Her work in Vienna, she believes, is one example of this approach.

> I am very much . . . at the juncture of inside and outside, but also I know how to bring people together for a common cause. And that's

what I did in Vienna—[it] was to create a framework in which feminists were working with each other across geographical borders but also with women in the human rights movement and in governments and from the UN system. We created an understanding that we had a common goal, with women from different parts of the world and sectors all having a role to play in our success. And I think that's been the style of my leadership.

According to Srilatha Batliwala's definition of feminist leadership, Bunch's leadership represents several elements shared by feminist leaders. First, she is a woman leading with a transformative agenda that connects gender power to social change. Over the decades, Bunch has exhibited "the ability to influence agendas even without the formal power or authority to do so, and the capacity to leverage larger-scale changes (in policy, legal rights, social attitudes, and power relations) with very marginal resources." In addition, Bunch has consistently emphasized the value of collective and multilayered leadership and the importance of relationship building within organizations, with constituencies, and with both allies and opponents.[38]

Today, Bunch continues her work at Rutgers University, where she is a senior scholar with the Center for Women's Global Leadership and a Board of Governors Distinguished Service Professor in the Department of Women's and Gender Studies. She is also a professor in the Leadership Scholars Program, which is sponsored by the Institute for Women's Leadership at Rutgers. Her course on women and leadership nurtures the next generation of women leaders, who look up to Bunch as the icon and generous mentor that she has become. A collaborative leader who rose to influence in the global human rights movement after involvement in the US civil rights and feminist movements, Bunch uses "we" instead of "I" when answering questions about her past activism. When told, "You saw an alternative," Bunch responds, "We saw an alternative."[39]

Notes

1   Institute for Women's Leadership, "An Interview with Charlotte Bunch—A Documentary by Suzan Sanal [Excerpt]," Vimeo, 2010, http://vimeo.com/10778207, video.

2 Ethel Brooks and Dorothy L. Hodgson, "'An Activist Temperament': An Interview with Charlotte Bunch," *Women's Studies Quarterly* 35, nos. 3–4 (2007): 63.
3 Charlotte Bunch, conversation with Mary Trigg, September 2, 2014, New Brunswick, NJ. All direct quotes are taken from this interview unless otherwise noted.
4 Duke University admitted its first African American undergraduate students in 1963. Today, its student body is still majority white but has significant numbers of Black, Asian American, and Latino students, compared to many other elite private universities.
5 Sara Evans went on to write an influential history of the New Left and the civil rights movement. Sara Evans, *Personal Politics: The Roots of Women's Liberation in the Civil Rights Movement and the New Left* (New York: Random House, 1979).
6 Quoted in "Bunch, Charlotte (b. 1944)," *glbtq*, 2004, http://www.glbtq.com/social-sciences/bunch_c.html.
7 *Passionate Politics: The Life and Work of Charlotte Bunch*, dir. Tami Gold (New York: AndersonGOLD Films, 2011), DVD.
8 Charlotte Bunch, "The Reform Tool Kit," *Quest: A Feminist Quarterly* 1 (1974): 37–51.
9 UN Women, "About UN Women," n.d., http://www.un.org/womenwatch/daw/daw/index.html (accessed July 9, 2014). The Beijing Declaration and Platform for Action was adopted by the Fourth World Conference on Women in 1995. The Platform for Action reaffirms the fundamental principle that the rights of women and girls are an "inalienable, integral and indivisible part of universal human rights," and requires all governments to develop strategies to implement the Program nationally. The eight Millennium Development Goals range from halving poverty rates to halting the spread of HIV/AIDS and providing universal primary education, by the target date of 2015. The Goals form a UN-supported blueprint agreed to by all the worlds' countries as well as leading development institutes.
10 Brooks and Hodgson, "Activist Temperament," 69.
11 *Passionate Politics*.
12 Brooks and Hodgson, "Activist Temperament," 70.
13 "GRITtv Interview: Charlotte Bunch," Blip, n.d., http://blip.tv/grittv/grittv-interview-charlotte-bunch-1869163 (accessed March 13, 2014), video.
14 Charlotte Bunch, "What Are We Talking About When We Say Women's Leadership?," in *Power for What? Women's Leadership: Why Should You Care?* (New Brunswick, NJ: Institute for Women's Leadership, Rutgers University, May 2002), 14, http://iwl.rutgers.edu/documents/research/RUWomens2002.pdf.
15 Charlotte Bunch, conversation with Mary Trigg, March 31, 2015.
16 Charlotte Bunch, "Legacy of Vienna: Feminism and Human Rights," paper presented at the International Expert Conference on Vienna + 20, Vienna, June 27, 2013, http://www.cwgl.rutgers.edu/docman/coalition-building/620-legacy-of-vienna-feminism-and-human-rights/file.
17 The UN World Conferences were held in 1992, 1993, 1994, 1995, and 1996. United Nations, "World Conferences Introduction," May 23, 1997, http://www.un.org/geninfo/bp/intro.html.

18 Elizabeth Reichert, "Women's Rights Are Human Rights: Platform for Action," *International Social Work* 41 (1995): 371–384.

19 Known as the Women's Campaign, hundreds of groups were involved in this coalition, with forty to fifty groups as key actors.

20 Bunch, "Legacy of Vienna," 1.

21 Ibid.

22 Charlotte Bunch and Roxanna Carrillo, "Draft Paper for 'Women and Girls' Rising' Conference" (working paper, September 2014), 9. In the author's possession.

23 Nongovernmental organizations (NGOs) are nonprofit, citizen-based groups that function independently of government.

24 United Nations Human Rights, "World Conference on Human Rights, 14–25 June 1993, Vienna, Austria," n.d., http://www.ohchr.org/EN/ABOUTUS/Pages/ViennaWC.aspx (accessed July 16, 2014).

25 Julie Mertus and Pamela Goldberg, "A Perspective on Women and International Human Rights after the Vienna Declaration: The Inside/Outside Construct," *International Law and Politics* 26, no. 20 (1994): 206.

26 Ibid., 214.

27 Bunch, "Legacy of Vienna," 2.

28 Charlotte Bunch and Niamh Reilly, *Demanding Accountability: The Global Campaign and Vienna Tribunal for Women's Human Rights* (New Brunswick, NJ: Center for Women's Global Leadership, 1994), 15.

29 Bunch and Carrillo, "Draft Paper," 11.

30 See Mary K. Trigg, *Feminism as Life's Work: Four Modern American Women through Two World Wars* (New Brunswick, NJ: Rutgers University Press, 2014).

31 Bunch, "Legacy of Vienna."

32 Charlotte Bunch, conversation with Mary K. Trigg, September 23, 2014, New Brunswick, NJ.

33 Bunch and Reilly, *Demanding Accountability*, 100–101.

34 Ibid., 103.

35 Ibid. See part 4, document D.

36 Quoted in Makers, "Makers Profile: Charlotte Bunch: International Women's Rights Activist," March 19, 2012, http://www.makers.com/charlotte-bunch, video.

37 Institute for Women's Leadership, "Interview with Charlotte Bunch."

38 Srilatha Batliwala, *Feminist Leadership for Social Transformation: Clearing the Conceptual Cloud* (New Delhi, India: Creating Resources for Empowerment in Action, 2011), 65–66, http://www.uc.edu/content/dam/uc/ucwc/docs/CREA.pdf.

39 Brooks and Hodgson, "Activist Temperament," 73.

Bibliography

Batliwala, Srilatha. *Feminist Leadership for Social Transformation: Clearing the Conceptual Cloud*. New Delhi, India: Creating Resources for Empowerment in Action, 2011. http://www.uc.edu/content/dam/uc/ucwc/docs/CREA.pdf.

Brooks, Ethel, and Dorothy L. Hodgson. "'An Activist Temperament': An Interview with Charlotte Bunch." *Women's Studies Quarterly* 35, nos. 3–4 (2007): 60–74.

Bunch, Charlotte. "Legacy of Vienna: Feminism and Human Rights." Paper presented at the International Expert Conference on Vienna + 20, Vienna, June 27, 2013. http://www.cwgl.rutgers.edu/docman/coalition-building/620-legacy-of -vienna-feminism-and-human-rights/file.

———. "The Reform Tool Kit." *Quest: A Feminist Quarterly* 1 (1974): 37–51.

———. "What Are We Talking About When We Say Women's Leadership?" In *Power for What? Women's Leadership: Why Should You Care?*, 13–20. New Brunswick, NJ: Institute for Women's Leadership, Rutgers University, May 2002. http://iwl .rutgers.edu/documents/research/RUWomens2002.pdf.

Bunch, Charlotte, and Roxanna Carrillo. "Draft Paper for 'Women and Girls' Rising' Conference." Working paper, September 2014. In the author's possession.

Bunch, Charlotte, and Niamh Reilly. *Demanding Accountability: The Global Campaign and Vienna Tribunal for Women's Human Rights.* New Brunswick, NJ: Center for Women's Global Leadership, 1994.

"Bunch, Charlotte (b. 1944)." *glbtq*, 2004. http://www.glbtq.com/social-sciences/ bunch_c.html.

Evans, Sara. *Personal Politics: The Roots of Women's Liberation in the Civil Rights Movement and the New Left.* New York: Random House, 1979.

"GRITtv Interview: Charlotte Bunch." Blip, n.d. http://blip.tv/grittv/grittv -interview-charlotte-bunch-1869163 (accessed March 13, 2014). Video.

Institute for Women's Leadership. "An Interview with Charlotte Bunch—A Documentary by Suzan Sanal." Vimeo, 2010. http://vimeo.com/10778207. Video.

Makers. "Makers Profile: Charlotte Bunch: International Women's Rights Activist." March 19, 2012. http://www.makers.com/charlotte-bunch. Video.

Mertus, Julie, and Pamela Goldberg. "A Perspective on Women and International Human Rights after the Vienna Declaration: The Inside/Outside Construct." *International Law and Politics* 26 no. 20 (1994): 201–234.

Passionate Politics: The Life and Work of Charlotte Bunch. Directed by Tami Gold. New York: AndersonGOLD Films, 2011. DVD.

Reichert, Elizabeth. "Women's Rights Are Human Rights: Platform for Action." *International Social Work* 41 (1995): 371–384.

Trigg, Mary K. *Feminism as Life's Work: Four Modern American Women through Two World Wars.* New Brunswick, NJ: Rutgers University Press, 2014.

United Nations. "World Conferences Introduction." May 23, 1997. http://www.un .org/geninfo/bp/intro.html.

United Nations Human Rights. "World Conference on Human Rights, 14–25 June 1993, Vienna, Austria." n.d. http://www.ohchr.org/EN/ABOUTUS/Pages/ ViennaWC.aspx (accessed July 16, 2014).

UN Women. "About UN Women." n.d. http://www.un.org/womenwatch/daw/daw/ index.html (accessed July 9, 2014).

Dázon Dixon Diallo
Feminism and the Fight to Combat HIV/AIDS

Stina Soderling and Alison R. Bernstein

Background

In the mid-1980s, Dázon Dixon Diallo, a recent graduate of Spelman College, landed an entry-level position at the local women's health center. There Dixon Diallo, the only woman-of-color health worker at the women's center and the youngest, noticed how many of the callers were Black women inquiring about a mysterious illness that later turned out to be HIV/AIDS. Dixon Diallo, like her heterosexual women callers, had previously thought themselves immune to the epidemic because it was presumed to be a gay white male affliction. Looking back after several decades, Dixon Diallo half jokingly and half seriously insists that it was Rock Hudson who got her into doing HIV/AIDS activism. The aging, closeted movie star's public statement in 1985 that he was living with AIDS, and his death soon thereafter, brought the virus into the living rooms of millions of Americans. In an instant, the message hit home: anyone could contract HIV. In Atlanta, a local, gay-male-dominated AIDS organization was overwhelmed with calls from worried Black women and reached out to the local women's health center for help. From then on, Dixon Diallo's time was devoted to helping Black women newly diagnosed with the disease.

It was a stressful period, the work seemingly endless, the resources never quite enough. Still, Dixon Diallo and her collaborators continued, knowing that this work had to be done. And if they did not do it, who would? Only a few years later, in the middle of this disastrous epidemic, the women's health center where Dixon

Diallo was based saw its governmental funding slashed, and as a result, it withdrew all money from its HIV/AIDS initiative. The budget cuts were due primarily to efforts by determined, obstructionist antiabortion activists and were thus not directly related to HIV/AIDS. Ironically, it was the HIV/AIDS initiative that was defunded due to the increased costs of security for the clinic and the legal expenses associated with maintaining abortion services.

Dixon Diallo saw that this decision was based on financial necessity, yet this decision also signified an inadequate racial and class analysis: it was the program that primarily benefited women of color that lost its funding. Dixon Diallo, in her midtwenties, with only a few years of experience, but armed with a strong background in women's studies and abundant energy, had to decide, "What do I do now?"

Early Life

Dázon Dixon (Diallo was the last name she took when she married her now ex-husband) was born on March 25, 1965, and grew up in Fort Valley, Georgia, the state where she still lives. Fort Valley is a small town a hundred miles south of Atlanta. It is a predominantly African American community and is home to the historically Black Fort Valley State University.

As with so many leaders, the values that have come to define Dixon Diallo's work were nurtured in her childhood. In an oral history, Dixon Diallo expresses that she was raised with "a very deep sense of justice," stemming in large part from the Episcopal church she attended as a kid and also from the role models she had at home. Her "parents . . . were activists and community service advocates."[1]

Through education, Dixon Diallo found ways of further developing the values she had from her family. School was important to the young Dixon Diallo. In an interview, she states, laughingly, "I loved school growing up. I know that sounds crazy. I was a nut for school."[2] Her love for education was encouraged at home. Her parents, aware of her love of learning, challenged her to constantly ask questions and explore where the answers may come from and what those solutions are. Her parents are now retired educators. But years ago, Dixon Diallo's mother was her science teacher, and in her class and others, Dixon Diallo learned to think critically and combine education with action.

Considering Dixon Diallo's love for schooling and the value her parents put on education, college was an obvious next step after high school for her. She was admitted to Spelman College, a distinguished Black women's college in Atlanta, where she began her studies in 1982. Spelman expected its women to be of service to their communities after graduation and has counted among its alumnae such notable women as Bernice Reagon, the founder of the singing group Sweet Honey in the Rock, and Marian Wright Edelman, the founder of the Children's Defense Fund. Dixon Diallo's time at Spelman did not turn out quite as she had expected. Her studies took the backseat to activism. During college, Dixon Diallo encountered new opportunities for putting the sense of justice she had been raised with into practical use.

Dixon Diallo stayed on campus to work during the summer between her first two years at Spelman. This proved to be fortuitous, leading her on a life-changing path. Her first summer on campus coincided with a conference held at Spelman, which led to the founding of the National Black Women's Health Project. The organization is still in existence, now under the name Black Women's Health Imperative. Dixon Diallo attended the conference and later recalled "seeing all these incredible black women": "Here they are, right in my presence, and I just had to join and see what was happening."[3] Dixon Diallo was not an official attendee at the conference, but the participation of so many strong Black women leaders left an indelible impression on her. Inspired by this experience, she started looking for work that related to Black women's health issues, and eventually she found her way as a volunteer in the Feminist Women's Health Center in Atlanta. The center "provided contraceptive care, family-planning assistance, [and] well-woman gynecological services," as well as abortions and, later on, artificial insemination.[4]

Dixon Diallo graduated in 1986. She had fulfilled all the college's academic requirements, but she admits, "I graduated from Spelman not with the greatest of honors, and that's mostly because I really put more of my college years' energy into the work and the organizing that I was doing through the feminist health movement, because I was already involved from my sophomore year in school."[5] This training would serve her well and has influenced her work until this day.

Dixon Diallo moved from volunteer to a paid employee and was the only woman of color on the Feminist Women's Health Center's staff; she ended up connecting with many of the women of color who came there. The situation speaks to a longer, complex history in feminist work, where differences between women, based on categories such as race, ethnicity, and class, were often overlooked by mainstream, predominantly white, feminist groups. Black feminist organizers, working in groups such as Black Women's Alliance, the Combahee River Collective, and the National Black Feminist Organization, addressed the need for Black women to claim space within feminism and for the importance of centering the lives of women of color in feminist work. As the Combahee River Collective once pointed out, because of the multiple oppressions Black women face, their issues are often marginalized within movements working on only one concern—racism, sexism, or homophobia. A more complex analysis was needed in order to address the situation facing many Black women. This insight was central to how Dixon Diallo approached her burgeoning HIV/AIDS work.

During Dixon Diallo's time as a health worker at Atlanta's busy Feminist Women's Health Center, a monumental change took place: HIV/AIDS for the first time received attention as a disease that affected not only gay men but also women and heterosexual individuals. In 1985, Rock Hudson, the 1950s movie heartthrob, came out and spoke about his battle with AIDS. Though Hudson was a white gay man and hence fit the profile of the gay male HIV/AIDS patient, because of his fame, his diagnosis and death opened the eyes of a broader general public to HIV/AIDS. This general public included women living in Atlanta, who started searching for answers to whether they might be affected by HIV/AIDS. One day, the Feminist Women's Health Center got a call from a local gay male AIDS organization, where the staff did not know how to respond to the large number of Black women seeking help. The Feminist Women's Health Center staff and volunteers agreed that HIV/AIDS was an important issue and that they should be involved in the work of addressing the situation of women living with the virus. Thus, the two organizations started collaborating.

Dixon Diallo began to focus her energies on this collaborative program, which was named the Women's AIDS Prevention Project (WAPP). Eventually, the people from the women's center ended up running the program singlehandedly. The break between the two organizations was due to the fact that most women at the AIDS organization left, and with a male-dominated leadership, women's issues, according to Dixon Diallo, "fell by the wayside."[6] This was by no means a scenario unique to the AIDS organization in Atlanta. In the early years of the epidemic, HIV/AIDS was widely considered an illness that predominantly, or even exclusively, affected men, and the circumstances of women were not considered central to fighting the epidemic.

Dixon Diallo and her colleagues ran the HIV/AIDS program at the women's center for three years. In 1988, however, a high-profile event took place in Atlanta that changed the climate for reproductive and health justice work. The city was chosen to host the 1988 Democratic National Convention (DNC). As big political conventions typically do, the DNC drew a large number of protestors, among them antiabortion activists from several groups, including Operation Rescue. While most protestors left at the end of the convention, Operation Rescue stayed, and for months, abortion centers and clinics in Atlanta were, in Dixon Diallo's words, "under siege."[7] As Dixon Diallo explains, the antiabortion activists were terrorizing women visiting these sites, and the women's clinics faced a new set of challenges, which included costs for court fees and overtime for staff. This was not a unique situation: for many clinics providing abortion services, attacks by groups who oppose abortion lead to increased costs for security and replacing broken facilities due to vandalism.

The women's center in Atlanta, faced with escalating costs, decided to reprioritize its budget. It chose to eliminate the HIV/AIDS program and reallocate the funding to other critical needs. In one respect, this decision made financial and strategic sense. The US Congress had passed legislation aimed at nongovernmental organizations receiving federal funding. These organizations were henceforth not allowed to perform abortions. The federal government and its Centers for Disease Control were, at the time, also the best sources of funding for HIV/AIDS work, but this money was not accessible to Dixon Diallo's HIV/AIDS project as long as it was part of the women's clinic that performed abortions.

The HIV program thus was cut because it was not income generating and also because HIV/AIDS, for the most part, did not affect white middle-class women, who were the majority of both clients and providers at the clinic. HIV/AIDS was a condition primarily affecting Black women in Atlanta. The broad analysis of health and reproductive justice that Dixon Diallo employs sees HIV/AIDS as a reproductive concern, the same way abortion is, but this analysis was not shared by most of her women's-health-activist colleagues. "[I] found that as a Black woman volunteering at that time, . . . as things rolled on, we were just really clear that this truly was going to be a Black woman's issue. . . . There was a commitment there I couldn't walk away from."[8]

HIV/AIDS in Atlanta

The mideighties were a volatile time to be doing HIV/AIDS work. While the virus had been in existence in humans for at least a couple of decades, it was first identified only in the early 1980s. The infection routes and risk factors of the virus were still largely unknown. Health care for HIV/AIDS patients was often poor, and those infected usually died within months, sometimes weeks, after their diagnosis. Understandably, the severity of the epidemic and the lack of knowledge about it caused panic among many health care providers. President Ronald Reagan infamously did not utter the word *AIDS* in public until 1987, seven years into his presidency and then only after the death of Rock Hudson.

HIV/AIDS work in the mid-1980s was difficult no matter the target population, but working for the rights of women living with HIV/AIDS entailed extra challenges. What is now called AIDS—acquired immune deficiency syndrome—was referred to as GRIDS—gay-related immune deficiency syndrome—in the early days of the epidemic. It was widely believed that only gay men could contract the virus. Soon, the group of people at risk was expanded to what was derogatorily referred to as "the 4Hs": homosexuals, Haitians, hemophiliacs, and heroin users.

It was not until 1993 that the US government, through the Centers for Disease Control's new guidelines, recognized that women can get HIV/AIDS. In response to the government's silence on women with HIV/AIDS, a coalition of women living with HIV/AIDS and ACT UP activists across the country came up with a campaign slogan: "Women Don't Get AIDS, We Just Die from It." Dixon Diallo was at the forefront of this campaign at the local level. Despite the pressure from protesters, it took more than decade to acknowledge that women, and in particular heterosexuals, were at risk and represented a growing population of AIDS patients.

Today, even though HIV/AIDS still is often viewed as a "gay disease," we now know that people of all genders and sexualities can contract the virus. In fact, in the United States, women are among the groups for which HIV infection rates are growing the fastest. Black women are especially hard hit. In Atlanta, where Dixon Diallo established the key Black women's AIDS and reproductive justice organization, SisterLove, and where it remains headquartered, the numbers are even more astounding: 20 percent of the 27,560 individuals living with HIV/AIDS in Atlanta are women,[9] and African American women in Atlanta are fourteen times more likely than white women to receive a positive diagnosis.[10]

Dixon Diallo has spoken out on the disproportionate effect that HIV/AIDS has had on Black communities in the United States: "More than 1.2 million people in America are living with HIV or AIDS. Almost 50% of the new HIV infections every year are in Black Americans. Among women, more than 60% of women with HIV are Black. Among gay and bisexual men, more than 40% of those living with HIV are Black. Among HIV positive youth between the ages of 15–29, nearly 70% are Black."[11]

From the women affected by the epidemic, whom Dixon Diallo first had met at the women's health clinic, she learned that HIV had a significant social component and that it affected people differently depending on factors such as class, race, and gender. For example, preventing HIV among women is intimately tied to stopping domestic violence: an abusive situation makes it harder for a woman to demand that a condom is used during sexual intercourse with an intimate partner. Unlike men, including African American men, women are not in total control of reproductive options—they are constantly forced to negotiate condom use. Equally important to the fate of Black women at risk for HIV/AIDS was the reality that frequently their socioeconomic conditions, including lack of health insurance, poverty, and inadequate education and housing, made access to preventative care even more challenging for them than for their more affluent white sisters.

Armed with knowledge about the impact of HIV/AIDS in the life of Black women in Atlanta and because of the health center's unfortunate decision to defund the HIV/AIDS program, Dixon Diallo was faced with a difficult challenge. She was passionate about the work she was doing and had shown herself to be a skilled organizer. Still, she was young and had limited experience. How could she continue to focus on reproductive justice for Black women? Would she leave the Feminist Women's Health Center? Would she find a solution working somewhere else? If so, what would that solution look like?

Resolution

Dixon Diallo knew that the work she and the others in the women's HIV/AIDS program were doing was of crucial importance. They did not want to admit defeat because their funding had been cut. But it was clear that the Feminist Women's Health Center was under attack. To keep providing services for clients at risk for HIV/AIDS and for those who had already contracted the deadly disease, something had to be done. A radical step had to be considered. Dixon Diallo and her colleagues left the center and took the first steps to start their own, nonprofit organization.

In 1989, when the Feminist Women's Health Center sunset the HIV program that was in its infancy, a women-of-color advisory group that Dixon Diallo had formed while doing that work concluded that Black communities in Atlanta still needed this service. It said to Dixon Diallo, "If you want to do that, we got your back": "And so that's when I left the center, and a few months later, we started SisterLove, which is the organization that I've been working with and running for the last twenty years."[12] With a $2,500 seed grant from the Fund for Southern Communities and unemployment benefits, Dixon Diallo began the process of building the organization, starting with a focus on the struggle for women's sexual and reproductive rights as part of the Black women's health movement.

Established in 1989, SisterLove faced many challenges. At this point, Dixon Diallo was only twenty-four years old and had never managed a department, let alone a free-standing institution. Dixon Diallo claims that the organization got started the way many community-based nonprofits start: there is an unmet need and a gap that needs to be filled. "I just found myself in the right place at the right time and facing the opportunity to make the right decision and to be involved."[13] From the beginning, the organization has focused on women with HIV/AIDS. Though others in the struggle to prevent and treat HIV/AIDS may not have seen it, Dixon Diallo was clear that HIV/AIDS was a Black and, later, Latina women's reproductive justice issue.

Reproductive justice is the paradigm that underlies the building not just of an organization like SisterLove but also of a social movement dedicated to the idea that all people should have the right to make decisions regarding their own reproduction. This includes avoiding risks of sexuality transmitted diseases and being able to make conscious, knowledgeable decisions about those risks. Women, who are often socialized not to speak up for themselves and to put their partners' needs and desires above their own, are especially vulnerable to the risks of nonconsensual, risky sex, such as contracting HIV/AIDS and other sexually transmitted diseases (STDs). Unlike men, women have to negotiate condom use, since they must rely on the willingness of their partners to agree to this form of protection. That puts women, and especially women of color, at a disadvantage. For these reasons, Dixon Diallo and others working on HIV from a reproductive justice perspective consider HIV prevention to be central to reproductive and sexual health work.

Looking back, it is possible that Dixon Diallo's relative inexperience at the time of the organization's founding may have advantaged her in forming SisterLove. In an interview, Dixon Diallo stated, "I didn't realize that I would have to literally build a business from the ground up."[14] She wanted to work in her community, with and for Black women, to provide services. "I got in this to bring some solutions to some serious problems, not to worry about grants and funding or whether or not I'm going to be able to make my payroll."[15] Sometimes, it may be valuable for a leader not to look too far ahead to all the pitfalls related to a start-up. A little myopia might be a good thing. Dixon Diallo was young but not naïve. And her most important asset was a deep commitment to and passion for serving her community. She knew that SisterLove would require a lot for work. She was not fully aware of the extent of the work, but she was open-minded enough to embrace this challenge. She was willing to make "bold, risky, controversial decisions" because there was a sense of urgency.[16] If not SisterLove, which organization would take on the complexity of preventing as well as treating HIV/AIDS among women of color?

It was clear to Dixon Diallo that an organizing model focused narrowly on HIV as a virus—a clinical, strictly medical issue—was not enough. While all humans are susceptible to the virus, the epidemic does not affect everyone equally, and it is as much a social issue as it is a medical one. For example, the reduction of risk to women needs to address issues such as the intersectionality of race, poverty, and class. Reduction of risk also needs to address violence against women, which, though widespread, is even more rampant among poorer women. A poor intravenous drug user who is dependent on others for a fix, cannot afford her own clean needles, and is forced to share needles with others runs a higher risk of being infected with HIV than does someone who does not share syringes for intravenous drugs. Incarcerated people, who, due to the ban on condoms in jails and prisons, often have unprotected sex, typically have infection rates higher than in the general population. And because the virus is spread through human interactions, an elevated infection level in a poor community, especially when combined with lack of health care, can easily lead to others in the community being infected. SisterLove would have to take factors such as these into consideration. SisterLove's work is specifically focused on the situation of HIV-positive women of color. The organization considers itself women centered and feminist based. What does that mean? To Dixon Diallo, it is clear that the issues around HIV/AIDS at it pertains to women is best understood as a gender-based, human rights issue. As she puts it, "All of the work we do whether it's in the delivery of services, education, training, capacity building, or even in partnership development is done so within the human rights framework even in its broadest definition with regard to gender."[17]

An important aspect of SisterLove's work, and a testament to the organization's commitment to feminist values, is its sex-positive approach. This means that while SisterLove acknowledges that sexual activity does come with a risk for HIV transmission, sexuality is also a positive force in people's lives, something to be encouraged, not feared. Positive sexuality, even for those who are HIV-positive, proved another leadership juncture for Dixon Diallo.

Sex can be a source of pleasure and intimacy, and SisterLove aims to help people have a safe and enjoyable sex life, regardless of HIV status. An individual can of course choose celibacy, but abstinence is not advocated as a universal policy. Rather, a sex-positive perspective supports teaching people about ways to make sex safer, such as using condoms. It also acknowledges that people take risks and does not seek to shame them for doing so. Sex positivity is important in removing the stigma around HIV/AIDS and all sexually transmitted diseases. Stigma and shame can raise infection rates, as people who are ashamed of their illness may not tell their sexual partners about it. This sex-positive approach does not always conform to the values of other institutions within Atlanta's Black communities, especially the largely male-led Black churches. As Dixon Diallo has diplomatically noted, "Black churches have been reluctant to come along."[18]

Even the Centers for Disease Control in Atlanta had problems acknowledging the presence of the HIV/AIDS epidemic among women, and specifically women of color, who are disproportionately at risk for the disease. This led Dixon Diallo to embrace and encourage the early 1990s activist slogan "Women do not get AIDS, they just die from it." In 1993, the official government stance changed, and the HIV/AIDS epidemic was finally seen as a women's issue.

Today, SisterLove has an annual operating budget of a little over $1 million. It has eleven full-time and three part-time staff members. In a world where large-scale HIV/AIDS work has gained increased attention from large funders and has moved from an activist to a service-provision model, SisterLove remains small. Even with its limited resources, however, SisterLove has an extensive agenda and, increasingly, national and international reach. The organization takes a trifold approach to HIV/AIDS work: service provision, policy advocacy, and movement building. Dixon Diallo views these three aspects as interrelated: each functions better if the other two are in place. This is an approach she learned from her early days in the AIDS movement, when she was involved in ACT UP (the AIDS Coalition to Unleash Power).

ACT UP is widely recognized as one of the most effective, albeit controversial, organizations in the AIDS movement. Remembered for its raucous demonstrations, there was also another side to ACT UP in the 1980s and 1990s: service provision. People who were too sick to leave their homes got meals delivered, and volunteers sat by the bedside of those dying. Dixon Diallo learned from ACT UP that if an organization takes care of its members, those members are more able to advocate and organize for change in their own lives. As Dixon Diallo points out, when women are hungry, homeless, or beaten, they are not fully able to participate in activism.[19] Thus, service provision can be a way of creating the conditions necessary for working and advocating for systemic change.

Over the course of three decades, and learning from experience, Dixon Diallo now takes a systemic and holistic approach to Sister-Love's work. This means that, as a leader, Dixon Diallo is not afraid to change course and challenge existing conventions. Rather than viewing HIV/AIDS prevention and care as solely a matter of medical interventions, she looks at the broad socioeconomic context. For example, in an article for the NAACP's blog, Dixon Diallo lists several things that must be part of the HIV/AIDS movement: "ending the prison industrial complex; ending violence in our communities (especially against women, children/youth, and lesbians and gay men); ending the stigma and discrimination associated with homophobia, HIV and AIDS in our communities; and being more inclusive in our houses of worship."[20]

In the mid-1990s, Dixon Diallo decided to take a more formal approach to her development as a leader and enrolled in graduate school. She earned her master's of public health from the University of Alabama at Birmingham in 1997. Working with SisterLove for a decade, she had come to understand that public health was a crucial component of the work the organization was doing, and she wanted to "put some theory into [her] practice."[21] The more scientific approach that graduate education provided gave her the means to communicate with a wider network of public health practitioners, thus assisting SisterLove to further its status as a scientifically based institution and to advance its coalition-building strategy among larger, more visible HIV/AIDS advocacy groups.

Importantly, getting a professional degree also helped Dixon Diallo to elevate SisterLove's capacity to conduct its own rigorous evaluation research, eventually achieving the inclusion of SisterLove's own HIV-prevention program, Healthy Love, into the CDC's national compendium of effective, evidence-based interventions. SisterLove has since become a recognized community-based participatory research partner, working primarily with Emory University's major National Institutes of Health–funded women's HIV research program.

While still grounded in Atlanta and focused on local work, Sister-Love has also recently internationalized and established a branch in Mpumalanga, South Africa. Southern Africa has been the region most heavily affected by the global HIV/AIDS epidemic; in some parts of the region, infection rates hover around 25 percent of the population. When Dixon Diallo was in college, she had a connection to struggles in South Africa, through her involvement in anti-apartheid work.[22] True to SisterLove's approach to practice locally specific work, the Mpumalanga branch's activities are not simply copies of those of the Atlanta branch but instead are sensitive to the needs of the Black women and families involved with the organization in South Africa. Access to land—a crucial resource in a society where many people survive through farming—is a central component of SisterLove's work in Mpumalanga. SisterLove has founded a cooperative entity called Thembuhlelo, which loosely translates as "Trust Your Program." Thembuhlelo operates a seven-hundred-acre dairy-producing farm. Says Dixon Diallo, "That happened because we bridged the notion of women's empowerment and rights with HIV and AIDS service delivery. And the land-reform policies that are going on to help restore the land that originally belonged to local people from the hands of the white farmers and the white government regime under apartheid—to reclaim that land and put it back in the hands of the people it should belong to."[23]

Dixon Diallo is still a leader in the HIV/AIDS movement, and SisterLove continues to serve as a role model for holistic thinking in care and prevention. Looking back at her college years, Dixon Diallo notes that her commitment to her activist work has had a lasting value and that she "was achieving something noteworthy."[24] After thirty years as one of the leading figures in the HIV/AIDS movement in the United States and the world, Dixon Diallo is still actively pursuing her work, serving as a role model for long-term, sustainable feminist leadership.

Dixon Diallo's integrative approach means that she engages in work with a multiplicity of networked organizations such as Sister-Song: Women of Color Reproductive Justice Collective. SisterLove is a founding member organization of SisterSong, and Dixon Diallo has served as part of its leadership, including the board of directors, for over fifteen years. She gives presentations at many different venues. SisterLove has also collaborated with ACT UP, the national yet grassroots organization that was started in the 1980s, and still works to lower infection rates and improve the conditions for those who are living with HIV/AIDS.

Over many years of engagement in the HIV/AIDS movement, Dixon Diallo has grown and changed. She now recognizes the importance of encouraging the next generation. She also engages in what she refers to as "leading from behind," which means encouraging those who are directly affected, namely, women who have tested positive for HIV/AIDS, to find the voice and agency to lead a movement for their own needs.

With a multifaceted, holistic, women-centered approach to HIV/
AIDS prevention and activism, Dázon Dixon Diallo serves as a role
model for other activists for women's reproductive health. After
three decades, Dixon Diallo is still active, leading the way for a new
generation of feminists. She has shown that it is possible to work
against the devastating results of an epidemic while at the same
time maintaining hope, dignity, and as the name of her organization implies, a great deal of love.

Notes

1 Dázon Dixon Diallo, "Dázon Dixon Diallo Interviewed by Loretta Ross,"
   transcript of video recording, April 4, 2009, 3, Voices of Feminism Oral History
   Project, Sophia Smith Collection, Smith College, Northampton, MA, http://
   www.smith.edu/libraries/libs/ssc/vof/transcripts/Diallo.pdf.
2 Ibid., 22.
3 Ibid., 4.
4 Ibid., 5.
5 Ibid., 24.
6 AIDS gov, "Dazon Dixon Diallo on HIV/AIDS," YouTube, August 30, 2011,
   https://youtu.be/52w_bnpfKAc, video.
7 Dázon Dixon Diallo, phone conversation with Alison Bernstein, February 25,
   2014.
8 "Dazon Dixon Diallo on HIV/AIDS."
9 Georgia Department of Public Health, Integrated Epidemiologic Profile
   of HIV/AIDS, Georgia (Division of Health Protection, Epidemiology
   Program, HIV/AIDS Epidemiology Section, 2011), 13, https://dph.georgia
   .gov/sites/dph.georgia.gov/files/HIV_Integrated_Epi_Profile_Georgia_2011
   .pdf.
10 AIDSVu, "Atlanta: Estimated HIV Prevalence Rate Ratios by Race/Ethnicity:
   2011," http://aidsvu.org/state/georgia/atlanta/ (accessed July 27, 2015).
11 Dázon Dixon Diallo, "Prevent Insanity and Stop Being Stupid—Change What
   You Do," NAACP Blog, January 3, 2012, http://www.naacp.org/blog/entry/
   prevent-insanity-and-stop-being-stupid-change-what-you-do.
12 Dixon Diallo, "Dázon Dixon Diallo Interviewed by Loretta Ross," 7.
13 AIDS gov, "Dazon Dixon Diallo on HIV/AIDS."
14 Keith R. Green, "Dazon Dixon Diallo: Sisterly Love at Its Best: Helping Those
   in Need," Positively Aware, March–April 2008, http://positivelyaware.com/
   archives/2008/08_02/dazon_dixon_diallo.shtml.
15 Ibid.
16 Dázon Dixon Diallo, phone conversation with Alison Bernstein, February 25,
   2014.
17 Dázon Dixon Diallo, "Special Needs: HIV-Positive Women: Speech from the
   Nexus Symposium: An Interdisciplinary Forum on the Impact of International

Patent & Trade Agreements in the Fight against HIV & AIDS," *Emory International Law Review* 17, no. 2 (2003): 566.

18 AIDS gov, "Dazon Dixon Diallo on HIV/AIDS."
19 Dázon Dixon Diallo, phone conversation with Alison Bernstein, February 25, 2014.
20 Dixon Diallo, "Prevent Insanity."
21 Dixon Diallo, "Dázon Dixon Diallo Interviewed by Loretta Ross," 24.
22 Ibid., ii.
23 Ibid., 43.
24 Ibid., 24.

Bibliography

AIDS gov. "Dazon Dixon Diallo on HIV/AIDS." YouTube, August 30, 2011. https://youtu.be/52w_bnpfKAc. Video.

AIDSVu. "Atlanta: Estimated HIV Prevalence Rate Ratios by Race/Ethnicity: 2011." http://aidsvu.org/state/georgia/atlanta/.

Dixon Diallo, Dázon. "Dázon Dixon Diallo Interviewed by Loretta Ross." Transcript of video recording, April 4, 2009. Voices of Feminism Oral History Project, Sophia Smith Collection, Smith College, Northampton, MA. http://www.smith.edu/libraries/libs/ssc/vof/transcripts/Diallo.pdf.

———. "Prevent Insanity and Stop Being Stupid—Change What You Do." *NAACP Blog*, January 3, 2012. http://www.naacp.org/blog/entry/prevent-insanity-and-stop-being-stupid-change-what-you-do.

———. "Special Needs: HIV-Positive Women: Speech from the Nexus Symposium: An Interdisciplinary Forum on the Impact of International Patent & Trade Agreements in the Fight against HIV & AIDS." *Emory International Law Review* 17, no. 2 (2003): 561–575.

Georgia Department of Public Health. *Integrated Epidemiologic Profile of HIV/AIDS, Georgia.* Division of Health Protection, Epidemiology Program, HIV/AIDS Epidemiology Section, 2011. https://dph.georgia.gov/sites/dph.georgia.gov/files/HIV_Integrated_Epi_Profile_Georgia_2011.pdf.

Green, Keith R. "Dazon Dixon Diallo: Sisterly Love at Its Best: Helping Those in Need." *Positively Aware*, March–April 2008. http://positivelyaware.com/archives/2008/08_02/dazon_dixon_diallo.shtml.

"Integrated Epidemiologic Profile of HIV/AIDS, Georgia," Georgia Department of Public Health, Division of Health Protection, Epidemiology Program, HIV/AIDS Epidemiology Section, 2011. https://dph.georgia.gov/sites/dph.georgia.gov/files/HIV_Integrated_Epi_Profile_Georgia_2011.pdf.

"Leadership For A Changing World: 2004 Awardees." *NYU Wagner*. http://wagner.nyu.edu/leadership/research/work/2004/Diallo.

Ross, Loretta. "Dázon Dixon Diallo interview." *Voices of Feminism Oral History Project*, Sophia Smith Collection, transcript of video recording, April 4, 2009. http://www.smith.edu/libraries/libs/ssc/vof/transcripts/Diallo.pdf.

Cecile Richards
Leading Planned Parenthood
in the New Millennium

Bridget Gurtler

Background

In 2006, the new CEO of Planned Parenthood, Cecile Richards, faced problems both within and outside her organization. On the one hand, the organization was well known and established, providing reproductive and sexual health advocacy and services to millions of women and families. On the other hand, it was facing a hostile governmental landscape under the Bush administration, including the loss of federal funding and legal challenges to many of the services and educational programs it offered. It was also coming to terms with a critical need to mobilize, connect with, and educate a new generation of women, many of whom did not come of age during the battle for *Roe. v. Wade* or were part of a newer and important demographic group using Planned Parenthood services, Latina youth.

Over the course of the organization's one-hundred-year history, Planned Parenthood Federation of America has become the most widely recognized provider of sexual and reproductive health care in the United States. Its services range from sex education and the production of contraceptive products (its own brand of condoms) to advocacy initiatives for women's health and women's rights. The organization emerged in 1916 under the leadership of Margaret Sanger and opened the first birth-control clinic in the United States. Contraception was illegal under the Comstock Laws at the time, and the history of Sanger and her organization was an embattled one in these early years. By 1938, the organization became incorporated as the American Birth Control League, and shortly thereafter, in 1941, it merged with Sanger's Birth Control Clinical Research Bureau to become the Planned Parenthood Federation of America (PPFA).

PPFA has been an advocate for the creation and funding of domestic and international family-planning programs and was integral in the development of the pill and intrauterine device (IUD). Although PPFA was successful in the early 1970s in its support of landmark decisions including *Roe v. Wade* (affirming the constitutional right to privacy and women's right to choose abortion), by the late 1970s and in the following decade, Planned Parenthood and its clinics faced increasing, and often violent, opposition. The intimidation of physicians, other medical personnel, and women seeking reproductive health care was heightened during this era as assassinations, clinic bombings, and arson attacks became realities for some Planned Parenthood clinics. It was during the Reagan era that the first effective steps at limiting teen sexual education and confidential access to contraceptives were taken at the federal level. The funding of "chastity education" programs began in Congress, and the so-called gag rule forbid public health clinics that were funded by the Title X federal reproductive health care program from counseling (largely low-income clients) about abortion. Although later removed during the Clinton administration, the gag rule is symbolic of politics that continue to effect women's, and especially young women's, reproductive health.

This was the long history of the organization that Cecile Richards was to guide as president of PPFA and the Planned Parenthood Action Fund (a political action committee). The latter was "committed to supporting pro-choice, pro-family planning candidates for federal office."[1] She knew that the organization was at a critical moment. It had faced huge challenges in the year before her arrival, and she struggled to find the most effective means to protect its achievements and to incorporate them into her future plans for the organization. She was dedicated to sustaining and expanding the important role that PPFA had played in the past, advocating for women's health and reproductive services. But the question was how to do so in the coming years.

The Landscape of Reproductive Health Care

By 2006, Planned Parenthood (PP) was providing services to over five million women, men, and teens worldwide.[2] Its mission was fourfold: to continue to provide trusted health care services; to educate women, teens, and families; to advance reproductive health and rights; and to promote global health. In the United States, the services it and other public health clinics offered actually encompassed a wider range of preventative care (including sexually transmitted infections, or STI, screening) than that found at private clinics.[3] Over three million clients used Planned Parenthood services in 2005. Eighty-one percent of clients received contraception services when they visited clinics. The distribution of services delivered by the organization in 2005 was 37 percent contraception, 29 percent STD/STI testing and treatment, 20 percent cancer screening and prevention, 10 percent other women's health services, and 3 percent abortion services.[4]

Planned Parenthood was facing many social, organizational, and technical issues as it attempted to provide services and fulfill its mission. These included rising teen pregnancy rates, a Supreme Court shifting toward conservative reproductive politics, and more generally a worldwide shift in information technologies that Planned Parenthood had yet to fully integrate into its client services. Teen pregnancies had dropped significantly throughout the 1990s because of more and better use of contraceptives and sex-education programs. However, by the middle of the first decade of the twenty-first century, when Richards arrived at Planned Parenthood, abstinence-only sex-education programs that were prohibited by law from discussing the benefits of contraception had become more widespread, and accordingly, contraceptive use had declined among teens. For the first time in more than a decade, teen pregnancy rates rose 3 percent in 2006. In 2005, there were 69.5 pregnancies per 1,000 women aged fifteen to nineteen; by 2006, there were 71.5. Put differently, about 7 percent of teen girls became pregnant in 2006. This increase was across all demographic groups—rates per

1,000 teens in 2006 were 126.3 among black teens, 126.6 among Hispanic teens, and 44.0 among non-Hispanic white teens.[5] The legislative landscape looked little better. Between 1995 and 2005, state legislatures adopted more than four hundred measures restricting abortion. By 2007, a downward-sliding economy in the wake of the bursting of the real estate bubble in the United States, shortly followed by a global financial crisis, pushed more people out of work and often out of access to, or the ability to afford, health insurance. Women were disproportionately bearing the burden of purchasing their own health insurance in this market, being charged at much higher rates than their male counterparts were (estimates ranged from 31 to 48 percent higher rates).[6] Furthermore, in 2007, the Eighth Federal Circuit Court reversed a prior decision that mandated birth control be covered under employers' health insurance plans (affecting women in Arkansas, Iowa, Minnesota, Missouri, Nebraska, North Dakota, and South Dakota).[7] Sandra Day O'Connor, a practical conservative who voted for *Roe v. Wade* and consistently protected women's reproductive rights, retired and was replaced by Samuel Alito, a conservative hardliner known for his decisions against basic reproductive rights.

The Food and Drug Administration (FDA) was also to release, after three long years of political feuding (2003–2006), its second decision on Plan B. Plan B, a synthetic form of progesterone (and the hormone most commonly used in birth-control pills), was an emergency contraceptive that when taken within 120 hours after unprotected intercourse or contraceptive failures (e.g., condom breakage), prevented both ovulation and fertilization of the egg as well as stopped the implantation of the egg in the uterine lining. Commonly known as the "morning-after pill" since its by-prescription-only release in 1999, it had been endorsed by almost all major medical and health care organizations, including the American College of Obstetricians and Gynecologists, the American Academy of Pediatrics, and the Society for Adolescent Medicine.[8] Moreover, these organizations shared the point of view that since the window of effectiveness was relatively short, a matter of days, timely access to the pill was critical and that, consequently, the pill needed to be available without a prescription.[9] On December 16,

2003, a joint hearing of the FDA Nonprescription Drugs and Reproductive Health Drugs Advisory Committees had previously voted twenty-three to four to recommend that the FDA make Plan B emergency contraception available over the counter. However, the debate about its regulation did not center around its effectiveness as a contraceptive—experts agreed that wider access to Plan B could prevent up to 1.7 million unintended pregnancies a year and eight hundred thousand abortions. The debate also did not focus on its safety. Rather, the central issue on the table at the FDA was whether teens should have access to the drug over the counter. On one side of the ethical debate were prolife groups and conservative organizations like the Family Research Council[10] that considered the drug practically the same as abortion, believing life begins at conception, and publicly argued that it would foster promiscuity.[11] On the other side were Planned Parenthood and other women's-health advocates, who argued that the leadership of the FDA was "playing politics with teens' lives" and in so doing had failed its public health responsibilities and failed women.[12] Planned Parenthood was particularly invested in this debate on behalf of its patients. Since it first began distributing emergency contraception "kits" eight years prior (in 1995), it had seen an astronomical 4,484 percent increase in their use. By 2003, it was distributing upon request almost eight hundred thousand kits per year.[13]

There were some welcome changes as well for the PP organization. In January 2006, the Supreme Court struck down, in *Ayotte v. Planned Parenthood of Northern New England, et al.*, a New Hampshire law that prevented doctors from performing abortions on pregnant teenagers until forty-eight hours after their parents were notified. The law had made no emergency exception to protect the life and health of the pregnant teenager. Thus, the decision reaffirmed that new abortion-restriction laws could not stand if they jeopardized a woman's health.

Leading and Learning

Cecile Richards began her political career early. In junior high, she helped her campaign-manager mother (and soon to be Texas governor), Ann Richards, in the state house race of Sarah Weddington.

Weddington was the lawyer who later successfully argued *Roe v. Wade* in the US Supreme Court. Cecile Richards's father, David Richards, was an important influence on her life as well. He was a respected labor and civil rights attorney who regularly took pro bono cases to support conscientious objection, freedom of speech, voting rights, and public education. During Cecile Richards's student days at Brown University, she majored in history, but she said, "I really kind of minored in agitating." Her first taste of a national campaign was to fight for Brown University to agree to divest its investments in apartheid-segregated South Africa. She said, "I missed the [Vietnam] anti-war movement, but for me and for young people who grew up when I did, that was Nelson Mandela, Robben Island. It was the first big national campaign that American students got involved in and of course was ultimately successful."[14]

After graduating in 1980, the young Texan launched her long career of campaigning for social justice. She began in her own backyard by organizing low-wage garment workers along the Rio Grande border. She went on to organize workers in the hotel and health care industries in Louisiana. Her passion for union organizing culminated in what she called "the best campaign I was ever involved with," the 1988 Justice for Janitors campaign. It was an effort that fought to help janitors in the Los Angeles area, workers primarily from Latin America who had seen their hourly wages drop to $4.50 an hour and the complete loss of their health care coverage. Their eventually successful efforts spurred a nationwide campaign to organize for janitors' rights. For Richards, the courage and resilience of the people she met on that campaign spurred a respect for a bottom-up model in which people are organized in their community, as well as a commitment to improving the lives of people in immigrant communities.[15]

In 2004, Richards served as the deputy chief of staff for Nancy Pelosi and was instrumental in her election as House of Representatives Democratic Leader. After this insider taste of holding a statewide office, Richards decided that her liberal politics and skills in mobilizing constituents were better suited to another forum. "I worked for Ms. Pelosi in the House," she said, "and I have such admiration for her and for the people who serve up there, but the hours and hours, and where did it ever lead?" When queried whether she might consider running for governor, she laughingly replied, "Texas is not quite ready for me."[16]

Also in 2004, two years before joining Planned Parenthood, she founded and directed America Votes, an organization that worked to increase voter registration, education, and participation through a coalition of numerous progressive, Democratic, grassroots interest groups. She successfully spearheaded this effort that ultimately raised $250 million to try to oust President George W. Bush from the White House.[17]

Planned Parenthood in 2006

With the experiences and skills that Cecile Richards gained from her political activities, she was brought into Planned Parenthood to mobilize the organization to meet the challenges of the new millennium. Planned Parenthood's chair Esperanza Garcia Walters, articulated the board of directors' perception of Richards upon her hire. "Planned Parenthood has recruited an experienced, proven leader who has the vision and skill to lead Planned Parenthood during a period of both opportunity and challenge."[18] PPFA's interim president, Karen Pearl, concurred: "Planned Parenthood has chosen a dynamic leader who will be an important voice in advocating for reproductive freedoms around the world."[19] When queried about Richards's abilities to lead Planned Parenthood, Speaker of the House Nancy Pelosi stated, "Cecile is a tenacious organizer, talented at both inside maneuvering and outside mobilization. She always wins. She leads with diplomacy and makes her case with facts, not hyperbole. That's what I saw when she served as my deputy chief of staff. . . . Cecile . . . is a proud mother of three, a devoted wife and gracious company. But make no mistake: her resolve is steadfast. And American women are the better for it."[20]

Richards accepted the position, stating, "It is a great honor to assume the leadership of an organization that stands for the very freedoms embraced by the majority of Americans; the ability to decide when and whether to have children; and the importance of privacy, safety and access to health care. I look forward to working with Planned Parenthood affiliates, staff and partners to realize the dream of access to reproductive health care for all."[21] Her past experiences in labor organizing, a family tradition of public service, and commitment to reproductive rights (she created and directed the Turner Foundation's national prochoice project and served on the boards of the Planned Parenthood Action Fund and NARAL Pro-Choice America) made the opportunity to lead at Planned Parenthood an unparalleled one for Richards. Unlike her time with Pelosi, at Planned Parenthood, Richards knew that she could see outcomes—direct results—of her efforts. "In good times and bad, we provide 3 million women with healthcare every year. I feel like I can take that home with me every night no matter what kind of day we've had."[22]

Although hopeful, Richards was to face many hurdles in her first year guiding this important organization, and she needed to hit the ground running. How best could she serve her constituents, her board of directors, and her donors in the United States but also with an eye toward global reproductive health? In addition to the afore-mentioned issues—a tough legislative and political landscape for reproductive rights, rising teen pregnancy rates, a backlash against abortion providers, and structural problems in ensuring insurance coverage for reproductive health care—Richards also knew that her organization needed to address the rising infant-mortality rate in the United States.

For the first time since the 1950s, the infant-mortality rate was increasing in the United States, which enjoyed the dubious privilege of having one of the highest rates in the industrialized world. Not only were more than five hundred thousand babies being born prematurely, but also an estimated twenty-eight thousand children in the United States were dying before their first birthday.[23] They were dying from an incredibly wide range of problems, so a narrow campaign about a particular disease or hazardous product, for instance, would not be effective. Fetal health was being affected adversely by a host of congenital and teratogenic birth defects, a lack of knowledge about or access to important immunizations for childhood disease, the lack of basic health care for mothers, as well as the seemingly innocuous but in reality deadly factors of safe sleep, seasonal flu, oral and mental health, and proper nutrition.

This was a public health crisis that needed to be attended to in PP clinics throughout the United States, in local communities, and in a broader way via a public health campaign at the national level. How could Richards reach pregnant women, new mothers, and families at high risk and help provide them the information that would help them lead healthier lives? And importantly, what resources could she draw on to face this issue and the host of other critical problems facing her clinics, the organization, and the status of reproductive health in the United States?

The financial position of the not-for-profit organization in June, five months after Richards, arrived was sound. Total revenue was $902.8 million, derived primarily from the organization's health centers and government grants and contracts ($345.1 million and $305.1 million, respectively). However, private contributions and bequests provided a substantial amount of revenue ($162.3 million) that year. When juxtaposed with the total expenses of Planned Parenthood, $847 million, it is clear that without the help of private donations, the organization would have been over $100 million in the red. A complex organization split into many divisions, Planned Parenthood had a broad range of expenses in 2005–2006.[24] As Richards and her senior management staff considered potential new programs, new directions, and new sites and means of providing reproductive care, they needed to carefully balance the organization's revenue and expenses—continuing to pursue relationships and policies that would increase income while also making tough decisions about the distribution of resources within the organization during a precarious economic environment.

Richards had many experts in medicine, sexual health, advocacy, law, communications, and fundraising to draw on as advisers who were already strategically placed throughout the organization. PPFA had national offices in New York City and Washington, DC, and its separately incorporated funding arm, the Planned Parenthood Action Fund, had a firm commitment to supporting and collaborating with the renowned Guttmacher Institute (a longstanding independent organization that worked to advance sexual and reproductive health through research, policy analysis, and public education). The PPFA had an Action Network composed of over

180 college chapters of VOX (Voices for Planned Parenthood), more than 350 leaders in the arts and entertainment on the PPFA Board of Advocates ready and willing to publicly support the organization, a Clergy Advisory Board mobilizing clergy and lay religious leaders, and advocates at the federal and state levels in PP Republicans for Choice.[25] And last but not least, PP Online had just launched months before Richards took the helm. PP Online represented a new attempt to provide online access to health information and services, to provide opportunities for people to get involved, and with the subsidiary website teenwire.com, to connect with young people and educate them about issues like birth control and body image. With all of this in mind—the political and legislative landscapes, the human and financial resources of PPFA, Richards's own leadership strengths and skills, and the needs of all who stepped through PP's clinics or benefited from its advocacy work—Richards needed to formulate a strategy to allow Planned Parenthood to grow into the new millennium.

Resolution

In the years since Cecile Richards began leading Planned Parenthood, the organization has expanded its services and outreach efforts. A relatively constant number of patients (three million) used Planned Parenthood annually between 2005 and 2011. By the close of 2010, it provided over eleven million services in its nearly eight hundred health centers.[26] For the first time, its total net assets topped $1 billion—a $100 million increase from 2005. What accounted for this growth and what strategies, programs, and methods did Richards use to reach out to youth and Spanish-speaking clients, to affect the legislative/judicial landscapes, and to meet the expectations of her board of directors?

One of the first and most important goals Richards had for PP was nationwide standardization. To achieve this, the organization moved to electronic medical records, enabling all clinics to access patients' information to ensure continuity of care. She implemented a brand-new web presence for the organization in English and Spanish, titled Planned Parenthood Online. It had a lofty goal: "to create the leading sexual and reproductive health care resource available to people 24 hours a day, seven days a week."[27] The website sought to address a world that was not only changing demographically and politically but also being transformed by the way information was transmitted and health care was delivered. In so doing, Richards and the Planned Parenthood staff made an anticipatory move to better interact with the potential patients, advocates, and supporters of the future as well as to address barriers to accessing Planned Parenthood information and services through the harnessing of interactive technology. One important measure of the success of this strategy is the number of visitors to the website. From fifteen million visitors in 2007, Planned Parenthood Online had over thirty-three million visitors by 2011.

More specifically, what were some of the factors that accounted for the growth of online users? There was a sleek user-friendly web design that was accompanied by innovative methods to reach out to clients. Mobile websites (Planned Parenthood Mobile and Planned Parenthood en Español Móvil) and an innovative texting service, called Text4Baby, were launched in 2009 and 2010.[28] About 16 percent of www.plannedparenthood.org traffic was from mobile devices (iPhones, BlackBerries, etc.). The texting service was also unique because it was part of an unprecedented public-private partnership. The White House Office on Science and Technology Policy, the US Department of Health and Human Services, Voxiva, CTIA–The Wireless Foundation, Grey Healthcare Group, Johnson & Johnson, Pfizer, CareFirst BlueCross BlueShield, and numerous wireless carriers all collaborated to provide this service. With this free texting service, PP was able to provide "timely health information for pregnant women and new moms, from pregnancy through a baby's first year."[29] These services were part of an effort to address the rising infant-mortality rates in the United States. Text4Baby provided three free SMS text messages per week with health information (from birth-defects prevention to immunization) timed to the due date or birthdate of the baby.

One of the other central goals that Richards had upon becoming president of PP was to mobilize, educate, and connect with youth in the United States. In order to do so, she used a multipronged approach—of organizing, training young leaders and activists, and launching a teen-focused web presence. By founding the PPFA Youth Initiatives Program, Planned Parenthood trained hundreds of young people in leadership skills and health care advocacy. An online community on Facebook[30] and a new section of the Planned Parenthood website dedicated to teens and their parents[31] were aimed to better educate young people about their bodies, sexuality, and medical services available at PP. Youth involvement included students at the collegiate level through VOX chapters—in which college students educated and mobilized their peers in support of health care access and reproductive rights.[32] Richards also instituted a now-annual Young Leaders Summit in 2007 linked to the PPFA's yearly national conference and its health care institute. Young participants meet to share strategies, network, and become involved in the effort to provide children access to comprehensive sex education and reproductive health care. Many of the participants are peer educators, working in their schools and communities to teach fellow teens about sexuality—an education that includes information about contraception, safe sex, and LGBTQ issues. This sexual-health education offers information that only an estimated 5 percent of American youth receive from their schools.[33] The young leaders from Planned Parenthood are also instrumental in advocating at the state and federal levels for expanding access to medically accurate sex education and health care.

Causality at the national level is difficult to assess, but at the close of the period in which these new PP services and outreach efforts were launched, in 2009–2010, teen birthrates fell for the third year in a row and reached a record low of approximately 750,000 pregnancies per year nationwide. This precipitous drop was accompanied by a two-year-long 10 percent increase in the use of hormonal contraceptives; 47.5 percent of sexually active teens used these contraceptives during this period.[34] A shift clearly occurred in the relationship between youth and sexual education/practices.

PPFA also moved toward a new strategy of engagement in its international programs. Reflecting its new name, Planned Parenthood Global (from PP International), the global arm of PP concentrated on developing viable working partnerships and creating pioneering new models for reproductive health care abroad that could be replicated and scaled up by national and local communities. This shift was enabled by a new freedom for PP Global and other organizations to offer critical reproductive care and education abroad, with President Barack Obama's removal of the "global gag rule."[35] Richards advocated the new direction of the international arm of PP. Believing health care to be a basic human right, she saw care of women and families at the global level to be an important part of her and the organization's overall mission. In her words, in the service of humanity, national borders are "artificial divides between people" struggling for the same basic rights.[36] In 2009–2010 alone, PP provided $1.6 million in grants to reproductive-health partners in Africa, Asia, Latin America, and the Caribbean, increasing their delivery of health care by more than 655,000 patients.[37]

In 2011, Richards also actively influenced policy by launching a sweeping nationwide campaign to maintain PP access to federal funding for preventative care. With the overall goals of achieving affordable, quality, comprehensive reproductive health care as part of any reform efforts and especially to expand access to care through Medicaid, Richards and the PP organization were also pivotal in shaping health care coverage and services for women under the Patient Protection and Affordable Care Act (ACA). This was accomplished through countless hours of campaigning—outreach through public speaking and publishing venues ranging from the Huffington Post, a presentation at the White House Health Care Summit, and an appearance on *The Daily Show* to fundraising and a YouTube campaign ("I Have a Say" campaign)—to defend the right of women to testify at a congressional hearing on women's health in the United States.[38] Articulating the perspective that was one of the foundations for these strategies, Richards said,

I think there are times [that are] very discouraging because there are huge political movements that you feel are out of your control and so sometimes we do just have to buckle down and ask, "What are the pieces that we can actually influence and how can I make a difference?" In my dream, every progressive finds something that makes their heart sing, and that's how they make a difference. . . . It's all going to add up to something greater than the sum of the parts. If we don't believe that, we're not going to make it.[39]

The ACA legislated that cancer screenings, birth control, and immunizations be provided with no copays. This was a particularly important victory for many PP patients, of whom 76 percent fell below the poverty line in 2010. The law also addressed discriminatory practices against women (for instance, that women could be charged higher premiums or be denied coverage for preexisting conditions) and expanded health care coverage for young adults by allowing them to stay on their parents' health plan until age twenty-six.[40] By 2011, the number of PP supporters had nearly doubled since 2006 to reach eleven million.

Notes

1 Planned Parenthood Action Fund, "About Us," http://www.plannedparent hoodaction.org/elections-politics/about-us/.

2 Planned Parenthood Federation of America, *Annual Report 2005–2006*, 1.

3 Planned Parenthood Federation of America, "American Journal of Public Health Study Shows Public Clinics Provide More Choice, More Care," press release, August 14, 2008, http://www.plannedparenthood.org/about-us/newsroom/press-releases/american-journal-public-health.

4 Planned Parenthood Federation of America, *Annual Report 2005–2006*, 4.

5 Rebecca Wind, "Following Decade-Long Decline, U.S. Teen Pregnancy Rate Increases as Both Births and Abortions Rise," Guttmacher Institute, January 26, 2010, https://guttmacher.org/media/nr/2010/01/26/index.html.

6 Robert Pear, "Women Buying Health Policies Pay a Penalty," *New York Times*, October 29, 2008, http://www.nytimes.com/2008/10/30/us/30insure.html?pagewanted=all&_r=0.

7 Tamar Lewin, "Court Says Health Coverage May Bar Birth-Control Pills," *New York Times*, March 17, 2007, http://www.nytimes.com/2007/03/17/health/17pill.html?_r=0.

8 For more on the politics of Plan B, see Heather Munro Prescott, *The Morning After: A History of Emergency Contraception in the United States* (New Brunswick, NJ: Rutgers University Press, 2011).

9 Laura Blue, "Why the Plan B Debate Won't Go Away," *Time*, August 25, 2006, http://content.time.com/time/nation/article/0,8599,1333925,00.html.

10 The Family Research Council's slogan is "advancing faith, family, and freedom," and its mission statement since its founding in 1983 has been, "[The Family

Research Council] champions marriage and family as the foundation of civilization, the seedbed of virtue, and the wellspring of society. FRC shapes public debate and formulates public policy that values human life and upholds the institutions of marriage and the family. Believing that God is the author of life, liberty, and the family, FRC promotes the Judeo-Christian worldview as the basis for a just, free, and stable society." Family Research Council, "Vision and Mission Statements," http://www.frc.org/mission-statement.

11 A study published in 2005 in *Obstetrics and Gynecology* found no increase in the sexual activity of its participants when they had access to Plan B. Curlin Fall and Daniel Hall, "Regarding Plan B: Science and Politics Cannot Be Separated," *Obstetrics and Gynecology* 105 (2005): 1148–1150.

12 Jackie Payne (government relations director for Planned Parenthood), quoted in Blue, "Why the Plan B Debate Won't Go Away."

13 Planned Parenthood Federation of America, "FDA Delay on EC," press release, August 26, 2005, http://www.plannedparenthood.org/about-us/newsroom/press-releases/fda-ec.

14 Neera Tanden, "Cecile Richards on How Progressives Can Make a Difference," Five Books, July 24, 2011, http://fivebooks.com/interviews/cecile-richards-on-how-progressives-can-make-difference.

15 Ibid.

16 Elizabeth Mitchell, "The Genius of Cecile Richards," *Nation*, March 7, 2012, http://www.thenation.com/article/166670/genius-cecile-richards.

17 Emily Ramshaw, "Texans Lead Battle for Women's Health," *New York Times*, February 4, 2012, http://www.nytimes.com/2012/02/05/us/texans-lead-battle-for-womens-health.html.

18 "Ann Richards' Daughter to Lead Planned Parenthood," *Austin Business Journal*, January 10, 2006, http://www.bizjournals.com/austin/stories/2006/01/09/daily14.html.

19 "Planned Parenthood Chooses New President," Feminist News, Feminist Majority Foundation, January 12, 2006, http://www.feminist.org/newsbyte/uswirestory.asp?id=9465.

20 Nancy Pelosi, "Cecile Richards," *Time*, April 21, 2011, http://content.time.com/time/specials/packages/article/0,28804,2066367_2066369_2066140,00.html.

21 Gustavo Suarez, "Planned Parenthood Names New President: Cecile Richards Will Head Organization," Planned Parenthood Federation of America, January 9, 2006, available at http://www.religiousconsultation.org/News_Tracker/Planned_Parenthood_announces_next_president.htm.

22 Mitchell, "Genius of Cecile Richards."

23 Planned Parenthood Federation of America, "Planned Parenthood Joins Unprecedented Public-Private Partnership to Address Rising U.S. Infant Mortality Rate," press release, February 5, 2010, http://www.plannedparenthood.org/about-us/newsroom/press-releases/planned-parenthood-joins-unprecedented-public-private-partnership-address-rising-us-infant-mort.

24 Planned Parenthood Federation of America, *Annual Report 2005–2006*, 14–15.

25 Ibid.

26 Planned Parenthood Federation of America, *Annual Report 2009–2010*, 5.

27 Planned Parenthood Federation of America, *Annual Report 2007–2008*, 8.

28 Planned Parenthood Mobile was launched in September 2009, Planned Parenthood en Español Móvil in November 2010, and Text4Baby in February of the same year. Planned Parenthood Federation of America, "Planned Parenthood Launches Essential and Innovative Resource for Latino Community: Mobile Website in Spanish Provides Medical Facts and Health Center Locator for Demographic Group Most Likely to Use Cell Phone to Look for Health Information," press release, November 9, 2010.

29 Text4baby, "Verizon Wireless Supports Text4baby Program," February 6, 2010, http://www.text4baby.org/index.php/news/42-verizon-wireless-supports -text4baby-program.

30 "Planned Parenthood Generation Action," Facebook, http://www.facebook .com/PlannedParenthoodYouth (accessed August 2015).

31 Planned Parenthood Federation of America, "Info for Teens," http://www .plannedparenthood.org/info-for-teens.

32 Although many campus action groups are still called VOX chapters, they are now currently under the umbrella of Generation Action Groups. Planned Parenthood Federation of America, "Find Your Planned Parenthood Generation Action Group," http://www.plannedparenthoodaction.org/get-involved/generation/ find-your-planned-parenthood-campus-group/ (accessed July 2015).

33 Planned Parenthood Federation of America, "Planned Parenthood Teen Summit Trains Youth Activists to Stand Up for Sex Education and Health Care," press release, March 30, 2007, http://www.plannedparenthood.org/about-us/ newsroom/press-releases/teen-summit.

34 Leslie Kantor, "Planned Parenthood Statement on New CDC Report Showing Drop in Teen Birthrate for Third Year in a Row," Planned Parenthood Federation of America, press release, December 2, 2011, http://www .plannedparenthood.org/about-us/newsroom/press-releases/planned -parenthood-statement-new-cdc-report-showing-drop-teen-birthrate-third -year-row.

35 The "global gag rule" was a policy that denied foreign organizations receiving US family-planning assistance the right to provide information, referrals, or services for legal abortion (or even to advocate for the legalization of abortion) in their country. The policy was instituted in 1984 by President Ronald Reagan, was rescinded in 1993 by President Bill Clinton, was reinstated in 2001 by President George W. Bush, and most recently, was (re)rescinded by President Barack Obama in 2009.

36 Tanden, "Cecile Richards on How Progressives Can Make a Difference."

37 Planned Parenthood Federation of America, *Annual Report 2009–2010*, 3.

38 Planned Parenthood Federation of America, "I Have a Say," http://www .womenarewatching.org/article/cecile-richards-i-have-a-say (accessed August 2013); TheCPWH's channel, "I Have a Say: Cecile Richards, President of Planned Parenthood Federation of America," YouTube, February 24, 2012, https://www .youtube.com/watch?v=HoRXKHg1Wzk, video.

39 Tanden, "Cecile Richards on How Progressives Can Make a Difference."
40 Tom Comar, "Viewpoint: Health Care Act Offers Critical Benefits," *Tribune*, March 18, 2012, http://www.sanluisobispo.com/2012/03/18/1995572_viewpoint -health-care-act-offers.html?rh=1.

Bibliography

"Ann Richards' Daughter to Lead Planned Parenthood." *Austin Business Journal*, January 10, 2006. http://www.bizjournals.com/austin/stories/2006/01/09/daily14.html.

Blue, Laura. "Why the Plan B Debate Won't Go Away." *Time*, August 25, 2006. http://content.time.com/time/nation/article/0,8599,1333925,00.html.

Comar, Tom. "Viewpoint: Health Care Act Offers Critical Benefits." *Tribune*, March 18, 2012. http://www.sanluisobispo.com/2012/03/18/1995572_viewpoint -health-care-act-offers.html?rh=1.

Fall, Curlin, and Daniel Hall. "Regarding Plan B: Science and Politics Cannot Be Separated." *Obstetrics and Gynecology* 105 (2005): 1148–1150.

Family Research Council. "Vision and Mission Statements." http://www.frc.org/ mission-statement.

Kantor, Leslie. "Planned Parenthood Statement on New CDC Report Showing Drop in Teen Birthrate for Third Year in a Row." Planned Parenthood Federation of America, press release, December 2, 2011. http://www.plannedparenthood.org/ about-us/newsroom/press-releases/planned-parenthood-statement-new-cdc -report-showing-drop-teen-birthrate-third-year-row.

Lewin, Tamar. "Court Says Health Coverage May Bar Birth-Control Pills." *New York Times*, March 17, 2007. http://www.nytimes.com/2007/03/17/health/17pill .html?_r=0.

Mitchell, Elizabeth. "The Genius of Cecile Richards." *Nation*, March 7, 2012. http:// www.thenation.com/article/166670/genius-cecile-richards.

Pear, Robert. "Women Buying Health Policies Pay a Penalty." *New York Times*, October 29, 2008. http://www.nytimes.com/2008/10/30/us/30insure.html ?pagewanted=all&_r=0.

Pelosi, Nancy. "Cecile Richards." *Time*, April 21, 2011. http://content.time.com/ time/specials/packages/article/0,28804,2066367_2066369_2066140,00.html.

Planned Parenthood Action Fund. "About Us." http://www.plannedparenthood action.org/elections-politics/about-us/.

"Planned Parenthood Chooses New President." *Feminist News*, Feminist Majority Foundation, January 12, 2006. http://www.feminist.org/newsbyte/uswirestory .asp?id=9465.

Planned Parenthood Federation of America. "American Journal of Public Health Study Shows Public Clinics Provide More Choice, More Care." Press release, August 14, 2008. http://www.plannedparenthood.org/about-us/newsroom/ press-releases/american-journal-public-health.

———. *Annual Report 2005–2006*.

———. *Annual Report 2007–2008*.

————. *Annual Report 2009–2010*.

————. "FDA Delay on EC." Press release, August 26, 2005. http://www.planned
parenthood.org/about-us/newsroom/press-releases/fda-ec.

————. "Find Your Planned Parenthood Generation Action Group." http://www
.plannedparenthoodaction.org/get-involved/generation/find-your-planned
-parenthood-campus-group/ (accessed July 2015).

————. "I Have a Say." http://www.womenarewatching.org/article/cecile-richards
-i-have-a-say (accessed August 2013).

————. "Info for Teens." http://www.plannedparenthood.org/info-for-teens.

————. "Planned Parenthood Joins Unprecedented Public-Private Partnership
to Address Rising U.S. Infant Mortality Rate." Press release, February 5, 2010.
http://www.plannedparenthood.org/about-us/newsroom/press-releases/
planned-parenthood-joins-unprecedented-public-private-partnership-address
-rising-us-infant-mort.

————. "Planned Parenthood Launches Essential and Innovative Resource for
Latino Community: Mobile Website in Spanish Provides Medical Facts and
Health Center Locator for Demographic Group Most Likely to Use Cell Phone to
Look for Health Information," press release, November 9, 2010.

————. "Planned Parenthood Teen Summit Trains Youth Activists to Stand Up
for Sex Education and Health Care." Press release, March 30, 2007. http://www
.plannedparenthood.org/about-us/newsroom/press-releases/teen-summit.

"Planned Parenthood Generation Action." Facebook. http://www.facebook.com/
PlannedParenthoodYouth (accessed August 2015).

Prescott, Heather Munro. *The Morning After: A History of Emergency Contraception in
the United States*. New Brunswick, NJ: Rutgers University Press, 2011.

Ramshaw, Emily. "Texans Lead Battle for Women's Health." *New York Times*, February 4, 2012. http://www.nytimes.com/2012/02/05/us/texans-lead-battle-for
-womens-health.html.

Suarez, Gustavo. "Planned Parenthood Names New President: Cecile Richards Will
Head Organization." press release, January 9, 2006. Available at http://www
.religiousconsultation.org/News_Tracker/Planned_Parenthood_announces
_next_president.htm.

Tanden, Neera. "Cecile Richards on How Progressives Can Make a Difference." Five
Books, July 24, 2011. http://fivebooks.com/interviews/cecile-richards-on-how
-progressives-can-make-difference.

Text4baby. "Verizon Wireless Supports Text4baby Program." February 6, 2010.
http://www.text4baby.org/index.php/news/42-verizon-wireless-supports
-text4baby-program.

TheCPWH's channel. "I Have a Say: Cecile Richards, President of Planned Parenthood Federation of America." YouTube, February 24, 2012. https://www
.youtube.com/watch?v=HoRXKHg1Wzk. Video.

Wind, Rebecca. "Following Decade-Long Decline, U.S. Teen Pregnancy Rate
Increases as Both Births and Abortions Rise." Guttmacher Institute, January 26, 2010. https://guttmacher.org/media/nr/2010/01/26/index.html.

Bhairavi Desai
Organizing Immigrant Labor through a Feminist Lens

C. Laura Lovin and Mary K. Trigg

Background

Bhairavi Desai cofounded the New York Taxi Workers Alliance in 1998, when she was twenty-six years old. She initiated a strike that year, to protest new rules imposed by then-mayor Rudolph Giuliani. The strike mobilized forty thousand licensed taxi drivers, who protested proposed regulations that sought to quadruple liability-insurance costs, increase fines, implement a longer probationary period, and mandate drug and alcohol testing. The strike kept the city's yellow cabs off the street for twenty-four hours. Desai fought to make the voices of the taxi workers heard and to reframe the drivers into knowledgeable and invested parties in conversation with the power brokers in the city. She queried, "Who, may I ask, knows more about safety and driving than a driver? . . . Who is most interested in driving being a safe occupation? Who is most affected by these rules? The answer to all these questions is 'the yellow-cab driver.'"[1]

Taxis are an integral part of the life, history, and culture of the city as well as one of the image brands of the New York metropolis. Ever present on postcards, T-shirts, films, and souvenirs, taxis are symbols of the speedy and ceaseless movement of the city of New York. From the perspective of the taxi drivers, the situation appears less dazzling. Taxi drivers' mobility and their presence on the streets are synchronous with their isolation from other workers and an unsurpassed vulnerability among the immigrant workforces in the city of New York. New York City taxi drivers work twelve-hour shifts in grueling conditions to provide a service that has been recognized for its "availability" and "value for money" and is ranked among the top two in the world, second only to London cabs. Taxing is monotonous, poorly paid, and dangerous.[2] How this young, immigrant, college-educated woman successfully mobilized a male-dominated workforce in an era of union downsizing is the leadership story told here.

Bhairavi Desai as an Advocate for Social Justice

Bhairavi Desai was born in 1973 in Bhadheli village in Gujarat, India. When she was six years old, she moved to New Jersey with her parents and two older brothers. Her family settled in Harrison, New Jersey, a suburb of Newark. Back in India, her father had been a lawyer and her mother a homemaker. In New Jersey, her father was unable to find work as a lawyer and consequently had to buy and run a two-aisle grocery store, while her mother worked the night shift in various factories. Desai later placed their experiences in a broader political and economic context: "We were part of that generation of Indian immigrants who came in 1979, during a recession. It felt like the beginning of the immigrant dream slipping away. . . . It was Reaganomics. It was the end of affirmative action, but it wasn't the end of racism."[3] Their apartment was connected to the family grocery store, and Desai's father had a little bell that he rang when he needed help. Desai and her brothers would come out and assist him. Labor was a family affair in Desai's childhood.

Politics and struggles for social justice were part of Desai's family history. Her grandmother's arrest during a fight for Indian independence and her father's legal work in India in defense of the underprivileged shaped and radicalized young Desai. From an early age, Desai loved politics. She always wanted to be an organizer: "Growing up for me social justice was as much a part of the menu as bread and butter," she told an interviewer in 2015. She recalled a childhood incident in New Jersey that politicized her: "I remember being chased down the road because of my colour."[4] The family also experienced poverty in the United States and were strong advocates of unions. Desai noted in 2005 that although no one in her family—including herself—ever drove professionally, they championed the disenfranchised. "I come from a line of union members and union supporters," she stated. "My mom was a union member. . . . Both of my parents are socially conscious. They raised us to hate poverty and to love the poor. We were poor."[5] Desai was "too busy dreaming of strikes and demonstrations," and as she grew into adolescence, she did not miss the dances or dates her parents strictly prohibited. She attended Rutgers University and graduated in 1994 with a degree in women's studies.[6]

After graduation, Desai continued her commitment to social justice by beginning a career in the nonprofit sector. First working with victims of domestic violence at Manavi, the South Asian women's organization in New Jersey, in 1996 she joined the Committee against Anti-Asian Violence (CAAAV). A pan-Asian community-based organization that works to build the power of low-income Asian immigrants and refugees in New York City, CAAAV was at the time seeking ways to address escalating violence against cab drivers. More than fifty South Asian cab drivers had been killed over the course of the past year. (At that time, South Asians made up 43 percent of the industry.)[7] At CAAAV, Desai was assigned to manage the organization's first workers' project, the Lease Drivers Coalition. During the drivers' breaks and shift changes, she would meet them at garages or call them to ask about their concerns.

Desai proved to be not only an attentive listener but an outstanding strategist and fearless organizer. She understood that the way to address the drivers' problems was not through social-service delivery but by forming a union. The New York City Taxi and Limousine Commission (TLC, the city agency responsible for licensing and regulating New York City's taxicabs), the garage owners and brokers, the New York Police Department, and taxi passengers became parties in the complex process of redefinition, negotiation, and struggle that Desai initiated.[8]

As early as August 1997, the Lease Drivers Coalition rallied two thousand yellow cabs in a demonstration at Fourteenth Street and Avenue D, taking the first step toward securing a bargaining position with the TLC. In February 1998, Desai, along with several other organizers and five hundred taxi workers, created the New York Taxi

Workers Alliance (NYTWA). While CAAAV incubated the NYTWA in its earliest incarnation, it was time for the alliance to spin off as its own organization.[9] Desai was convinced that improving the lives of immigrant communities depended on transforming the landscape of workers' struggles and their labor rights. Organizing immigrant labor was especially meaningful to her because it reflected her own family's struggle.

> I had been politicized most of my life, by my experience as a poor person and immigrant. . . . I wanted to work around issues of class and labor, and what is a better community than taxi drivers. . . . There's a lie about immigrants in America: You don't get handed jobs: you work very hard to find jobs. A grocery store is almost the same as a taxi; you work 70 to 80 hours a week. . . . It's the nature of immigrant life in America. Labor becomes a family activity. I think it's much more revealing of economic need than of individual personality. That's probably why I'm much more drawn to Marx than to Freud.[10]

When Desai was asked in a *New York Times* interview why a college-educated woman like herself, whose parents went through hardship to secure better lives for their children, was "working like, well, a taxi driver," she responded, "It's the sacrifice of the working men and women in the country, of the immigrants in this country. I think I owe them something in return."[11]

Work and Labor Organizing through an Intersectional Lens

The NYTWA became a multiracial, multinational, and multiethnic worker-led organization. Workers from countries in Africa, the Caribbean, South America, East Asia, and Europe and white and African American workers from the United States joined the South Asian drivers in an organization that expanded its representation to all strata of yellow-cab drivers. The union's membership brought together citizens, permanent residents, and undocumented immigrants. Desai was intent on attracting to the alliance women drivers, who have specific needs as women workers in the taxi industry.[12]

Desai was twenty-three when she started organizing taxi workers, whom she considered "the ultimate outsiders on the inside."[13] Taxi drivers are players situated at the bottom of an intricate industry with a complicated system of ownership, exploitative labor relations, and a multilayered power structure. This structure is populated by garage owners, medallion-leasing agents, and city regulators, all interested parties in determining the governing and profit-making rules of the industry. Taxi drivers' work conditions materialized at the intersection of power trends in global capitalism. These include the deunionization of the taxi industry, the transnational mobility of capital and labor, and the relegation of immigrant labor to the least desirable jobs of the new service economies of contemporary global cities.[14] Organizing taxi drivers was and continues to be particularly difficult given the following facts: (1) the status of the drivers is closer to that of independent contractors than employees;[15] (2) traditional union models require substantial altering in response to the special status of taxi workers, including an individualist ethos and the powerful capitalist dream—and mythology—of small business ownership; and (3) 90 percent of the New York City taxi drivers are transnational and immigrant workers who represent a wide range of ethnicities and nationalities,[16] together speak more than sixty languages, and do not necessarily represent themselves as a sociopolitical unit.[17] In spite of these challenges, Desai and the NYTWA were able to reposition immigrant taxi drivers as laborers within the terrain of US work and labor politics and thus to formulate demands for workers' rights.

Desai began her organizing by spending time at garages, hanging around airports during the day, stopping by South Asian restaurants at night, and during afternoons, visiting a gas station at the corner of Houston Street and Broadway, where the yellow-cab taxi workers changed shifts. The question that she asked the drivers over and over again was, "What are the biggest problems you face in your job?" Within a year, Desai had amassed seven hundred entries in her notebooks. Each entry documented the concerns and problems of a taxi worker. She learned that the drivers are divided not just by lines and nationality but also by the intersections of their work.

Social divisions arise among taxi drivers who cover the airport and those who work in the city and among those who drive during the day and those who labor at night. Desai's observations showed that older drivers tend to prefer the airport and avoid the hustle and bustle of Manhattan streets; taxi workers who drive during daytime have to cope with congested traffic and provide emotional labor for stressed-out clients who are late for meetings or work. Taxi drivers who work at night enjoy lighter traffic and can join a friend for dinner or stop by the gym, yet they face more danger.

By analyzing these notes, Desai learned that the taxi drivers' schedules were shaped by their domestic obligations, which varied by country of origin. In the South Asian community, for instance, Bangladeshis tended to immigrate to the United States with their families, while Pakistanis tended to leave their families back home. Thus, the Bangladeshis generally opt for a six-day workweek. To achieve this, they would work with a partner, which allowed them to alternate twenty-four-hour shifts on Sundays and Mondays. Pakistanis tended to have seven-day workweeks, with shorter workdays on Saturdays and Sundays. West African taxi workers, more frequently students, opted for alternating shifts of twenty-four hours on and twenty-four hours off. Finally, over and over, the drivers talked about the isolation they felt while in the midst of the busiest city. Most of the time ignored or patronized by passengers, in an occupation with no inherent grid for sociability, they described taxiing as "a job that can be excruciatingly isolating, and it really lends itself to a lot of analysis."[18] Desai put her careful research to good use in her organizing efforts. These conversations about the ups and downs of a taxi driver's job constituted the first step in a long journey of assiduous efforts, sustained mobilizations, incremental organizational development, and political victories.

Transformations in the New York City Taxi Industry

Larger economic changes, premised on the dismantling of unions, job security, and employee benefits, reshaped the structure of the New York City taxi industry during the 1970s. Unionized taxi work morphed into work performed by independent contractors or small business owners. The racial composition of the workforce changed as well, transforming taxi driving from a job performed by a "white majority" into an "immigrant job." Labor and occupational safety laws, the right to bargain collectively, and identifiable bargaining counterparts, such as "the owners" or "the management," were also lost in the process.[19] Through the institutionalization of the medallion—a number issued by the city that gives a vehicle the right to operate as a cab—the industry developed further, following a corporate model. The majority of New York City medallions are owned by garages and nondriving individuals. Brokers mediate the relation between medallion owners and taxi drivers who own their cars, while garages lease out to drivers both medallions and cars on a daily or weekly basis. The shift to leasing created opportunity for a range of exploitative practices such as requirements to pay up-front for the lease and gas expenses, which transferred the risks of business fluctuation onto the shoulders of the drivers. Although cab drivers are told they are independent contractors, the majority own neither the tools of their trade (the car) nor the permit to operate it (the medallion).[20] Furthermore, at the initiative of Rudolph Giuliani, mayor of New York from 1993 through 2001, the TLC and the New York Police Department became the state power instruments whose reach extended well into the taxi drivers' day-to-day working lives. This was a paradoxical gesture given drivers' repositioning from unionized workers into the "deregulated" space of small business ownership.

Desai entered the scene in the 1990s, during years of high turnover, a lack of stable worksites, and a transitioning industry. While at the time it appeared particularly difficult for the taxi movement to organize across ethnic, racial, and national lines, Desai created a new environment of mobilization that enabled drivers from Haiti, West African countries, Iran, South American, and East Asian countries to take leadership positions and to place on the table the issue of cultural diversity and ethnic barriers. In fact, these factors came to benefit the new organization, which took stock of the skills that many drivers had developed and refined when participating in resistance movements in their own countries.

A Pivotal Moment

On May 2, 1998, the NYTWA's Organizing Committee (OC) called an emergency meeting to respond to the TLC's newly proposed rules. Organizers recognized that the TLC's motivation was to increase its revenue rather than to increase the safety of the taxi passengers, taxi drivers, and other New York City drivers and passengers. The TLC never consulted any taxi drivers while it was crafting the changes. According to the scholar and NYTWA activist Biju Mathew, the TLC based its new rules "on little more than a patchwork of ill-informed assumptions about taxi driving, including racist stereotypes about immigrant taxi drivers as well as deliberately obfuscated statistics."[21]

Sixteen NYTWA members showed up at the May 2 emergency meeting. The members launched into an emotionally charged analysis of the new regulations; their angry comments demonstrated their shared frustrations. Desai listened with intent concentration to the drivers' cogent assessments of the new rules. She made her points only after she was sure that everyone's ideas were on the table. When discussions got heated, she transformed the mood of the meeting, "moving from anger and analysis to the idea of action." "We need to respond. . . . What do you think we should do?" she asked.[22] The OC members agreed that it was time for the taxi workers to strike. In those early days, about five hundred drivers belonged to the NYTWA. While this was a good starting point for a union, the numbers also indicated that the NYTWA reached only a small fraction of the total New York City population of taxi drivers. Questions pertaining to logistics and the practical aspects of organizing flooded the next two hours of the meeting.

Labor Organizing in the Global City

Mayor Giuliani's rules and regulations were not altogether his invention. Their genealogy could be traced to the moment when the industry turned to immigrant labor. For the NYTWA, claiming economic rights could thus not be separated from the racist and xenophobic violence that passengers and the police directed at the drivers. Giuliani's need to regulate yellow-cab drivers was intricately linked with vocabularies and practices of gender and racialization: "The drivers' brown bodies, language, and ethnic practices, just by being what they are, have been seen as posing a threat to law and order. The racialization of these bodies as threatening is deeply gendered. The difficulty in coding these South Asian bodies as docile, feminized, and compliant—attributes often ascribed to East Asian men—leads to their representation as hypermasculine and therefore dangerous and belligerent."[23] In the meantime, passengers, because of their role as consumers, become the only subjects deserving protection, safety, and quality service. Desai expressed the connection cogently in her analysis of space, power, race, and citizenship:

> [For] drivers, their factory floor is out on the street. Who's their supervisor? The cops. Who's their second supervisor? It is the passengers in the back who tell them what to do. Who has armed them? The city. The city has armed both sets of people to make sure that this group of workers follows all the rules just like any good worker would in one controlled geographic location, right? That's one thing about the history of enforcement against the taxi industry. . . . Police brutality is historically a tool which has been used by property-owning white people to control non-white people, primarily working-class and poor non-white people, which also includes immigrants.[24]

In order to reach out and mobilize, NYTWA members talked to other taxi drivers about the strike, distributed flyers and asked the taxi drivers to distribute even more and to translate them if needed, and used CB radio and cell-phone networks to spread the word. The organizing work began on May 3, 1998. Desai talked with as many drivers as she could reach. Wherever she arrived, discussion became more animated, the crowds grew larger, and stacks of flyers got distributed. The NYTWA also reached out to small driver-welfare organizations. They all endorsed the strike call. At the Organizing Committee meeting on May 6, members drew an outreach map and assigned tasks for the next four days. Despite the fact that many OC members had started incurring debt and felt the lack of income while they redirected their time from driving to organizing, their commitment was unwavering. The same day, the NYTWA reached out to Local 3036, the AFL-CIO union in the industry. The NYTWA asked Local 3036 for a gesture of solidarity and to endorse the strike by putting its name on the strike bill as one of the sponsoring organizations. Local 3036 refused, not believing that the taxi drivers in the city "had progressed past the point where the Local 3036 had abandoned them in the mid-1980s."[25]

The TLC and Mayor Giuliani first chose to ignore the NYTWA's call to strike. Many garage owners advised the drivers against the strike. The media was generating a growing wave of news coverage of the impending strike. Passengers themselves started to react. Reactions ranged from irritation, hostility, and concern about potential inconvenience to willingness to help. In general, passengers were misinformed, imagining taxiing to be a lucrative job: one driver commented, "I dropped somebody . . . who had no idea we leased the taxi, that we paid rent on it, that we didn't own it, that we hardly made any money."[26]

Mayor Giuliani took a stand on May 11 and stated that the desire of a small group of drivers to maintain their option to drive at reckless speeds without losing their driving privileges was the fuel igniting the strike. The rhetoric got really inflated when Police Commissioner Howard Safir called those who were planning to strike or demonstrate "taxi terrorists," which underscored the threat he sensed in the NYTWA's rising power as well as the racist approach the Giuliani administration took to the taxi drivers.[27] These rhetorical excesses struck a sensitive nerve with the garage owners, who changed course and began encouraging drivers to strike.

On May 12, 1998, Desai, on behalf of the entire taxi community, sent a letter to Mayor Giuliani, confirming the strike for the next day and officially submitting its demands.[28] By that evening, the city of New York understood that the strike was about to occur. Journalists from mainstream media flooded the NYTWA office. Desai was attending to pressing issues about the upcoming strike, including the safety of the striking drivers and the protection of nonparticipating drivers. Late that night, she encouraged NYTWA members to be careful to withstand any provocation from the police to incite violence against nonstriking drivers. "We know that we can have a good and peaceful strike tomorrow," she told them. "Our single most important concern will be those few drivers who may try and come into work. There will be hundreds of people looking for cabs and the trouble that can start will surely be exploited by the cops. Cabs may be confiscated, drivers harassed, arrested, and beaten up. . . . Our task is to protect the drivers who do not join the strike, whatever their reasons might be."[29] The strikers were reluctant to show solidarity with nonstriking drivers. An antagonistic mood was in the air, and some drivers threatened to flatten the tires of nonstriking cabbies in order to immobilize traffic. At this critical juncture, how could twenty-six-year-old Bhairavi Desai convince the taxi drivers to remain disciplined and conduct a strike that could have the potential to change workers' rights in the taxi industry for decades to come?

Resolution

Desai's remarkably clear vision and extraordinary capacity to create productive dialogue shifted the mood once again from "antagonism into one of concern and solidarity." The NYTWA devised a detailed plan to ensure the presence of teams at critical points in the city, such as the bridges connecting the boroughs of Queens and Brooklyn to Manhattan. They hoped to encourage dialogue with nonstriking taxi drivers: "Our task was to convince them [the nonstriking drivers] to turn around by pointing out that they would be sitting targets for cops and angry passengers."[30] The second critical goal on the strike day was informing the passengers. Teams of volunteers assembled and fanned out to airports and train and bus stations. They explained to stranded passengers the conditions that had led to the strike and encouraged them to direct their frustrations not toward the taxi workers but toward the mayor and the TLC.

On the morning of May 13, 1998, no yellow taxis could be seen on the streets of New York. More than twenty-four thousand New York City yellow-cab drivers, amounting to over 98 percent of the active workforce of the yellow-cab industry, went on strike from five A.M. that day to five A.M. the next day, May 14. The striking drivers arrived at their spots in groups of friends or neighbors. They took turns chanting slogans and making speeches. They complained about Giuliani's plethora of rules. The striking yellow-cab drivers challenged their position in relation to the legal system, which they claimed operated on the assumption of "found guilty until proven innocent." The taxi drivers peacefully demonstrated for better working conditions and pay under circumstances that made it nearly impossible for them to keep up with rising leasing and gasoline costs.

The power of the strike took TLC by surprise: "This was somewhat bigger than anticipated," their spokesperson remarked. Giuliani was resolute in not acknowledging the strikers' action and demands: "If they would like to stay home forever, they can stay home forever. The city will function very well without them. It [already] functioned very well without them."[31]

Building Momentum: Another Strike to Come

Drivers, enthused and encouraged by their success, gathered at the NYTWA headquarters in the days that followed, in order to decide the next course of action. On May 16, the NYTWA called an open meeting. More than eight hundred drivers responded, and by the end of the night, they had reached a consensus: they would call a second strike for May 21.[32] Giuliani shifted gears and this time portentously framed the strike as "an imminent threat to the delivery of a necessary service in the City of New York."[33] The mayor also attempted a diversion, by collaborating with the United Yellow Cab Association and persuading it to convene a United taxicab procession across the Queensboro Bridge at the same time as the NYTWA strike.[34] Desai recognized this for what it was, a strike-breaking tactic. In her negotiations with the leadership of United, Desai was steadfast and crystal-clear:

> A procession across the bridge would be a gift to Giuliani in a public
> relations war. What is crucial at this moment is to strike the city
> with the same vehemence as we did on May 13—bring the city to a
> standstill. Each successful day of strike will expose Giuliani more,
> and the day will come when we can take a procession and he will be

powerless against it. Already just with one strike, public perception has begun to shift in favor of drivers, especially since Giuliani was so way off in his understanding of the mobilization. If we go ahead with a procession across the bridge, every car that appears on the streets would be subject to intense harassment if it refused to pick up passengers.[35]

On May 21, when the drivers gathered at the bridge, the riot police met them. On the bridge, the police force broke the taxicab procession. The NYTWA refused to call off the strike, and when the bridge was cleared, the taxi workers marched on foot. More than twenty thousand drivers observed the strike call, and the police harassed or arrested a number of them. The city administration continued the deployment of a racist rhetoric in relation to the city's immigrant labor force. Advertisements sponsored by garage owners and brokers were aired on the radio, reiterating that the drivers were well paid but failing to note that they had to cover the pricey costs of cab leases. Giuliani described the drivers as "uncaring, brutal men who would not hesitate to block the passage of ambulances carrying dying old women."[36]

On May 28, the TLC eventually passed fifteen of the seventeen new rules in a closed-door meeting that violated its own procedural grounds. However, the strikes of May 1998 proved momentous to the broader worker struggles in New York City. The 1998 taxi drivers' strike represented the single largest worker mobilization the city had witnessed in two decades. From a base of only five hundred active members, the NYTWA under Desai's leadership utilized traditional organizing tactics—dispensing flyers, one-on-one conversations with drivers—to mobilize enough of New York's taxi drivers to stop work and gain credibility.[37] The strike put the New York Taxi Workers Alliance on the map and made it a popular organization with taxi drivers. "Drivers started to come to us," Desai stated.[38] Second, the strike had a significant impact on New Yorkers and tourists, who were finally able to see taxi drivers as a united and organized workforce. Third, the media, old and new, started to voice the taxi workers' perspectives and interests, enriching the public discourse with analyses of workers' rights that accounted for the subjugating power of gender, nation, and race hierarchies. The power elite in the city took notice. The organizer and labor studies expert Mischa Gaus has argued that the NYTWA's capacity to mount effective strikes made it a daunting presence from the start, an organization that the TLC and other city leaders viewed as potentially powerful.[39] The 1998 strikes established the NYTWA as a fearless union in touch with its members, with a clear vision for change and the strategic ingenuity to move its agenda forward.

The 1998 strikes opened the way to numerous struggles and quite a few victories. Over the course of a decade, the NYTWA transformed the TLC from an organization that used intimidation and fine extraction as its primary approach into one in which drivers participate in policy decisions. In 2001, the TLC raised the fee for rides to and from John F. Kennedy Airport in response to the NYTWA's economic-justice petitions and resulting hearings. In 2004, after a two-year campaign, the NYTWA won a resounding victory when the TLC agreed to increase taxi fares by 26 percent, the first increase since 1996. For the first time in the taxi industry, a significant part of the fare-raise revenue was directed toward drivers' wages. Whereas back in 1996 the workers received only 14 percent of the fare increase negotiated at the time, the NYTWA's organizing brought them 60 to 75 percent of the fare increase in 2004.[40] Again in 2012, the NYTWA won the majority of a 17 percent fare increase, defeating intense pressure from the taxi lobby to boost lease rates at the same time. According to Gaus, for long-term taxi drivers, "the wave of activism initiated by the alliance among the 'hacks' who drive cabs is the most exciting development in a generation, stretching beyond the boundaries of a fragmented workforce to create a cultural and political unity unseen for decades."[41]

In 2011, the NYTWA was chartered to build the National Taxi Workers Alliance (NTWA), which is now the fifty-seventh union of the AFL-CIO. Although the NTWA lacks formalized collective bargaining and does not sign contracts with employers, it "engages in virtually all forms of typical union bargaining, negotiating over income, grievances, benefits, and the conditions of the job."[42] Most notably, this is the first charter for nontraditional workers since the farm workers' charter in the 1960s, as well as the first union of independent contractors that has ever joined the AFL-CIO. Not being a traditional union is not stopping Desai or members of the NTWA. In a 2011 interview, Desai stated, "We're not waiting to win collective bargaining recognition. We are establishing ourselves as a mass-base, independent, democratic workers' organization and, through our affiliation with the AFL-CIO, building our political power, our numbers, our strength, our resources, to one day win collective bargaining."[43]

In 2013, Bhairavi Desai was elected onto the AFL-CIO Executive Council, and the taxi workers' movement thus won a seat on labor's governing body. That same year, NWTA members won their campaign to set up the first New York City regulations designed to protect drivers from the violence that is endemic to their work. Desai told a Rutgers University audience in 2012, "I've been organizing in this industry for 17 years. I've never had a year when I didn't have to go to a funeral or an emergency room."[44] In fact, taxi drivers face extraordinary rates of violence on the job. According to the Bureau of Labor Statistics, taxi drivers are thirty-six times more likely than the average worker to be killed on the job.[45] After a ten-year campaign, as of May 2015, the successful passage of the Taxi and Livery Driver Protection Act required all yellow and green taxis in New York City to be equipped with warning signs that read, "Attention— Assaulting a driver is punishable [with] up to twenty-five years in prison." These are similar to the stickers required on Metropolitan Transit Authority buses and subways.[46]

In 2015, the members of NYTWA came from over thirty countries that spread across three continents. Multinational, multiethnic, and multigenerational, the alliance brings together taxi workers from "every community, garage, and neighborhood."[47] The NYTWA has currently over fifty thousand members and an internal culture that is a "more rollicking and flexible affair" than the formality of more mainstream unions.[48] The organization has no plans to stop, and neither does its leader. "We had demonstrations, work stoppages, and strikes. And that sense of militancy—we need to set that ablaze throughout all the industries in our country. And working people have that spirit," Desai proclaimed.[49] Next on the NYTWA's agenda is winning collective bargaining rights and a fare increase that will enable it to establish a health fund for drivers. Very soon, six cents from every trip will go toward a fund to provide disability insurance and health care services to drivers, the first health fund ever implemented for taxi workers. All these victories were set in motion by Desai's astute organizing in the late spring of 1998. Yet she is alert to the dangers that on-demand rides from start-up companies like Uber and Lyft represent to taxi drivers. In a recent interview, she described Uber as "Wal-Mart on wheels" and criticized the "erosion of work" that she believes Uber epitomizes.[50]

Desai, Gender, and Leadership

Over the years, Desai, along with the NYTWA, has won acclaim and accolades from labor organizers, progressive agencies, and other social justice counterparts.[51] She has won the Ford Foundation's Leadership for a Changing World Award, has been invited to the White House twice, and is widely respected as a still-young leader who embraces worker leadership in the organization she heads.[52] Desai's leadership demonstrates her skills in using media, along with political and grassroots campaigning, to raise awareness about workers' rights in an era in which unions and collective bargaining have been increasingly under attack. She was able to reach across boundaries of gender, age, and nationality to convince taxi workers in New York City to join together, form a union, and strike. Her journey has not been without challenges. In her early years, Desai recalled, some taxi drivers, officers from the old union, and supervisors told her she could not "embody worker power" because she was an immigrant woman of color. Some even invoked an offensive stereotype to suggest that she created her path to power by sleeping her way to the top. "That was the expectations of what I should be doing," Desai said. Yet her commitment to transformative social change is unwavering. "In organizing the working class, the real beauty is transformation," Desai explained. "The people you're organizing change because of you, and you change because of them."[53]

Desai considers one-on-one interactions with those men who feel voiceless as crucial to base building for a union that strives to influence the collective consciousness of drivers. "Drivers appreciated that somebody gave a damn, that somebody recognized what the conditions were, and that they needed to change," Desai said.[54] "It was the graciousness of taxi drivers to engage me in conversation," she explained, "to want to organize, to want to unionize."[55] Desai views her role as a leader as a conduit and illustrated her leadership philosophy when she remarked, "The primary role of a leader in a mass organization is to produce a framework for the workers to engage through, in which they can meaningfully participate and build every part of the organization, from its campaign ideas to benefit plans, from its decision-making model to the organization's shape and structure."[56]

Desai is fueled by the commitment to social justice she had witnessed in her immigrant parents, and her bottom-up leadership is grassroots oriented and focused on building alliances and gaining the respect of diverse partners. The legal advocate Chaumtoil Huaq said of Desai, "The Port Authority has been extremely supportive of her work; they've distributed pamphlets for the health fairs. The TLC respects her. These are unlikely governmental allies. People enjoy working with her; they respect her. People want to work with her because she is committed to social change and gets things done."[57] In addition, her vision is global. When asked whether a peaceful taxi strike she called could be considered "a Gandhian protest in New York," Desai responded, "It did bear all the Gandhian hallmarks of being a peaceful, mass protest. But I would say that whether it is in India or the U.S. the labour movement knows no borders."[58]

Many people have asked what it is that a woman activist does to successfully lead a virtually male-dominated constituency of workers. The scholar Ed Ott calls Desai "the most interesting and the most accomplished union leader of her generation" and deems that "her great strength is that the drivers really respect her."[59] Desai has built a reputation among drivers as a fearless, effective, and committed organizer with an unprecedented capacity to create collaborative spaces of political dialogue and alliance. The historian Graham Russel Gao Hodges, the author of *Taxi! A Social History of New York City Cabdrivers*, suggests that lending her "female ear" to "the lives and struggles of the immigrant taxi men" gained her acceptance.

In addition, her status as a college graduate gave her legitimacy.[60] Gaus writes, "Although she shuns her media tag as the taxi drivers' 'confessor,' Desai's gender puts the taxi driver population—which is 97 percent male, according to 2010 census ACS data—at ease."[61] Monisha Das Gupta attributes Desai's accomplishments to an approach to organizing that is strongly shaped by feminist understandings of gender, power, class inequality, and social change. Moreover, the impact of Desai's struggles reach beyond the triumph of her personal leadership, as her efforts have made it possible for women to be taken seriously as organizers and outreach workers in a male-dominated industry.[62] Her passion for social justice motivates her advocacy and leadership. "If you believe in justice you fight for it wherever you are," Desai said in 2012. "The battleground is beneath your feet."[63] Fueled by her commitment to give back to her community and to empower workers to build the union organization themselves, this informed, youthful leader transformed the scene of labor politics.

Notes

1   Bhairavi Desai, quoted in Biju Mathew, *Taxi! Cabs and Capitalism in New York City* (New York: New Press, 2005), 19–20.

2   Alex Nopoliello, "NYC Cabs Seen as Second Best in the World, Report Says," *NJ.com*, November 4, 2012, http://www.nj.com/news/index.ssf/2013/11/nyc _cab_drivers_rank_second_in_the_world.html; Diego Gambetta and Heather Hamill, *Streetwise: How Taxi Drivers Establish Their Customers' Trustworthiness* (New York: Russell Sage Foundation, 2005), 109.

3   Bhairavi Desai, quoted in Lizze Widdicombe, "Thin Yellow Line," *New Yorker*, April 18, 2011, http://www.newyorker.com/magazine/2011/04/18/thin-yellow -line.

4   Uttera Choudhury, "Meet Firebrand Social Activist: Bhairavi Desai," *braingainmag.com*, http://www.braingainmag.com/meet-firebrand-social-activist -bhairavi-desai.htm.

5   Elaine G. Flores, "Desi Making Waves: On the Shy: For Thousands of New Yorkers, Bhairavi Desai Is a Reluctant Star," *ABCD Lady*, n.d., http://www.abcdlady.com/2005–06/art1.php (accessed February 18, 2015).

6   Ibid.; Angela Delli Santi, "Cabbin' It," *Rutgers Magazine*, Winter 2012, http:// urwebsrv.rutgers.edu/magazine/archive1013/departments/winter-2012/on -the-banks/cabbin-it.

7   In 2010, the national origin, race, and ethnicity of New York City taxi drivers was South Asian 55 percent, Haitian 15 percent, African 10 percent, Arab 10 percent, Latino 5 percent, eastern European 5 percent. See Mischa

Gaus, "Not Waiting for Permission: The New York Taxi Workers Alliance and Twenty-First-Century Bargaining," in *New Labor in New York: Precarious Workers and the Future of the Labor Movement*, ed. Ruth Milkman and Ed Ott (Ithaca, NY: Cornell University Press, 2014), 252.

8 Monisha Das Gupta, *Unruly Immigrants: Rights, Activism, and Transnational South Asian Politics in the United States* (Durham, NC: Duke University Press, 2006), 229.

9 CAAV, "History of CAAAV," n.d., http://caaav.org/about-us/history-of-caaav (accessed October 4, 2014).

10 Bhairavi Desai, quoted in Joyce Wadler, "Public Lives: An Unlikely Organizer as Cabdrivers Unite," *New York Times*, December 8, 1999, http://www.nytimes.com/1999/12/08/nyregion/public-lives-an-unlikely-organizer-as-cabdrivers-unite.html.

11 Ibid.

12 Taxi driving is a male-dominated occupation. The number of women limo/taxi drivers has increased from 11 to 13 percent between 1990 and 2000, yet it also varies geographically, with higher representation in Boston (11 percent of all drivers) than in the New York metropolitan area (3 percent) in 2000.

13 Bhairavi Desai, quoted in Widdicombe, "Thin Yellow Line."

14 Das Gupta, *Unruly Immigrants*, 210.

15 For a historical analysis of labor relations across time in relation to ownership, the setting of salaries, and licensing, see Mathew, *Taxi!*.

16 For an analysis of the transnational composition of the taxi workers contingent during the 1990s, see Graham Russel Gao Hodges, *Taxi! A Social History of the New York City Cabdriver* (Baltimore: John Hopkins University Press, 2007), 158–168.

17 Das Gupta, *Unruly Immigrants*; Hodges, *Taxi!*; Mathew, *Taxi!*; Widdicombe, "Thin Yellow Line."

18 Bhairavi Desai, quoted in Widdicombe, "Thin Yellow Line."

19 Mathew, *Taxi!*, 118.

20 Gaus, "Not Waiting for Permission," 264. In 1971, medallions were valued around $30,000, but by 2001, the price of an individual medallion soared to about $1 million. See ibid., 250.

21 Mathew, *Taxi!*, 20.

22 Ibid., 20–21.

23 Das Gupta, *Unruly Immigrants*, 239.

24 Ibid., 242.

25 Ibid.

26 Mathew, *Taxi!*, 25.

27 Ibid., 26; Gaus, "Not Waiting for Permission," 252.

28 For the full letter, see NYTWA, "Lease Driver Coalition Letter to Giuliani," May 12, 1998, available at the South Asian American Digital Archive, http://www.saadigitalarchive.org/item/20130703-2968.

29 Mathew, *Taxi!*, 28.

30 Ibid.

31 Ibid., 31.
32 Ibid., 32.
33 Widdicombe, "Thin Yellow Line."
34 United tried to negotiate a deal with the mayor in exchange for its participation in this strategy.
35 Bhairavi Desai, quoted in Mathew, *Taxi!*, 34.
36 Ibid., 35–36. See also Benjamin Weiser, "Cabbies Denied Free Speech, a Judge Rules," *New York Times*, May 27, 1998, http://www.nytimes.com/1998/05/27/nyregion/cabbies-denied-free-speech-a-judge-rules.html.
37 Gaus, "Not Waiting for Permission," 252.
38 Naomi Grossman, "Cab Calling: Desai Drives N.Y. Taxi Alliance; Group Gives 6,700 Members a Unified Voice," *IndUS Business Journal*, December 1, 2005, http://www.indusbusinessjournal.com/ME2/dirmod.asp?sid=&nm=&type=Publishing&mod=Publications%3A%3AArticle&mid=8F3A70274218419 78F18BE895F87F791&tier=4&id=908871415CBD4D1C8B8593E62EA16454.
39 Gaus, "Not Waiting for Permission," 252.
40 Ibid., 253; Bhairavi Desai, "New York Taxi Workers Alliance: Adapting Worker Representation to New Models of Employment, a Union of 'Independent Contractors' with an AFL-CIO Organizing Charter," presentation for the panel discussion "Building Bridges: Discussing Innovative Partnerships and Types of Organizations That Bridge the Gap between 'Formal' and 'Informal' Sectors to Secure Decent Work for All Workers," at the Organizing Workers in the Informal Economy Conference, Cape Town, South Africa, December 2011.
41 Gaus, "Not Waiting for Permission," 253.
42 Ibid., 247.
43 "Making History: Bhairavi Desai Elected AFL-CIO Executive Council," *The Laura Flanders Show*, GRITtv, blip, November 13, 2013, http://blip.tv/grittv/making-history-bhairavi-desai-elected-to-afl-cio-executive-council-6642900, video.
44 Hannah Schroer, "Alumna Shares Taxi Drivers' Trials," *Daily Targum*, November 15, 2012, 1.
45 Cited in Gaus, "Not Waiting for Permission," 260.
46 NYTWA, "Events and Actions: TDPA Warning Stickers against Driver Assaults—May 4th, 2015," n.d., http://www.nytwa.org/events-and-actions (accessed August 5, 2014); "Bhairavi Desai," *Leadership for a Changing World*, November 18, 2005, http://www.leadershipforchange.org/talks/desai/.
47 NYTWA, "Mission & History," n.d., http://www.nytwa.org/mission-and-history/ (accessed August 5, 2014).
48 Gaus, "Not Waiting for Permission," 259.
49 "Making History."
50 GRITtv, "Uber: Wal-Mart on Wheels? | Bhairavi Desai on #GRITtv," YouTube, February 17, 2015, http://youtu.be/ICSZg9EGsSE, video.
51 For a complete list of awards given to the NYTWA and its leader, Bhairavi Desai, see NYTWA, "Awards & Honors," n.d., http://www.nytwa.org/awards-and-honors/ (accessed August 5, 2014).

52 Santi, "Cabbin' It"; Gaus, "Not Waiting for Permission," 258.
53 Bhairavi Desai, quoted in Gaus, "Not Waiting for Permission," 259.
54 Bhairavi Desai, quoted in ibid., 258–259.
55 Schroer, "Alumna Shares Taxi Drivers' Trials."
56 "Bhairavi Desai."
57 Ibid.
58 Choudhury, "Meet Firebrand Social Activist."
59 Daniel Massey, "Where Is Bhairavi Desai Now?," *Crain's New York Business*, October 12, 2012, http://mycrains.crainsnewyork.com/40under40/profiles/2012/bhairavi-desai.
60 Hodges, *Taxi!*.
61 Gaus, "Not Waiting for Permission," 258. Lizze Widdicombe used the term "confessor" in "Thin Yellow Line."
62 Gaus, "Not Waiting for Permission," 230–231.
63 Schroer, "Alumna Shares Taxi Drivers' Trials."

Bibliography

"Bhairavi Desai." *Leadership for a Changing World*, November 18, 2005. http://www.leadershipforchange.org/talks/desai/.

CAAV. "History of CAAAV." n.d. http://caaav.org/about-us/history-of-caaav (accessed October 4, 2014).

Choudhury, Uttera. "Meet Firebrand Social Activist: Bhairavi Desai." *braingainmag.com*. http://www.braingainmag.com/meet-firebrand-social-activist-bhairavi-desai.htm.

Das Gupta, Monisha. *Unruly Immigrants: Rights, Activism, and Transnational South Asian Politics in the United States*. Durham, NC: Duke University Press, 2006.

Desai, Bhairavi. "New York Taxi Workers Alliance: Adapting Worker Representation to New Models of Employment, a Union of 'Independent Contractors' with an AFL-CIO Organizing Charter." Presentation for the panel discussion "Building Bridges: Discussing Innovative Partnerships and Types of Organizations That Bridge the Gap between 'Formal' and 'Informal' Sectors to Secure Decent Work for All Workers," at the Organizing Workers in the Informal Economy Conference, Cape Town, South Africa, December 2011.

Flores, Elaine G. "Desi Making Waves: On the Shy: For Thousands of New Yorkers, Bhairavi Desai Is a Reluctant Star." *ABCD Lady*. http://www.abcdlady.com/2005-06/art1.php.

Gambetta, Diego, and Heather Hamill. *Streetwise: How Taxi Drivers Establish Their Customers' Trustworthiness*. New York: Russell Sage Foundation, 2005.

Gaus, Mischa. "Not Waiting for Permission: The New York Taxi Workers Alliance and Twenty-First-Century Bargaining." In *New Labor in New York: Precarious Workers and the Future of the Labor Movement*, edited by Ruth Milkman and Ed Ott, 246–265. Ithaca, NY: Cornell University Press, 2014.

GRITtv. "Uber: Wal-Mart on Wheels? | Bhairavi Desai on #GRITtv." YouTube, February 17, 2015. http://youtu.be/ICSZg9EGsSE. Video.

Grossman, Naomi. "Cab Calling: Desai Drives N.Y. Taxi Alliance; Group Gives 6,700 Members a Unified Voice." *IndUS Business Journal*, December 1, 2005. http://www.indusbusinessjournal.com/ME2/dirmod.asp?sid=&nm=&type=Publishing&mod=Publications%3A%3AArticle&mid=8F3A7027421841978F18BE895F87F791&tier=4&id=908871415CBD4D1C8B8593E62EA16454.

Hodges, Graham Russel Gao. *Taxi! A Social History of the New York City Cabdriver*. Baltimore: John Hopkins University Press, 2007.

"Making History: Bhairavi Desai Elected ALF-CIO Executive Council." *The Laura Flanders Show*, GRITtv, blip, November 13, 2013. http://blip.tv/grittv/making-history-bhairavi-desai-elected-to-afl-cio-executive-council-6642900, video.

Massey, Daniel. "Where Is Bhairavi Desai Now?" *Crain's New York Business*, October 12, 2012. http://mycrains.crainsnewyork.com/40under40/profiles/2012/bhairavi-desai.

Mathew, Biju. *Taxi! Cabs and Capitalism in New York City*. New York: New Press, 2005.

Nopoliello, Alex. "NYC Cabs Seen as Second Best in the World, Report Says." *NJ.com*, November 4, 2012. http://www.nj.com/news/index.ssf/2013/11/nyc_cab_drivers_rank_second_in_the_world.html.

NYTWA (New York Taxi Worker Alliance). "Awards & Honors." n.d. http://www.nytwa.org/awards-and-honors/ (accessed August 5, 2014).

———. "Events and Actions: TDPA Warning Stickers against Driver Assaults—May 4th, 2015." n.d. http://www.nytwa.org/events-and-actions (accessed August 5, 2014).

———. "Lease Driver Coalition Letter to Giuliani." May 12, 1998. Available at the South Asian American Digital Archive, http://www.saadigitalarchive.org/item/20130703-2968.

———. "Mission & History." n.d. http://www.nytwa.org/mission-and-history/ (accessed August 5, 2014).

Santi, Angela Delli. "Cabbin' It." *Rutgers Magazine*, Winter 2012. http://magazine.rutgers.edu/departments/winter-2012/on-the-banks/cabbin-it.

Schroer, Hannah. "Alumna Shares Taxi Drivers' Trials." *Daily Targum*, November 15, 2012.

Wadler, Joyce. "Public Lives: An Unlikely Organizer as Cabdrivers Unite." *New York Times*, December 8, 1999. http://www.nytimes.com/1999/12/08/nyregion/public-lives-an-unlikely-organizer-as-cabdrivers-unite.html.

Weiser, Benjamin. "Cabbies Denied Free Speech, a Judge Rules." *New York Times*, May 27, 1998. http://www.nytimes.com/1998/05/27/nyregion/cabbies-denied-free-speech-a-judge-rules.html.

Widdicombe, Lizze. "Thin Yellow Line." *New Yorker*, April 18, 2011. http://www.newyorker.com/magazine/2011/04/18/thin-yellow-line.

Thuli Madonsela
Whispering Truth to Power

Taida Wolfe and Alison R. Bernstein

Background

On April 23, 2014, *Time* magazine named Thuli Madonsela of South
Africa as one of its one hundred most influential people of 2014 for
her work in addressing corruption in public office, advocating land
reform, and protecting human rights.[1] Upon learning the news of
the *Time* magazine nomination, Madonsela thought it was a Nige-
rian scam. In an interview with the South African reporter Leanne
Manas, Madonsela said that she thought the "wildly ecstatic" reactions of South Africans to the news that she was named to the *Time*
list was because of a hunger for good leadership.[2]

In the role of the public protector (PP), Thuli Madonsela has relied
on her beliefs in "justice, humanity, integrity, high morals, and public service," beliefs cultivated from growing up poor and black during apartheid in South Africa.[3] During the media conference where
she released the Nkandla report—a report on presidential corruption that catapulted her to the international stage—Madonsela likened her role as PP to that of the Makhadzi, a figure of the Venda
people of South Africa.[4] In Venda culture, the Makhadzi is responsible for the well-being of the people—the mediator who connects
the people to God.[5] Madonsela states, "The Makhadzi is an aunt or
non-political figure who serves as a buffer between the ruler and the
people. . . . [The Makhadzi] enhances the voice of the people while
serving as the king's eyes, ears, and conscience."[6] From working
with trade unions during her early career to her work at the Office
of the Public Protector, Thuli Madonsela has been a buffer between

some of South Africa's most powerful figures and the most vulnerable parts of its population. And she has done so by quietly speaking with knowledge, truth, and conviction. As she reminds us, "sometimes we just let the loudest among us become leaders of society."[7]

Personal History

Thuli Madonsela was born on September 28, 1962, in Soweto—an acronym for South West African Township—located outside Johannesburg. Born in the midst of apartheid, South Africa's system of racial discrimination, Madonsela grew up in a town famous for its 1976 student uprising protesting the implementation of Afrikaans, the language of white South Africans, into its segregated education system. The daughter of informal traders, Madonsela excelled academically at such places as Evelyn Baring High School in Swaziland but often experienced the insecurities that plague many young people. In a letter she wrote as an adult to her sixteen-year-old self, Madonsela recalled that although she felt socially awkward, ugly, and unlovable, she felt sure in her academic ability.[8]

Growing up with the segregation, injustices, and brutality common during the apartheid era heavily influenced Madonsela's young life and led her to a career in law. In an interview with the *New Age Online*, Madonsela remembered, "Growing up from a poor background and having experienced injustices and the brutality of apartheid, where Blackjacks would come to your house and remove you because you don't have permits. I experienced my parents being arrested for being informal traders. I experienced the injustices, interpersonal disputes, and the Black Administration Act. My soul just resonated with those issues."[9] The Black/Native Administration Act allowed the South African state to set up a separate legal system for African or Native affairs so that the state could rule natives by proclamation—effectively bypassing the judicial system. This limited nonwhites seeking justice through the judicial process.

Madonsela says her passion for the law and justice started because she witnessed such injustices perpetrated by the Black/Native Administration Act and the Natives Act of 1952, which forced Black South Africans to carry several documents or suffer arrest.[10]

She states, "My passion for law and justice was ignited when I was growing up during the 1970's era when I witnessed some of my family members hiding from the police because they didn't have their passes."[11] This drove her to protect the most vulnerable of the population from those in power who would abuse them for self-interest.

Madonsela pursued law, teaching, and political life—a departure from an early decision to study medicine. She completed her BA in law in 1987 at the University of Swaziland and an LLB (law degree) from the University of Witwatersrand in Johannesburg in 1990. In the early 1980s, Madonsela taught high school, but some of her first political work began when she became involved with union work at the National Union of Printers and Allied Workers, where she helped union workers and community members with legal disputes.[12] She went on to work in a number of organizations that strengthened her commitment to human rights, labor reform, and the empowerment of women in South Africa. When asked if she thought her experiences in organizing helped her with her job as a PP, Madonsela replied, "I think so. . . . It has helped me to understand the shoes of the complainant but also to be able to advocate, to play the role of an advocate, when it comes to interrupting the government when somebody's rights have been violated."[13]

Madonsela's passion for human rights and social justice led her to be chosen as one of eleven technical experts who helped South Africa's Constitutional Assembly draft and pass the final constitution in 1994 and 1995. To this day, it is one of the most liberal constitutions in the world.

In 2009, she assumed the Office of the Public Protector after being appointed by Jacob Zuma, the man whom she eventually investigated. Her investigation into the security upgrades made at the president's private home in Nkandla in KwaZulu-Natal province moved her from the national stage to international recognition. In 2011, the *Daily Maverick*, a South African news outlet, named her "Person of the Year," and in 2012, she was awarded the South Africa's Most Influential Women Award.[14] Madonsela is the mother of two children: a daughter, Wenzile Una; and a son, Mbusowbantu Fidel. She is a member of the South African Women Lawyers Association and the Business Women's Association of South Africa.

Half a Century of Segregation: South Africa, Apartheid, and the Newly Democratic State

The human rights and social justice interventions of Thuli Madonsela must be seen through the complicated history of South Africa—a history that led to the creation, and finally the dismantling, of the infamous racial segregation policy called apartheid. Madonsela's staunch advocacy for the rights of the South African public is intimately connected with her past, with the development of a newly democratic government in the country, and with its ultimate promise of governmental transparency.[15]

Apartheid, which translates to "apart-hood," was a system of racial segregation enacted and enforced by the Afrikaner Nationalist Party in 1948. Although apartheid is the racial segregation system most often associated with the modern history of South Africa, South Africa has a long history of slavery, discrimination, and segregation dating back to the settlement of the Dutch in the seventeenth century.[16] This long history of racial segregation culminated in the implementation of a particularly brutal set of policies that sought to regulate the movement, labor, and living arrangements of South Africa's nonwhite populations.[17] Seeking to ensure a continual Black laboring class for the new capitalist economy, apartheid also set up a complicated caste system to separate people into groups based on their racial and ethnic heritage. From 1960 to 1983, over three and a half million nonwhite South Africans were removed from their homes and placed in racially and ethnically separated neighborhoods such as Soweto, where Thuli Madonsela was born in 1962.[18]

The dismantling of apartheid as an official system of racial segregation began in 1990 after decades of regional, national, and international protests, economic sanctions, and sports bans that made "apartheid unworkable" and South Africa "ungovernable."[19] In 1994, after almost half a century of racially repressive rule, the first multiracial democratic elections were held in South Africa. The African National Congress (ANC), the organization at the forefront of the decades-long struggle against apartheid, gained power, and Nelson Mandela, one of apartheid's most famous political prisoners, became president of the newly democratic state in 1994—ending forty-six years of apartheid in the country.

In 1996, a new constitution was finalized that was distinct from previous ones that entrenched racial discrimination within the country. In contrast, the 1996 constitution sought to acknowledge and protect the equal rights of South Africa's diverse population.[20] Importantly, Thuli Madonsela participated in the drafting of this new South African constitution, which undergirded the newly democratic nation and led to the creation of the Office of the Public Protector—the office that catapulted Madonsela onto the international stage as an advocate for human rights and a foe of public corruption and maladministration.

The Office of the Public Protector of South Africa

The new South African constitution created the Office of the Public Protector to ensure just public administration within the country. The Office of the Public Protector is based on similar offices, often called the Office of the Ombudsman, that have arisen in a number of European governments. These offices not only attempt to provide a more just public administration but also seek to protect the human rights of the country's citizens.[21]

The term *ombudsman* originates from the Scandinavian term for "representative," but the earliest iterations of such an office may be traced back to China and Korea.[22] Modern uses of the term began, however, in nineteenth-century Sweden. The New York City Public Advocate and Los Angeles County Ombudsman are administrative offices that have similar functions in the United States. While the goal of the ombudsman or public protector is not to punish people or public organizations, the office can provide recommendations or attempt mediation after its investigations. In certain countries, like South Africa, the Office of the Public Protector is also charged with protecting the human rights of the country's citizens.[23]

In South Africa, the public protector (PP) is appointed by the president on the recommendation of the National Assembly and must provide a report to the National Assembly once a year. As written in the constitution, the PP is subject only to the constitution and the law, and the office operates as an impartial entity that ensures proper public administration and strives to protect the human rights of South African citizens. The PP is empowered to investigate a wide range of public entities, state offices, and any part of the South African government that is accused or alleged to have engaged in improper conduct. Anyone in South Africa can make an appeal to the Office of the Public Protector, and the PP can compel a person to give evidence and/or produce documents that will assist with the investigation. Once an investigation has been conducted, the PP can provide recommendations to the government, and to any other actors, and take remedial action.[24] The person appointed as the PP serves a nonrenewable seven-year term and may only be removed through evidence of misconduct or incompetence.

The first PP to be appointed in South Africa was Selby Baqwa, who left the office in 2002 to become the head of corporate governance at a private company. Lawrence Mushwana, a former ANC member of parliament ascended to the Office of the Public Protector in 2002, and during his term, he was accused of being little more than a tool of the ANC and of being selective in what his office investigated.[25] Mushwana was suspected of whitewashing reports that would have called into question some of the policies and practices of the ANC, the ruling political party. In 2009, Mushwana left the Office of the Public Protector amid a scandal in which he claimed that a R7 million payout he was given at the end of his term was the gratuity he was owed—indicating that the money was part of his initial contract upon taking office in 2002.[26] He stated to the *Mail & Guardian*, "People just want to see my name rubbished in the newspapers."[27] In 2009, Jacob Zuma appointed Thuli Madonsela to the Office of the Public Protector, an appointment that led to a critical juncture for public accountability in the South African political landscape. Madonsela not only became universally acclaimed but also became a shining example of women's leadership and a "symbol for [South Africa's] moral transformation."[28]

A Critical Juncture: Advocate Madonsela
Answering the Call for Public Accountability

When Madonsela was appointed to serve as the PP, Jacob Zuma said to the National Assembly, "Advocate Madonsela takes on an important responsibility, having to protect South Africans against any abuse of power by state organs or officials. She will need to ensure that this office continues to be accessible to ordinary citizens and undertakes its work without fear or favour."[29]

Corruption, or maladministration, is the unscheduled use of public resources for private ends.[30] There is the perception, and often the reality, that political corruption is especially apparent in the governments of developing countries or postcolonial governments. However, in many developing countries, the state may be the major player within the economy, giving those who are in power greater control over economic and material resources. Political office may, for those who have been historically disenfranchised, become an avenue for personal wealth as well as power.[31] South Africa, however, is not a typical developing African country. For example, the state plays a minor role in the economy and is not the main path for economic or material wealth. The question for South Africa, then, is not one of modernization but of *democratization.*[32]

The newly democratic government of South Africa was committed to transparency, and the creation of the Office of the Public Protector was one way to demonstrate that commitment to transparency and public accountability. Corruption probes became officially embedded within government. As Madonsela notes, "The issue of governing properly was always part of the understanding that apartheid was a bad state not only because it violated human rights but because it was a government that was arbitrary and a government that was not accountable. . . . The idea was then to create a better government."[33]

The investigations done by the Office of the Public Protector allowed the media to report on government corruption in ways that the apartheid state did not allow. In addition, the affirmative action policies of the newly democratic South Africa, through policies such as Black economic-empowerment initiatives, not only enabled a growing Black middle class but also opened up such initiatives to public comment and critique. In other words, the democratization of South Africa and the destruction of racially and ethnically separate administrations also opened up the government, its actors, and its actions to public scrutiny.

It may seem that many of the instances of corruption or maladministration that are happening in the central government are remnants of the apartheid state—especially in such areas as social welfare and the police. However, there are new forms of corruption emerging in democratic South Africa, such as nepotism and political cronyism arising from political solidarity.[34] Understanding these new forms of maladministration becomes important when we examine the impact that Advocate Madonsela has had in the area of government accountability in the first five years of her tenure as South Africa's PP and what her actions signify for women's leadership.

Against the Rules

In August 2010, the *Sunday Times* accused Police Chief Bheki Cele of participating in a "dodgy" business deal with Roux Shabangu, a wealthy businessman who was well connected politically.[35] The newspaper reported that Cele made a deal with Shabangu to move the headquarters of the South African Police Service (SAPS) to the Middestad building in Pretoria, a building that would be owned by Shabangu. A letter leaked to the *Sunday Times* outlined how Chief Cele agreed to move SAPS to Shabangu's Pretoria building almost two months before Shabangu bought it. The police chief argued at the time that the new building was needed to house new units of the police force. SAPS had a ten-year lease agreement in its current building, an agreement that would have had to be prematurely canceled, potentially costing the public a significant amount of money to break the current lease.[36] The transaction proposed between the police chief and Shabangu never underwent the competitive bid process, which violated treasury regulations that state that government contracts over R500,000 must be open to such a process. In addition to the building in Pretoria, Cele had also signed a deal to move the police in Durban to the Transnet building, another building that Shabangu was planning to buy.[37]

In response to the formal complaint being lodged with the Office of the Public Protector, Madonsela and her team initiated a three-month investigation into the two lease deals between the SAPS and Roux Shabangu. In a report titled *Against the Rules*, Madonsela and her team found that there was no legitimate reason for Police Chief Cele to deviate from treasury regulations. In addition, her office found that both buildings were in need of upgrade that would cost the public taxpayers a significant amount and that the rental for the spaces were higher than the market rate.[38] The PP also accused Police Chief Cele and the Department of Public Works of maladministration when the investigation revealed that Cele (and others) had agreed to lease the new police headquarters from the politically connected real estate magnate for inflated prices (one source quotes an inflation rate of 300 percent).[39] With these findings, Madonsela and her team concluded that the SAPS and officials in the Department of Public Works engaged in maladministration with regard to the lease deals in Pretoria and Durban.[40]

The reaction from the police was swift. One of the reporters responsible for the exposé in the *Sunday Times*, Mzilikazi wa Afrika, was arrested four days after printing the article. Eight days after Madonsela released the report, SAPS raided her offices.[41] When Madonsela was asked if she was surprised by the raid, she said, "I was definitely surprised. I was. They did more than that; they told the media they were about to arrest me for corruption."[42] Police Chief Cele maintained that he did not directly participate with the lease deals.[43] However, in October 2011, President Zuma suspended Police Chief Cele, and in June 2012, Cele was let go from office.[44]

Inappropriate Moves

In 2013, Madonsela became embroiled in a dispute with the Independent Electoral Commission (IEC) chairwoman Pansy Tlakula. In a report, titled *Inappropriate Moves*, the PP office charged that Tlakula engaged in maladministration when she did not recuse herself from a deal in which her business partner was attempting to supply the IEC with a new head office at the Riverside Office Park in Pretoria. Advocate Madonsela recommended that parliament consider taking action against Tlakula.

The IEC is a chapter 9 institution similar to the Office of the Public Protector and is charge of running South Africa's elections. The Office of the Public Protector accused Tlakula of having a conflict of interest when she gave the contract to Abland, a company in which her business partner, Thaba Mufamadi, owned 20 percent. Madonsela also accused Tlakula of having not only a business relationship with Mufamadi but also a romantic one. Tlakula denied any conflict of interest and said that Madonsela did not have jurisdiction to investigate her or the IEC since they are both chapter 9 institutions and not part of the formal government.

Tlakula accused Madonsela of overstepping the mandate of the Office of the Public Protector, which is to investigate the government and other public institutions. Parliament agreed with Tlakula and found that Madonsela had made technical mistakes. As a result of this finding, parliament decided that it could not act on Madonsela's recommendation to take action against Tlakula because doing so would interfere with the separation of powers between the government and chapter 9 institutions outlined in the 1996 constitution. The ad hoc committee that was formed to investigate Madonsela's report concluded that all the PP office could do was to suggest that Home Affairs needed to strengthen the procurement processes at the IEC. The fallout of the IEC situation heavily influenced Madonsela's actions with regard to the PP's 2012–2014 investigation into the president's actions. Her critique of the president's actions gained Madonsela international recognition and resulted in *Time* magazine recognizing her as one of its one hundred most influential leaders.

Resolution

Radio, newspaper, and TV stories began to surface reporting that President Zuma, the man who had appointed Madonsela to the Office of Public Protector, was spending public monies to remodel his private residence above and beyond the security updates that public policy allowed. Madonsela decided to examine the security upgrades at the president's residence. If she chose to pursue this investigation and if she found evidence of maladministration, Madonsela would be going against not only the president of the country but also the ANC, the ruling party—a party of which she was a member. However, if she refused to pursue the investigation or found evidence of maladministration and was not transparent about her findings, Madonsela could be seen as condoning or even participating in corrupt government practices. This dilemma proved to be a critical juncture in her leadership. Madonsela ultimately investigated the security upgrades done at the private residence of President Zuma. At that moment, Thuli Madonsela distinguished herself from her predecessors by showing that she was unafraid to tackle the harder issues of corruption or maladministration within the government and other public organizations.

The Nkandla Report

In order to understand the significance of the Nkandla report and why this investigation became the juncture through which Thuli Madonsela gained international praise and recognition, some background on Jacob Zuma, then president of South Africa and the man at the center of the Nkandla report, is crucial. Zuma, whose Zulu name, Gedleyihlekisa, means "one who smiles while grinding his enemies," was born into poverty in 1942 in Inkandla, KwaZulu-Natal province, to a policeman father and a mother who did domestic work.[45] Zuma joined the ANC in 1959 and the South African Communist Party in 1963.[46] In 1963, he was arrested and convicted on charges of trying to overthrow the apartheid government and was sentenced to ten years' imprisonment on Robben Island with other antiapartheid prisoners including Nelson Mandela. Zuma eventually went into exile and returned to South Africa in 1990, when the ban on the ANC was lifted, and became involved in the process of postapartheid negotiations.[47] In 2007, after a lifetime of being in politics, Zuma became president of the ANC and went on to become president of South Africa after the ANC won general elections in 2009.

However, the political career of Zuma after the dismantling of apartheid has been plagued by a number of controversies and scandals. In 2003, Zuma was investigated alongside Tony Yengeni, the chief whip of the ANC. Both were accused of abuse of power. Zuma was charged with exerting improper influence in an arms deal from which he ultimately financially benefited. Yengeni was found guilty of the crimes, but the charges against Zuma were dropped.[48] In 2005, Zuma was accused of raping a woman in his Gauteng home. Zuma claimed that the sex was consensual, and in 2006, after a trial, he was found not guilty of rape.[49]

In 2004, Zuma became embroiled in political corruption charges with his financial adviser, Schabir Shaik, a Durban businessman. Shaik was investigated for bribery in connection with the purchase of a waterfront development in Durban for the South African navy and for excessive spending on Zuma's residence in Nkandla.[50] During the trial, evidence was presented that showed that Shaik had provided R4 million in bribes to Zuma over the years in return for support of a defense contract.[51] After Shaik was found guilty, formal charges of corruption were then leveled against Zuma. Zuma was indicted by the Directorate of Special Operations to stand trial in the High Court and was accused of racketeering, money laundering, corruption, and fraud. If convicted and sentenced to more than one year, Zuma would have become ineligible to serve as the president of South Africa. In September 2008, however, a judge cleared Zuma of corruption charges, citing political interference from his opponents. Zuma's supporters had claimed that he was the "victim of a political witch-hunt by his rival, South African President Thabo Mbeki."[52] In 2009, the National Prosecuting Authority dropped all charges against Zuma. Thus, despite multiple accusations of corruption and ethics violations, Zuma was never found guilty and remains a popular figure among many South Africans.

In 2009, Zuma once again became embroiled in accusations of maladministration with regard to excessive spending on the security upgrades to his home in Nkandla in KwaZulu-Natal province. These accusations catapulted Thuli Madonsela and her office onto the international stage.

In November 2011, an article in the *Mail & Guardian* charged that President Zuma was expanding his homestead at Nkandla at the cost of the taxpayer. On the basis of interviews with workers at the site, the article claimed that the expansion included a police station, military clinic, and visitor center. When the *Mail & Guardian* asked for comment on the allegations, Zuma at first claimed that the expansion was undertaken before he was elected and that he was paying for it. Although he claimed that no government money was being used, accusations of corruption and maladministration persisted.[53]

In 2012, in response to several requests by private citizens and charges in the press, Public Protector Madonsela began an investigation into the allegations of corruption and overspending for security installations at Nkandla. She investigated allegations that the president had used state funds to undertake more than security installations; it was alleged that he had completed a total remodeling of his private residence.[54]

In 2014, after several delays and two years, the Office of the Public Protector released its final report, titled *Secure in Comfort*. On the basis of its own investigations, the office's report found that approximately R246 million had been used to complete the "security installations" (US$23 million).[55] The report described several ethical breaches including excessive expenditure beyond what was permitted for such security installations. It also found that the final approval process for such expenditures was never followed. In addition, Zuma's private architect had been appointed to the Department of Public Works and had approved the most expensive options for improvements to Zuma's home.[56]

Madonsela's report recommended that President Zuma pay back the money that did not go to security upgrades, including such "improvements" as the installation of an amphitheater, a visitor center, a chicken run, and a swimming pool.[57] The *Mail & Guardian* calculated that Zuma would need to return about R20 million (approximately US$2 million).[58]

The Fallout

The release of the Nkandla report detailing the ethical violations and excessive expenditures for the upgrades to Zuma's private estate sent a shockwave through South Africa's political circles.

The Democratic Alliance (DA), the ANC's chief rival, called for the impeachment of the president.[59] Other political parties that have a strong Zulu power base, like the Inkatha Freedom Party (IFP), thought that an impeachment strategy was a good idea but that it would likely not work.[60] The ANC very quickly moved to discredit Madonsela and thus her report. After the preliminary release of the report, Madonsela was accused of being a DA agent by the ANC's Youth League (ANCYL).[61]

Two weeks after the report was released, President Zuma informally responded to it, stating, "I did not use the public's money in Nkandla. . . . What I am saying is I'm not guilty. Even if they look for me under a tree, they can't find me. I did nothing wrong. I did not do anything."[62] Zuma continued to claim he had little knowledge of the government's decisions about Nkandla.

Zuma had fourteen days after the release of the report to make a formal response, during which time Madonsela and her team at the Office of the Public Protector prepared for the reaction to its findings from the South African parliament.[63] The attacks against Madonsela were vicious, with some detractors going so far as to level sexist attacks by commenting on her looks.[64] Others claimed that she had not followed proper procedure by not first submitting her report to parliament before awaiting a response from the president.[65] But Madonsela defended her decision. In an interview with the *Star*, Madonsela said, "In this case, learning from the lessons of the IEC fiasco, I decided to follow the law."[66]

Despite international recognition for Madonsela's work in exposing corruption at the highest level, in May 2014, the *Mail & Guardian* reported that the Cabinet security cluster was going to request that the report undergo judicial review. It called her findings "irrational" and "contradictory" and argued that the report was informed by material errors of law.[67] The ANC continued to level attacks against Madonsela, accusing her of having a personal vendetta against President Zuma, undermining parliament and the constitution, and spreading rumors.[68] Madonsela said in a press conference, "I have served the ANC, I have taken [up] arms under the ANC. A lot of the people who are insulting me, some of them are old enough to have been in the trenches with me, but they were not there when it was tough." She continued, "I am not fazed by these people because, when there were no benefits of being in the struggle, they were not there."[69]

As late as August 2014, Madonsela maintained that Zuma had not formally replied to the report despite his office putting out a twenty-page response. Madonsela argued that Zuma and his team failed to address the content of her report and disregarded some of her findings and suggestions for remedial actions.[70] Minenhle Makhanya, who played the dual role of architect of Nkandla and member of the Department of Public Works committee that authorized much of the spending on Nkandla, became embroiled in a civil lawsuit brought by the Special Investigating Unit (SIU). The unit claimed that Makhanya engaged in excessive spending on security upgrades on the property. Makhanya is also bound by a nondisclosure clause that limits what he can say about the entire process.[71] Zuma maintains that he has responded to the Nkandla report, going so far as to write a hip hop song titled "99 Problems but Nkandla Ain't One," parodying a song with a similar title written and performed by Jay Z.[72]

Conclusions: Thuli Madonsela—Human Rights Activist

What are the moments that shape women leaders? Madonsela asserts,

> Within my own personal actions, I qualify to be called a leader—it
> is up to the observer to say you have influenced change, you have
> enabled groups in society to define a better life for themselves and
> to pursue that life effectively. What makes an effective leader is
> one that is able to help clarify a vision for a group or a society and
> mobilize others to pursue that vision or goal with them. Leadership
> is about the many ways that people or groups influence, socially or
> politically, change within the communities they live.[73]

Madonsela's strong belief in social justice and human rights led her to seek out government corruption as a way to secure justice for the most vulnerable of South Africa's people. Madonsela has championed the rights of all South African citizens. In her early actions in organizing and ultimately as public protector, Madonsela has strived to "make a difference towards the change you want to see."[74] Madonsela's investigation into government corruption is connected to her commitment to human rights and social justice. It has allowed her to demand public accountability for the actions of South Africa's public officials, including President Zuma himself. As she observed, "I see a link between human rights and corruption because, firstly, a corrupt administrative process may deny somebody the rights that they have, and a corrupt justice system may deny rights. But secondly, when corruption steals resources away from the state, it undermines service delivery and social and economic rights. . . . Lives depend on state resources."[75] Madonsela's actions demonstrate what it means to lead, even when it means challenging your political allies and colleagues. Leaders are shaped by junctures that require courage and intelligence, framed by a passion for social justice. Thuli Madonsela exemplifies a person who believes that good government requires just behavior. Instead of looking the other way in the face of government corruption, she has publicly taken on prominent figures in the antiapartheid struggle, powerful government officials, and well-known business leaders to enact change. Madonsela embodies the idea that "everyone is called upon to lead everywhere they are."[76]

Notes

1 Lamido Sanusi, "South Africa's Fearless Public Advocate," *Time*, April 23, 2014, http://time.com/70854/thuli-madonsela-2014-time-100/.

2 University of Johannesburg Strategic Communications, "Advocate Thuli Madonsela in Conversation with Leanne Manas UJ's Alumni Day," YouTube, May 19, 2014, https://youtu.be/fZBItuY6rjk, video.

3 Ranjeni Munusamy, "Thuli's Time: SA's Protector, Sentinel, Makhadzi Gets Global Recognition," *Daily Maverick*, April 25, 2014, http://www.dailymaverick.co.za/article/2014-04-24-thulis-time-sas-protector-sentinel-makhadzi-gets-global-recognition/#.VSsYSxBdVZf.

4 Ibid.

5 Mphatheleni Makaulule, "The Role of Makhadzi—Passing Knowledge to Future Generations," Mupo Foundation, May 1, 2013, http://mupofoundation.org/2013/the-role-of-makhadzi/.

6 Quoted in Munusamy, "Thuli's Time."
7 University of Johannesburg Strategic Communications, "Advocate Thuli Madonsela in Conversation."
8 Thuli Madonsela, "Thuli Madonsela's Letter to Her 16-Year Old Self," O: The Oprah Magazine, April 26, 2012, http://www.oprahmag.co.za/live-your -best-life/self-development/thuli-madonsela%27s-letter-to-her-16-year -old-self.
9 Xolani Mbanjwa, "The Big Interview: Madonsela's," New Age Online, September 21, 2011.
10 "Pass Laws in South Africa 1800–1994," South African History Online, n.d., http://www.sahistory.org.za/south-africa-1806–1899/pass-laws-south-africa-1800–1994 (accessed July 27, 2015).
11 Mbanjwa, "Big Interview."
12 Ibid.
13 Thuli Madonsela, conversation with Alison Bernstein, August 28, 2014.
14 Sipho Hlongwane, "Thuli Madonsela, 2011 South African Person of the Year," Daily Maverick, December 5, 2011, http://www.dailymaverick.co.za/article/2011 -12-05-thuli-madonsela-2011-south-african-person-of-the-year#.VSsg4xB dVZc; Who's Who Southern Africa, "Thuli Madonsela," n.d., http://whoswho .co.za/thulisile-madonsela-9068.
15 Eric P. Louw, The Rise, Fall, and Legacy of Apartheid (Westport, CT: Praeger, 2004).
16 Nancy L. Clark and William H. Worger, South Africa: The Rise and Fall of Apartheid (Abingdon, UK: Routledge, 2013).
17 Louw, Rise, Fall, and Legacy of Apartheid; Clark and Worger, South Africa.
18 Clark and Worger, South Africa.
19 Oliver Tambo, "Address by Oliver Tambo to the Nation on Radio Freedom," July 22, 1985, available at http://www.anc.org.za/show.php?id=4470.
20 Clark and Worger, South Africa.
21 Office of the Public Prosecutor South Africa, "History and Background to the Office of the Public Protector," 2009, http://www.pprotect.org/about_us/ history_background.asp.
22 Sangyil Park, Korean Preaching, Han, and Narrative (New York: Peter Lang, 2008).
23 Office of the Public Prosecutor South Africa, "History and Background to the Office of the Public Protector."
24 Ibid.
25 Phakathi Bekezela, "DA Call to Reopen Oilgate Probe," Business Day BDlive, August 6, 2012, http://www.bdlive.co.za/articles/2010/09/20/da-call-to-reopen -oilgate-probe; Ernest Mabuza, "Court Orders New Probe of Oilgate," Business Day BDlive, July 31, 2009, http://www.bdlive.co.za/articles/2009/07/31/court -orders-new-probe-of-oilgate.
26 Mmanaledi Mataboge, "Shock R7m Payout for Mushwana," Mail & Guardian, October 30, 2009, http://mg.co.za/article/2009–10–30-shock-r7m-payout-for -mushwana.
27 Ibid.

28 Adriaan Groenewald, "Public Protector Is in One of Her Finest Hours," *Star* (Johannesburg, South Africa), August 29, 2014, http://www.iol.co.za/business/opinion/columnists/public-protector-is-in-one-of-her-finest-hours-1.1742755#.VSsu2BBdVZc.

29 South African Government, "Appointment by President Zuma of Public Protector," October 18, 2009, http://www.gov.za/appointment-president-zuma-public-protector.

30 Tom Lodge, "Political Corruption in South Africa," *African Affairs* 97, no. 387 (1998): 157–187.

31 Ibid.

32 Ibid.

33 Thuli Madonsela, conversation with Alison Bernstein, August 28, 2014.

34 Lodge, "Political Corruption in South Africa."

35 Mzilikazi wa Afrika and Hofstatter Stephan, "Bheki Celeís R500m Police Rental Deal," *Citizen Alert Za* (blog), *Sunday Times* (Johannesburg, South Africa), August 1, 2010, http://citizenalertzablogspotcom-tango.blogspot.com/2010/08/bheki-celes-r500m-police-rental-deal.html.

36 Ibid.

37 "Cele Was 'Solely Responsible,'" *Sunday Times* (Johannesburg, South Africa), June 19, 2011, http://www.timeslive.co.za/sundaytimes/2011/06/19/cele-was-solely-responsible.

38 Office of the Public Protector South Africa, *Against the Rules*, report 33, February 22, 2011, http://www.pprotect.org/library/investigation_report/2011/Report%20no%2033%20of%202010–11.pdf.

39 Ibid.; "Shooting the Messenger," *Business Day BDlive*, June 22, 2011, http://www.bdlive.co.za/articles/2011/06/22/editorial-shooting-the-messenger.

40 Office of the Public Protector South Africa, *Against the Rules*.

41 Dianne Kohler Barnard, "Zuma Should Dismiss Commissioner Cele," Politicsweb, July 14, 2011, http://www.politicsweb.co.za/politics/zuma-should-dismiss-commissioner-cele—kohler-barn.

42 Thuli Madonsela, conversation with Alison Bernstein, August 28, 2014.

43 Ido Lekota, "Cele Suspended over Police Leases," Sowetan Live, October 25, 2011, http://www.sowetanlive.co.za/news/2011/10/25/cele-suspended-over-police-leases.

44 Ibid.

45 "South Africa's President Jacob Zuma—a Profile," BBC, April 25, 2014, http://www.bbc.co.uk/news/world-africa-17450447; Jeremy Gordin, *Zuma, a Biography* (Johannesburg, South Africa: Jonathan Ball, 2008).

46 David Beresford, "Zuma's Missing Years Come to Light," *Times* (UK), February 22, 2009, available at http://www.armsdeal-vpo.co.za/articles14/glimmers.html.

47 The Presidency: Republic of South Africa, "President Jacob Zuma," n.d., http://www.thepresidency.gov.za/pebble.asp?relid=7 (accessed July 27, 2015).

48 "Ngcuka Accused of 'Derailing Justice,'" iafrica.com, August 24, 2003, http://news.iafrica.com/specialreport/armsdeal_ocus/265106.htm.

49 "South Africa's President Jacob Zuma."
50 Andrew Fowler, "Jacob Zuma," ABC News, July 4, 2009, http://www.abc.net
.au/foreign/content/2009/s2538726.htm.
51 Ibid.
52 Muchena Zigomo, "S. African Judge Dismisses Zuma Corruption Case," China
Post, September 13, 2008, http://www.chinapost.com.tw/international/africa/
2008/09/13/174479/S-African.htm.
53 Matuma Letsoalo and Charles Molele, "Bunker Bunker Time: Zuma's Lavish
Nkandla Upgrade," Mail & Guardian, November 11, 2011, http://mg.co.za/
article/2011-11-11-bunker-time-for-zuma.
54 Office of the Public Prosecutor South Africa, Secure in Comfort, March 2014,
http://www.pprotect.org/library/investigation_report/2013-14/SECURE%20
IN%20COMFORT.pdf.
55 Ibid.
56 AmaBhungane team, "Nkandla Report: Payback Time, Zuma," Mail & Guardian,
November 29, 2013, http://mg.co.za/article/2013-11-28-payback-time-mr
-president.
57 Office of the Public Prosecutor South Africa, Secure in Comfort.
58 AmaBhungane team, "Nkandla Report."
59 Bongani Hans, "Calling for Zuma's Impeachment Futile, Says Buthelezi," Star
(Johannesburg, South Africa), March 24, 2014, http://www.highbeam.com/
doc/1G1-362543228.html.
60 Ibid.
61 "ANCYL Calls Madonsela a 'DA Agent,'" News24, February 20, 2014, http://www
.news24.com/SouthAfrica/Politics/ANCYL-calls-Madonsela-a-DA-agent-20140220.
62 Cobus Coetzee and Bongani Hans, "There Is Simply No Case against Me,
President Insists," Star (Johannesburg, South Africa), March 31, 2014,
http://www.highbeam.com/doc/1G1-363325951.html.
63 Ibid.
64 Matuma Letsoalo, "Mapisa-Nqakula Defends Madonsela against 'Sexist'
Remarks," Mail & Guardian, March 24, 2014, http://mg.co.za/article/2014-03
-24-mapisa-nqakula-defends-madonsela-against-sexist-remarks.
65 Babalo Ndenze, "Madonsela Slams 'Electioneering' Nkandla Criticism—
ANC Members Advised to Read Provisions in Public Protector Act before
Attacking Her," Star (Johannesburg, South Africa), March 31, 2014,
http://www.highbeam.com/doc/1G1-363325948.html.
66 Ibid.
67 "Security Cluster to Take Madonsela's Nkandla Report to Court," Mail & Guardian, May 15, 2014, http://mg.co.za/article/2014-05-15-cabinet-to-go-to-court
-with-nkandla-report.
68 Phillip De Wet, "Will Madonsela Press the Big Red Button after ANC
Remarks?," Mail & Guardian, August 27, 2014, http://mg.co.za/article/2014-08
-27-nkandla-will-madonsela-press-the-big-red-button.
69 Phillip De Wet, "Madonsela Talks Tough," Mail & Guardian, August 29, 2014,
http://mg.co.za/article/2014-08-28-madonsela-talks-tough.

70   Phillip De Wet, "Nkandla Could Be Heading for Courtroom," *Mail & Guardian*, August 29, 2014, http://mg.co.za/article/2014–08–29-nkandla-set-to-go-to-court.
71   Glynnis Underhill, "Nkandla Architect Bound by Non-disclosure Agreement," *Mail & Guardian*, September 5, 2014, http://mg.co.za/article/2014–09–05-nkan dla-architect-bound-by-non-disclosure-agreement.
72   Haji Mohamed Dawjee, "Jacob Zuma—99 Problems but Nkandla Ain't One," *Mail & Guardian*, August 20, 2014, http://mg.co.za/article/2014–08–19-jacob-z uma-99-problems-but-nkandla-aint-one.
73   Ken W. Parry, "Grounded Theory and Social Process: A New Direction for Leadership Research," *Leadership Quarterly* 9, no. 1 (1998): 85.
74   University of Johannesburg Strategic Communications, "Advocate Thuli Madonsela in Conversation."
75   Thuli Madonsela, conversation with Alison Bernstein, August 28, 2014.
76   Thuli Madonsela, "Address by Public Protector Adv. Thuli Madonsela during the Quality Life Women's Leadership Conference at the Peninsula Hotel in Cape Town," South African Government, August 7, 2014, http://www.gov.za/ address-public-protector-adv-thuli-madonsela-during-quality-life-womens -leadership-conference.

Bibliography

Afrika, Mzilikazi wa, and Stephan Hofstatter. "Bheki Celeís R500m Police Rental Deal." *Citizen Alert Za* (blog), *Sunday Times* (Johannesburg, South Africa), August 1, 2010. http://citizenalertzablogspotcom-tango.blogspot.com/2010/ 08/bheki-celes-r500m-police-rental-deal.html.
AmaBhungane team. "Nkandla Report: Payback Time, Zuma." *Mail & Guardian*, November 29, 2013. http://mg.co.za/article/2013–11–28-payback-time-mr -president.
"ANCYL Calls Madonsela a 'DA agent.'" News24, February 20, 2014. http://www .news24.com/SouthAfrica/Politics/ANCYL-calls-Madonsela-a-DA-agent -20140220.
"Axed S. African police chief vows to clear his name." *Agence France-Presse*, June 13, 2012. http://en.starafrica.com/news/axed-safrican-police-chief-vows-to-clea -237487.html.
Barnard, Dianne Kohler. "Zuma Should Dismiss Commissioner Cele." Politicsweb, July 14, 2011. http://www.politicsweb.co.za/politics/zuma-should-dismiss -commissioner-cele—kohler-barn.
Bekezela, Phakathi. "DA Call to Reopen Oilgate Probe." *Business Day BDlive*, September 20, 2010. http://www.bdlive.co.za/articles/2010/09/20/da-call-to -reopen-oilgate-probe.
Beresford, David. "Zuma's Missing Years Come to Light." *Times* (UK), February 22, 2009. Available at http://www.armsdeal-vpo.co.za/articles14/glimmers.html.
"Cele Was 'Solely Responsible.'" *Sunday Times* (Johannesburg, South Africa), June 19, 2011. http://www.timeslive.co.za/sundaytimes/2011/06/19/cele-was -solely-responsible.

Clark, Nancy L., and William H. Worger. *South Africa: The Rise and Fall of Apartheid*. Abingdon, UK: Routledge, 2013.

Coetzee, Cobus, and Bongani Hans. "There Is Simply No Case against Me, President Insists." *Star* (Johannesburg, South Africa), March 31, 2014. http://www.highbeam.com/doc/1G1-363325951.html.

Dawjee, Haji Mohamed. "Jacob Zuma—99 Problems but Nkandla Ain't One." *Mail & Guardian*, August 20, 2014. http://mg.co.za/article/2014-08-19-jacob-zuma-99-problems-but-nkandla-aint-one.

De Wet, Phillip. "Madonsela Talks Tough." *Mail & Guardian*, August 29, 2014. http://mg.co.za/article/2014-08-28-madonsela-talks-tough.

———. "Nkandla Could Be Heading for Courtroom." *Mail & Guardian*, August 29, 2014. http://mg.co.za/article/2014-08-29-nkandla-set-to-go-to-court.

———. "Will Madonsela Press the Big Red Button after ANC Remarks?" *Mail & Guardian*, August 27, 2014. http://mg.co.za/article/2014-08-27-nkandla-will-madonsela-press-the-big-red-button.

Fowler, Andrew. "Jacob Zuma." ABC News, July 4, 2009. http://www.abc.net.au/foreign/content/2009/s2538726.htm.

Gordin, Jeremy. *Zuma, a Biography*. Johannesburg, South Africa: Jonathan Ball, 2008.

Groenewald, Adriaan. "Public Protector Is in One of Her Finest Hours." *Star* (Johannesburg, South Africa), August 29, 2014. http://www.iol.co.za/business/opinion/columnists/public-protector-is-in-one-of-her-finest-hours-1.1742755#.VSsu2BBdVZc.

Hans, Bongani. "Calling for Zuma's Impeachment Futile, Says Buthelezi." *Star* (Johannesburg, South Africa), March 24, 2014. http://www.highbeam.com/doc/1G1-362543228.html.

Hlongwane, Sipho. "Thuli Madonsela, 2011 South African Person of the Year." *Daily Maverick*, December 5, 2011. http://www.dailymaverick.co.za/article/2011-12-05-thuli-madonsela-2011-south-african-person-of-the-year#.VSsg4xBdVZc.

Lekota, Ido. "Cele Suspended over Police Leases." Sowetan Live, October 25, 2011. http://www.sowetanlive.co.za/news/2011/10/25/cele-suspended-over-police-leases.

Letsoalo, Matuma. "Mapisa-Nqakula Defends Madonsela against 'Sexist' Remarks." *Mail & Guardian*, March 24, 2014. http://mg.co.za/article/2014-03-24-mapisa-nqakula-defends-madonsela-against-sexist-remarks.

Letsoalo, Matuma, and Charles Molele. "Bunker Bunker Time: Zuma's Lavish Nkandla Upgrade." *Mail & Guardian*, November 11, 2011. http://mg.co.za/article/2011-11-11-bunker-time-for-zuma.

Lodge, Tom. "Political Corruption in South Africa." *African Affairs* 97, no. 387 (1998): 157–187.

Louw, P. Eric. *The Rise, Fall, and Legacy of Apartheid*. Westport, CT: Praeger, 2004.

Mabuza, Ernest. "Court Orders New Probe of Oilgate." *Business Day BDlive*, July 31, 2009. http://www.bdlive.co.za/articles/2009/07/31/court-orders-new-probe-of-oilgate.

Madonsela, Thuli. "Address by Public Protector Adv. Thuli Madonsela during the Quality Life Women's Leadership Conference at the Peninsula Hotel in Cape

Town." South African Government, August 7, 2014. http://www.gov.za/address
-public-protector-adv-thuli-madonsela-during-quality-life-womens-leadership
-conference.

———. "Thuli Madonsela's Letter to Her 16-Year Old Self." *O: The Oprah Magazine*, April 26, 2012. http://www.oprahmag.co.za/live-your-best-life/self
-development/thuli-madonsela%27s-letter-to-her-16-year-old-self.

Makaulule, Mphatheleni. "The Role of Makhadzi—Passing Knowledge to Future
Generations." Mupo Foundation, May 1, 2013. http://mupofoundation.org/
2013/the-role-of-makhadzi/.

Mataboge, Mmanaledi. "Shock R7m Payout for Mushwana." *Mail & Guardian*, October 30, 2009. http://mg.co.za/article/2009–10–30-shock-r7m-payout-for
-mushwana.

Mbanjwa, Xolani. "The Big Interview: Madonsela's." *New Age Online*, September 21, 2011.

Munusamy, Ranjeni. "Thuli's Time: SA's Protector, Sentinel, Makhadzi Gets Global
Recognition." *Daily Maverick*, April 25, 2014. http://www.dailymaverick.co.za/
article/2014–04–24-thulis-time-sas-protector-sentinel-makhadzi-gets-global
-recognition/#.VSsYSxBdVZf.

Ndenze, Babalo. "Madonsela Slams 'Electioneering' Nkandla Criticism—ANC
Members Advised to Read Provisions in Public Protector Act before Attacking
Her." *Star* (Johannesburg, South Africa), March 31, 2014. http://www.highbeam
.com/doc/1G1–363325948.html.

"Ngcuka Accused of 'Derailing Justice.'" iafrica.com, August 24, 2003. http://news
.iafrica.com/specialreport/armsdeal_ocus/265106.htm.

Office of the Public Protector South Africa. *Against the Rules*. Report 33. February 22, 2011. http://www.pprotect.org/library/investigation_report/2011/
Report%20no%2033%20of%202010–11.pdf

———. "History and Background to the Office of the Public Protector." 2009.
http://www.pprotect.org/about_us/history_background.asp.

———. *Secure in Comfort*. March 2014. http://www.pprotect.org/library/
investigation_report/2013–14/SECURE%20IN%20COMFORT.pdf.

Park, Sangyil. *Korean Preaching, Han, and Narrative*. New York: Peter Lang,
2008.

Parry, Ken W. "Grounded Theory and Social Process: A New Direction for Leadership Research." *Leadership Quarterly* 9, no. 1 (1998): 85–105.

"Pass Laws in South Africa 1800–1994." South African History Online. n.d. http://
www.sahistory.org.za/south-africa-1806–1899/pass-laws-south-africa
-1800–1994 (accessed July 27, 2015).

Presidency, The: Republic of South Africa. "President Jacob Zuma." n.d. http://www
.thepresidency.gov.za/pebble.asp?relid=7 (accessed July 27, 2015).

Sanusi, Lamido. "South Africa's Fearless Public Advocate." *Time*, April 23, 2014.
http://time.com/70854/thuli-madonsela-2014-time-100/.

"Security Cluster to Take Madonsela's Nkandla Report to Court." *Mail & Guardian*,
May 15, 2014. http://mg.co.za/article/2014–05–15-cabinet-to-go-to-court-with
-nkandla-report.

"Shooting the Messenger." *Business Day BDlive*, June 22, 2011. http://www.bdlive.co .za/articles/2011/06/22/editorial-shooting-the-messenger.

South African Government. "Appointment by President Zuma of Public Protec- tor." October 18, 2009. http://www.gov.za/appointment-president-zuma-public -protector.

"South Africa's President Jacob Zuma—a Profile." BBC, April 25, 2014. http://www .bbc.co.uk/news/world-africa-17450447.

Tambo, Oliver. "Address by Oliver Tambo to the Nation on Radio Freedom." July 22, 1985. Available at http://www.anc.org.za/show.php?id=4470.

Underhill, Glynnis, "Nkandla Architect Bound by Non-disclosure Agreement." *Mail & Guardian*, September 5, 2014. http://mg.co.za/article/2014–09–05-nkand la-architect-bound-by-non-disclosure-agreement.

University of Johannesburg Strategic Communications. "Advocate Thuli Madonsela in conversation with Leanne Manas UJ's Alumni Day." YouTube, May 19, 2014. https://youtu.be/fZBItuY6rjk. Video.

Who's Who Southern Africa. "Thuli Madonsela." n.d. http://whoswho.co.za/ thulisile-madonsela-9068.

Zigomo, Muchena. "S. African Judge Dismisses Zuma Corruption Case." *China Post*, September 13, 2008. http://www.chinapost.com.tw/international/africa/2008/ 09/13/174479/S-African.htm.

Contributors

CAROLINA ALONSO BEJARANO holds a law degree from Los Andes University in Bogota, and a master's in gender and social politics from the London School of Economics and Political Science. She is a collective owner, editor, and translator of *Sangria Legibilities*, a bilingual publishing house based in New York City and Santiago de Chile. She is currently pursuing her Ph.D. in women's and gender studies at Rutgers University, where she explores the intersection of decolonial theory and migration studies, specifically as it relates to the production of immigrant illegality in the United States. In her doctoral work, she examines how the colonial history of New Jersey influences current anti-immigration legislation in the state, while conducting ethnographic and organizing work with the undocumented Latin American community in Freehold, New Jersey.

ALISON R. BERNSTEIN assumed the position of director of the Institute for Women's Leadership (IWL) Consortium in July 2011. In this role, she has initiated two new areas of focus for IWL: women and health, and women and media. Previously, Bernstein served as a vice president for the Ford Foundation's Knowledge, Creativity, and Free Expression program for fourteen years. A former associate dean of faculty at Princeton University, Bernstein is the author of four books: *American Indians and World War II: Towards a New Era in Indian Affairs*; *The Impersonal Campus* (with Virginia B. Smith); *Funding the Future: Philanthropy in Higher Education*; and *Melting Pots and Rainbow Nations: Conversations about Difference in the United States and South Africa* (with Jacklyn Cock). Bernstein has taught at Princeton University, Teachers College / Columbia University, Sangamon State University (now the University of Illinois, Springfield), Spelman College, and Staten Island Community College. She graduated from Vassar College and received a Ph.D. and an M.A. in history from Columbia University. Bernstein is currently on the Board of Trustees at Bates College and serves on the boards of the Samuel Rubin Foundation and the News Literacy Project.

JO E. BUTTERFIELD is a visiting assistant professor of history at the University of Iowa, where she earned her Ph.D. in 2012. Her research examines the history of modern human rights by exploring the intersections between policy, ideology, and activism. Her book manuscript (in progress), "Social Justice, Not Charity: International Women's Activism, Gender Politics, and the Making of Modern Human Rights," examines how feminist activists and ideas about gender shaped the post–World War II international human rights project in fundamental ways. She currently teaches courses on the world since 1945, the United States in world affairs, the history of human rights, and Cold War America.

BLANCHE WIESEN COOK is a distinguished professor of history and women's studies at John Jay College of Criminal Justice and the Graduate Center of the City University of New York. She is the author of *Eleanor Roosevelt: Volumes I & II*, with *Volume III* forthcoming. She is a frequent contributor of reviews and columns in many newspapers and journals, and her other books include *Crystal Eastman on Women and Revolution* and *The Declassified Eisenhower*. For more than twenty years, she produced and hosted her own program for Radio Pacifica, originally called *Activists and Agitators* and renamed *Women and the World in the 1990s*. Cook is the former vice president for research of the American Historical Association and was vice president and chair of the Fund for Open Information and Accountability (FOIA, Inc.) She was also cofounder and cochair of the Freedom of Information and Access Committee of the Organization of American Historians, which was actively committed to maintaining the integrity of the Freedom of Information Act.

BRIDGET GURTLER is a postdoctoral research fellow at Princeton University's Woodrow Wilson School for Public & International Affairs and is a visiting fellow at the Center for Health and Wellbeing. Her research examines a broad host of issues in the history of medicine, science, and public health and the role of gender, identity, and race in shaping health care practices and policies. Her current book project examines the evolution of assisted reproduction in American medicine, families, and society. Focusing on the two-hundred-year history of artificial insemination, the book investigates how popular and scientific ideas about gendered bodies, heredity, and risk shaped the transformation of sperm into a (frozen) commodity, were pivotal to separating the act of sex from reproduction, and laid the institutional foundations for the modern fertility industry. Her publications include "From 'Fructification' to 'Insemination': Nomenclature and the Practice of Artificial Insemination," in *A Handbook of Infertility in History: Approaches, Contexts and Perspectives*, ed. Gayle Davis and Tracey Loughran, and numerous leadership case studies coauthored with Nitin Nohria. She received her Ph.D. in 2013 in history from Rutgers University, where she was an Andrew W. Mellon Dissertation Fellow and holds an M.A. in history from the University of Massachusetts–Amherst and a B.A. from Wellesley College.

BEVERLY GUY-SHEFTALL is the founding director of the Women's Research and Resource Center (since 1981) and Anna Julia Cooper Professor of Women's Studies at Spelman College. She was for many years an adjunct professor at Emory University's Institute for Women's Studies, where she taught graduate courses in its doctoral program. Guy-Sheftall holds a B.A. from Spelman College and did graduate work in English at Wellesley College before earning her master's degree at Atlanta University and her Ph.D. from Emory University. She has taught at Alabama State University and has been on the faculty of Spelman College since 1971. Guy-Sheftall has published a number of texts within African American and women's studies, including the first anthology on Black women's literature, *Sturdy Black Bridges: Visions of Black Women in Literature*, which she coedited with Roseann P. Bell and Bettye Parker Smith; her Ph.D. dissertation, *Daughters of Sorrow: Attitudes toward Black Women, 1880–1920*; and *Words of Fire: An Anthology of African American Feminist Thought*. Additional anthologies include *Traps: African American Men on Gender and Sexuality*, coedited with Rudolph P.

Byrd; *I Am Your Sister: Collected and Unpublished Writings of Audre Lorde*, with Rudolph P. Byrd and Johnnetta Betsch Cole; and *Still Brave: The Evolution of Black Women's Studies*, coedited with Stanlie James and Frances Smith Foster. She has also completed, with Johnnetta Betsch Cole, a monograph, *Gender Talk: The Struggle for Equality in African American Communities*, and *Who Should Be First? Feminists Speak Out on the 2008 Presidential Election.* In 1983, she became the founding editor of *Sage: A Scholarly Journal on Black Women.* Guy-Sheftall is the recipient of numerous fellowships and awards, among them a National Kellogg Fellowship, a Woodrow Wilson Dissertation Fellowship in Women's Studies, and Spelman's Presidential Faculty Award for outstanding scholarship. She has been involved with the national women's studies movement since its inception and provided leadership for the establishment of the first women's studies major at a historically Black college. She is also a past president of the National Women's Studies Association (NWSA).

JEREMY LAMASTER is a higher-education professional and adjunct faculty member at Rutgers University and holds an M.A. in women's and gender studies from Rutgers. LaMaster serves as the director of the Community Leadership, Action and Service Program (CLASP) at the Institute for Women's Leadership, an academic service-learning and leadership-development program. LaMaster's research interests include feminist and critical-thinking pedagogy, antiracist education, comprehensive sexuality education, Black feminisms, and disability studies.

KIM LEMOON is an honors student in the Department of Women's and Gender Studies at Rutgers University. In 2015, she completed an internship at the Institute for Women's Leadership at Rutgers as research assistant for the *Junctures: Women in Leadership* series. She has also worked as an intern for *SIGNS: Journal of Women in Culture and Society*, where she initiated the development of the journal's new website in 2012. LeMoon won the 2013 Aresty Undergraduate Research Award in the Humanities for her research on multicultural motherhood at Seabrook Farms, New Jersey, in the

1940s and 1950s. In 2014, she completed an honors thesis defending the sex researcher John Money against allegations of misconduct. LeMoon has maintained an evidence-based medical massage therapy practice since 1997. She was the 2007 Massage Therapy Foundation Practitioner Case Report Contest Silver Award Winner for her report *Clinical Reasoning in Massage Therapy*, which was subsequently published in the *International Journal of Therapeutic Massage & Bodywork*.

C. LAURA LOVIN is a researcher at the Weeks Centre for Social and Policy Research–London South Bank University, where she studies the transnational journeys, the quests for employment, and the trials of resettlement of immigrant workers from Romania in two major sites of global capitalism, London and New York City. Her project was awarded the 2015 Marie Skłodowska-Curie Fellowship by the European Commission. She received her Ph.D. in women's and gender studies from Rutgers University. Her areas of specialization include contemporary feminist theories, transnational mobilities, cultural politics and policy, and eastern European feminisms. Lovin's articles and reviews have appeared in anthologies and journals published in the United States and Europe. She has taught women's and gender studies courses at Rutgers–New Brunswick and Rutgers–Newark.

ROSEMARY NDUBUIZU is a fifth-year Ph.D. candidate in Rutgers University's Women and Gender Studies program. Her research interests are Black feminism, multifamily affordable housing policy, political economy, social movements, and the nonprofit industrial complex. Her dissertation explores how Black female domestic space is a privileged site for creative destruction. She argues that the United States' recent public and subsidized multifamily housing reforms cloak creative destruction within politically uncontroversial interventionist discourses such as concentrated poverty, culture of poverty, and undeserving poor, all of which figure Black female domestic space as an incubator of deviance and social waste. She ethnographically explores this phenomenon by analyzing how Washington, DC's housing advocates respond to creative destruction's three interventionist arguments. Committed to community-engaged scholarship, Ndubuizu remains connected to community organizing through her active involvement with Organizing Neighborhood Equity (ONE DC).

KATHE SANDLER is a Guggenheim Award–winning documentary filmmaker. Her credits include *A Question of Color*, the first nationally aired PBS documentary to explore attitudes about skin color, hair texture, and facial features in African American communities, as well as *Remembering Thelma*, on the late dancer, teacher, and mentor Thelma Hill, which screened at the New York Film Festival. She later adapted and directed Rosa Guy's classic Harlem novel *The Friends* as a short film, which won awards from the Black Filmmaker's Hall of Fame. Sandler received filmmaking grants from the Ford Foundation, MacArthur Foundation, National Endowment for the Arts, and Independent Television Service. She is a founding member of the Black Documentary Collective, where she worked closely with her mentor, the late St. Clair Bourne. She also served on the Artists Advisory Board for the New York Foundation for the Arts. Sandler wrote "Rediscovering Audre" for the Feminist Wire's 2014 Audre Lorde Forum. Her essays have been published in *Nka: A Review of African Art* and in the Infinity Award–winning anthology *Picturing Us: African American Identity in Photography*, edited by Deborah Willis. Sandler received her master's degree from New York University's Department of Social and Cultural Analysis with a concentration in Africana studies. Currently a Ph.D. candidate in the Department of Women's and Gender Studies at Rutgers University, she is completing her dissertation, "How Black Feminism Takes Place: Intergenerational Activism and Cultural Production in the New Millennium." She is also in progress on a similarly themed documentary film.

STINA SODERLING is a Ph.D. candidate in the Department of Women's and Gender Studies at Rutgers University. She has a bachelor's degree from Smith College in women's studies and international relations. Her research and teaching interests include queer theory, environmental justice and ecofeminism, and feminist perspectives on the prison system. Her dissertation, "In the Crevices of Global Capitalism: Rural Queer Community Formation," is an interdisciplinary study of the phenomenon of rural intentional queer communities in North America, focusing on questions of access to land. The project is based on ethnographic fieldwork in rural Tennessee, as well as archival research and oral histories. It draws on queer theory, feminist environmental studies, new materialism, and settler colonial studies. Teaching is a central component of Soderling's work as a scholar, and she has taught both introductory and upper-level undergraduate courses at Rutgers University and Mount Holyoke College on topics including queer studies, environmental justice, and feminist food politics. She has also been the coordinator for the prison-to-college efforts of the Progressive Education Initiative, a volunteer-run organization providing education to incarcerated women.

MIRIAM TOLA is a Ph.D. candidate in the Department of Women's and Gender Studies at Rutgers University. She is currently completing work on a dissertation that examines how anthropocentrism and hierarchies of gender and race inflect modern conceptions of politics. Her work has appeared or is forthcoming in *Hypatia*, *Theory & Event*, and *philoSOPHIA*. She has worked as a journalist for various Italian media outlets, as a programmer for nonprofit arts organizations, and as a documentary producer.

MARY K. TRIGG is an associate professor in the Department of Women's and Gender Studies at Rutgers University and the director of leadership programs and research at the Institute for Women's Leadership. She has published two books: *Feminism as Life's Work: Four Modern American Women through Two World Wars* and *Leading the Way: Young Women's Activism for Social Change*. She is at work on a new book examining representations of motherhood and ideas about time/temporality in the United States between 1920 and 1960. Trigg is the founding director of the Leadership Scholars Certificate Program, a leadership education honors program for undergraduate women, and has cofounded four additional leadership programs for women at Rutgers. She has published articles in *Liberal Education*, the *Journal of Women's History*, *Initiatives*, *Transformations*, *American National Biography*, and *Community, Work &*

Family. Her research has been supported by grants and fellowships from the National Historical and Publications Records Commission, the Woodrow Wilson Foundation, the AAUW, the Alfred P. Sloan Foundation, and the Bonner Foundation. She holds a Ph.D. and an M.A. in American civilization from Brown University, an M.A. in English from Carnegie-Mellon University, and a B.S. from the University of Michigan.

TAIDA WOLFE grew up in northern New Jersey and, after a summer enrichment program at Rutgers during high school, decided to pursue a career in medicine. She received her undergraduate degree at Dartmouth and her medical doctorate from Tufts University School of Medicine. She did her OB/GYN residency at Saint Barnabas Medical Center in Livingston, New Jersey, and a postresidency fellowship in family planning at the University of Michigan, where she also received her master's degree in public health. She currently is a Ph.D. candidate in the Department of Women's and Gender Studies at Rutgers University, where her research focuses on understanding the connection between Black female geographies and reproductive justice. She also has been the interim medical director at Planned Parenthood of Delaware and is a staff physician at Philadelphia Women's Center. She is a member of the Society of Family Planning and the National Abortion Federation.

Index

Bates, Daisy (Daisy Lee Gatson), xv, xii, 23–38
Bates, L. C. (Lucius Christopher), 25–26, 28, 32, 34
Batliwala, Srilatha, xvi, 157
Bay Area Rapid Transit District, 73
Bayh, Evan, 71
Bay Ridge High School (Brooklyn, New York), 62
Beal, Frances, 125
Beam, Joseph, 129
Beijing Platform, 76, 144, 158n9
Belli, Gioconda, 84
Berkshire Conference on the History of Women, 128
Berlin, Germany, 132
Berlin Conference, 42
Bernardino, Minerva, 6, 13
Bilwaskarma, Nicaragua, 84, 87–88
Bilwi, Nicaragua, 95
biological diversity, 46, 57
"biomythography," 119
birth control. *See* contraception
Birth Control Clinical Research Bureau, 178. *See also* Planned Parenthood
Black Administrative Act (South Africa), 218
Black Arts/Black Consciousness movement, 124
Black feminist movement. *See* feminism
"Black Feminist Statement," 127
"Black is beautiful" movement, 122
Blackjacks, 218
Black liberation movement, 73–74, 79n49, 124. *See also* civil rights, movement
Black Macho and the Myth of the Superwoman (Wallace), 126
Black nationalism, 79n49
Black/Native Administrative Act (South Africa), 218
Black Panthers, 79n49, 102
Black Power movement, 123
Blacks: female leadership development, xiv, 74–76; health issues, 163–175;

HIV/AIDS, 161–175; newspapers, 25; population migrations, 120; racial justice, 4; women and civil rights movement, 73–74; women writers' literary movement, 124, 125
Black Unicorn, The (Lorde), 125, 126
Black Woman, The (anthology), 124
Black Women Organized for Action (BWOA), xiv, 74, 75–76
Black Women's Alliance, 164
Black Women's Health Imperative, 163
Black Women Stirring the Waters, 76
"Black Women: Toward a Strategy for the Twenty-first Century," 76
Blossom, Virgil, 27–28, 30, 33
Blossom Plan, 28, 29
Bluest Eye, The (Morrison), 125
Borge, Tomás, 83
Bosnian War, 148
Bradley, Patricia, 110
Brauer, Carl, 66
"bridge leader," 35, 139
Brooklyn, New York, 62
Brown, Edmund "Pat," 65
Brown University, xiii, 124, 182
Brown v. Board of Education, 27
Bunch, Charlotte, xii, xiii, 139–160
Bundtland, Gro, vii
"bunny law," 66. *See also* Title VII
"A Bunny's Tale: *Show*'s First Exposé for Intelligent People" (Steinem), 101
Burst of Light, A (Lorde), 132
Bush, George H. W., 15
Bush, George W., 177, 183, 192n35
Business Women's Association of South Africa, 219
Butegwa, Florence, 153
Byelorussian Soviet Social Republic, 17n2

Cables to Rage (Lorde), 125
Cade, Toni. *See* Bambara, Toni Cade
California: Department of Health Services, 73; Division of Fair Employment Practices, 65, 70

Los Angeles (California) County
  Ombudsman, 221
"Love Poem" (Lorde), 125
Luisa Amanda Espinosa Association
  of Nicaraguan Women (AMNLAE),
  86
Lukas Clinik (Switzerland), 131
lunch counter sit-ins, 63, 70
Lutz, Bertha, 6
Lyft, 210

Maathai, Wangari (Miriam), xiii, xiv,
  xv–xvi, 39–59
machismo, 86
Madonsela, Mbusowbantu Fidel, 219
Madonsela, Thuli, xiii, 217–239
Madonsela, Wenzile Una, 219
MADRE (women's rights organization),
  92
Mail & Guardian, 222, 228–229, 230
Makhanya, Minenhle, 231
malnutrition, 46
"Mamas, the," xv, 51–52
Managua earthquake, 84
Manas, Leanne, 217
Manavi (South Asian women's organi-
  zation), 197
Mandela, Nelson, 182, 220, 227
Mann High School, Horace (Little Rock,
  Arkansas), 28
March on Washington: 1963, xii, 35, 123;
  1983, 119, 130
marriage restriction, hiring practice, 72
Marvelous Arithmetics of Distance: Poems
  1987–1992, The (Lorde), 133
masculinist nationalism, 119
maternity leave, 13, 16
Mathai, Mwangi, 44
Mathew, Biju, 202
Mau Mau rebellion, 42
Mayorga, Silvio, 83
Mbaya, Vertistine, 45
Mbeki, Thabo, 228
McCarthyism, 120
McGovern, George, 102

medallion, taxi, 201
Medgar Evers College, 130
Medicaid, 189
Mehta, Hansa, 14
Meriwether, Louise, 125
Methodist student movement (MSM),
  140
Mfume, Kweisi, 36
Millennium Development Goals, 144,
  158n9
misogyny, 110
Metropolitan Baptist Church, Annual
  Woman's Day, 35
Miskitu Indians, 82–83, 85, 87, 89, 90
MISURASATA (autonomist Indian
  organization) 85, 87–88
Modern Language Association, 128
Moi, Daniel arap, 39, 50, 51, 53–55
Moraga, Cherrie, 129–130
"morning-after pill," 180–181
Morrison, Toni, 125
motherhood, xv, 44–45, 119
Mother Teresa, 100
Mount Holyoke College, 128
Mpumalanga, South Africa, 173–174
Ms. (magazine), viii, 100, 110, 111, 125
Ms. Foundation for Women, 111
Mufamadi, Thaba, 226
Munich, Germany, 132
Murray, Pauli, 63–64, 69
Mushwana, Lawrence, 222
"My Day" column (Roosevelt), 9

Nakuru, Kenya, 42
NARAL Pro-Choice America, 184
Nation, The, 54
National Association for the Advance-
  ment of Colored People (NAACP),
  xiii, 4–5, 12, 15, 26, 28, 63, 69: Arkan-
  sas chapter, 23–24, 28–36; HIV/AIDS
  movement, 172; politics of exclusion,
  35; question of militancy, 26; State
  Conference of Branches, 26; State
  Conference Committee for Fair
  Employment Practices, 26

CPSIA information can be obtained
at www.ICGtesting.com
Printed in the USA
LVOW13s2127080817
544266LV00018B/343/P